Planning War with a Nuclear China

Planning War with a Nuclear China

US Military Strategy and Mainland Strikes

John Speed Meyers

Rapid Communications in Conflict and Security Series
General Editor: Thomas G. Mahnken
Founding Editor: Geoffrey R.H. Burn

Amherst, New York

Copyright 2023 Cambria Press.

All rights reserved.

Library of Congress Cataloging-in-Publication Data

Names: Meyers, John Speed, author.

Title: Planning war with a nuclear China : US military strategy and mainland strikes / John Speed Meyers.

Description: Amherst, New York : Cambria Press, [2023] | Series: Rapid communications in conflict and security series | Includes bibliographical references and index. | Summary: "Beginning in 2010, a public debate emerged about the role of so-called mainland strikes in any US military strategy toward China. Mainland strikes refer to wartime attacks on military targets located on the Chinese mainland with non-nuclear (conventional) weapons. This debate arose as American military strategists began to confront the implications of growing Chinese military power. Potential strategies were often defined, at least partially, by their relationship to and views toward mainland strikes. Some strategies assumed that an American president, and their advisers, would be willing to authorize or recommend mainland strikes in a future war with China. This course of action emphasized the procurement of a military force optimized to carry out these mainland strikes. Other strategies assumed an extreme unwillingness to recommend mainland strikes. These strategies called for building and training a military force capable of operational tasks other than mainland strikes. This book investigates the soundness of these two contradictory assumptions about mainland strikes so that strategists and American military planners can better understand the course of a future US-China war"-- Provided by publisher.

Identifiers: LCCN 2023031506 (print) | LCCN 2023031507 (ebook) | ISBN 9781621966777 (library binding) | ISBN 9781621966784 (paperback) | ISBN 9781638571858 (pdf) | ISBN 9781638571865 (epub)

Subjects: LCSH: United States--Military policy. | United States--Military relations--China. | China--Military relations--United States.

Classification: LCC UA23 .M515 2023 (print) | LCC UA23 (ebook) | DDC 355/.033573--dc23/eng/20230823

LC record available at https://lccn.loc.gov/2023031506

LC ebook record available at https://lccn.loc.gov/2023031507

Table of Contents

List of Tables vii

List of Figures ix

Acknowledgments xi

Chapter 1: Mainland Strikes and US Military Strategy 1

Chapter 2: The Theoretical Backdrop 15

Chapter 3: Sanctuary and the Korean War 49

Chapter 4: Operation Rolling Thunder and the Vietnam War 69

Chapter 5: Peering into the Future, Part I 105

Chapter 6: Peering into the Future, Part II 131

Chapter 7: Policy Recommendations 165

Appendices 183

Bibliography 215

Index 237

About the Author 245

Cambria Rapid Communications in Conflict and Security Series 247

List of Tables

Table 1: Number of Potential Participants Contacted by
Organization and Method 133

Table 2: The Four Scenarios and Associated Scenario
Characteristics 136

Table 3: Positive and Alternative Framing of Foreign-Policy Belief
and Attitude Questions 138

Table 4: Demographic and Professional Background Questions
and Response Options 139

List of Figures

Figure 1: Survey Respondents by Age Group 142

Figure 2: Survey Respondents by Career Length 143

Figure 3: Survey Respondents by Professional Background 144

Figure 4: Survey Respondents by Political Party (Self-Identified) 145

Figure 5: Survey Respondents by Gender 146

Figure 6: Survey Respondents by Level of Asia Expertise 147

Figure 7: Willingness to Recommend Mainland Strikes by Scenario 150

Figure 8: Relationship between Individual Characteristics and Willingness to Recommend Mainland Strikes by Scenario 153

Figure 9: Relationship between Foreign Policy Beliefs and Attitudes and Willingness to Recommend Mainland Strikes 156

Acknowledgments

This work started around a water cooler in the office kitchen of an American think tank over ten years ago. Thank you to the legions of people who tolerated me and nurtured my interests since then: Dave Baiocchi, Ellie Bartels, Julie Brown, Jim Chow, Mark Clodfelter, Zack Cooper, Natalie Crawford, Chris Dougherty, Derek Grossman, Dick Hallion, Eugene Han, Todd Harrison, Dung Huynh, Jennifer Kavanagh, Omair Khan, Kurt Klein, Paul Light, Sherrill Lingel, Michael Mazarr, Susan Marquis, Nick Martin, Tim McDonald, Forrest Morgan, David Ochmanek, Claire O'Hanlon, Michael O'Hanlon, Angel O'Mahony, Sara Turner, David Ronfeldt, Gery Ryan, Phillip Saunders, Travis Sharp, Rachel Swanger, Alex Utsey, Alan Vick, Hank Waggy, Russ Williams, Jon Wong, and Dakota Wood. Thank you also to those institutions that made this work possible: the Pardee RAND Graduate School, the RAND Corporation, especially Project Air Force and the National Security Research Division, the LBJ Foundation, and the Truman Library Institute. Some people also nurtured me before that water cooler conversation and are, for better or worse, stuck with me: John Burton Meyers, Anne McNaughton, Colin McNaughton, Austin Speed, and Andrew Wolford. There are also too many cousins, aunts, and uncles for me to list. But this book is really for two people: Jing and Carter, who are my everything.

Planning War with a Nuclear China

CHAPTER 1

MAINLAND STRIKES AND US MILITARY STRATEGY

Beginning in 2010, a public debate emerged about the role of so-called mainland strikes in any US military strategy toward China. Mainland strikes refer to wartime attacks on military targets located on the Chinese mainland with non-nuclear ("conventional") weapons. This debate arose as American military strategists began to confront the implications of growing Chinese military power. Potential strategies were often defined, at least partially, by their relationship to and views toward mainland strikes. Some strategies assumed that an American president, and their advisors, would be willing to authorize or recommend mainland strikes in a future war with China. This course of action emphasized the procurement of a military force optimized to carry out these mainland strikes. Other strategies assumed an extreme unwillingness to recommend mainland strikes. These strategies called for building and training a military force capable of operational tasks other than mainland strikes.

This book investigates the soundness of these two contradictory assumptions about mainland strikes so that strategists and American military planners can better understand the course of a future US-China war. This is a war that will hopefully never occur due, in part, to sound American military planning that maintains deterrence. Armed with knowledge about the conditions that make mainland strikes more or less likely, both military and civilian decision-makers can create better military strategy toward China.

GROWING CHINESE MILITARY POWER

Nearly all writers, strategists, analysts, and researchers interested in the Chinese military and in US military strategy toward China agree that Chinese military power has grown significantly over the past three decades and could pose formidable problems for the American military during a war in Asia between American and Chinese military forces.

Beginning in the mid-1990s, the Chinese military initiated a radical transformation. By focusing on building a force capable of challenging American intervention, Chinese leaders created an advanced military able to greatly complicate the task of US forces coming to the defense of a Pacific ally or partner. Eric Heginbotham and his coauthors in a 2015 RAND report entitled *The US-China Military Scorecard* documented the shifting military balance by evaluating the outcome of US-China combat in ten different mission areas. By assessing the relative balance in each mission area from 1996 to 2017, Heginbotham and his authors concluded that "trends in the military balance are running against the United States."[1] RAND analyst David Shlapak and his coauthors' widely cited 2009 report *A Question of Balance* came to a similar analytical result. Employing theater-level combat modeling in conjunction with historical analysis, they found a "growing imbalance of military power" between China and the United States.[2] These broad analytical reports complement the pessimistic findings of other, more policy-oriented reports and narrower, usually more technical, assessments of particular military domains.[3] Broader treatments of Chinese military power have also documented the growth of Chinese military capabilities.[4]

Mainland Strikes and US Military Strategy

To illustrate the effect of growing Chinese military power, this section describes the Chinese operational threat to US air bases and surface navy forces in the region. Because many strategists believe that US military dominance in East Asia rests on the US ability to deploy its conventional forces to East Asia, these sections reveal why American military strategists have viewed current trends as ominous for the US-China military balance and so have begun to debate different potential American military strategies toward China.

American air bases in Asia are presently vulnerable to attack by China's growing arsenal of accurate, long-range cruise and ballistic missiles. Eric Heginbotham and his coauthors in the 2015 *US-China Military Scorecard* RAND report devoted the first of their ten "scorecards" to assessing China's ability to attack American air bases.[5] In a scenario set in 2017, the authors found that Chinese attacks on Kadena Air Base in Okinawa, Japan could lead to a closure of "two weeks or more" in military operations and that attacks on Andersen Air Force Base on Guam would constitute a "significant threat."[6] RAND analyst Jeff Hagen, who has devoted considerable professional attention to air base vulnerability, has testified before the congressionally-sponsored U.S.-China Economic and Security Review Commission that "clearly the US could face extended periods of time when few, if any, of our bases near China are operating."[7]

A notable operational analysis of the missile threat to US bases in Asia was conducted by two US navy officers and published by the Center for New American Security in 2017. Their findings, which they describe as "deeply concerning," include that a large-scale Chinese missile attack on American bases in East Asia could overwhelm American air defenses and destroy over two hundred American aircraft on the ground in the first hours of the conflict.[8] This threat to the operation of American air bases creates a major problem for the post–Cold War "American way of war."[9] In particular, American forces will likely no longer be able to treat bases as "sanctuaries" where they can efficiently amass material and forces and then strike the enemy at a place and time of America's choosing.[10] The operational implications of air base vulnerability have led many analysts to conclude that preparing for a war with China requires a large dose of new thinking.[11]

In comparison to the situation prevailing in the 1990s, the surface forces of the US Navy, including American aircraft carriers, have also become more vulnerable to a Chinese attack. China's anti-ship ballistic missiles, cruise missiles, and submarines all pose threats to American surface forces operating close to China. This trend results from the growing range of Chinese surveillance and precision-strike capabilities and the relatively short range of the modern American carrier air wing. For instance, China's DF-21D anti-ship ballistic missile can travel approximately one-thousand nautical miles; the F-35C, the Navy's newest combat aircraft designed for takeoff and landing on aircraft carriers, has an unrefueled combat radius of 550 nautical miles.[12] Of course, the exact distance at which China's missiles pose a credible threat to American aircraft carriers is subject to debate.[13] There are limits to Chinese surveillance of the ocean through, for instance, over-the-horizon radars. The US Navy also does have formidable defensive capabilities, but the analytical debate has converged on the premise that American aircraft carriers can no longer operate with impunity.

To be sure, some scholars argue that Chinese military power, relative to the US, has not actually grown over the past few decades. Michael Beckley has made exactly this case.[14] Other analysis highlights persistent Chinese military weaknesses.[15] Nonetheless, most American observers of the US-China military balance have perceived a worsening situation for the US military and so have begun to devise and assess different means of reversing this shift.

Potential American Military Strategies toward China

In response to the growth of the Chinese military and the perception of a military balance tilting in favor of China, American strategists have devised and compared a number of alternative military strategies. There are three fundamental military strategies.[16] Each military strategy combines a problem framing and a solution involving military forces.

The first focuses on mainland strikes. Occasionally labeled AirSea Battle, this approach requires US military forces that can penetrate China's so-called anti-access/area-denial capabilities promptly during a conflict and conduct conventional strikes throughout the Chinese mainland.[17] The Center for Strategic and Budgetary Assessment's (CSBA) 2010 *AirSea Battle: A Point-of-Departure Operational Concept* report typifies this approach and its prescription for how the American military should adapt to Chinese military modernization.[18] The authors focused on the Chinese development of anti-access/area-denial capabilities, a suite of military weapon systems designed to prevent American forces from entering and maneuvering in the western Pacific, and they called for a major rethinking of both procurement priorities and war planning. In arguing that the United States should implement a blinding campaign against Chinese intelligence, surveillance, and reconnaissance capabilities at the outset of hostilities, the authors assumed that a president and their advisors would authorize strikes on a wide range of targets on the Chinese mainland.[19] In fact, the authors noted that a critical assumption underlying their proposed approach is that "neither US nor Chinese territory will be accorded sanctuary status" and that "US conventional counterforce strikes—both kinetic and non-kinetic (e.g., cyber)—inside China will be authorized from the conflict's outset."[20] The air base vulnerability problem and also China's anti-satellite capabilities and anti-ship ballistic missiles are all at the base of this strategic thinking. Some strategists argue that strikes on military targets located on the Chinese mainland are essential: only by reducing Chinese combat aircraft sortie generation, destroying or suppressing Chinese ballistic and cruise missiles, and disrupting Chinese targeting can American forces avoid heavy losses and possibly defeat. Broadly speaking, this strategy entails developing, at a minimum, the ability to perform reconnaissance throughout the Chinese mainland and strike capabilities able to penetrate deeply into Chinese airspace. The air force's new manned bomber is often associated with these missions, but in reality, many other weapon systems—reconnaissance satellites, fighter escorts, a range of munitions, among many other systems—would be needed to adequately perform this mission. Finally, it is worth pointing out that there are a number of thinkers beyond those formerly associated with CSBA who are loosely affiliated with this strategy.[21]

A maritime denial strategy presents a second option. The central idea of a maritime denial strategy is to target all Chinese power projection forces, especially ships and planes, that are attacking American forces or the forces of an American partner or ally. T. X. Hammes of the National Defense University has notably staked out a public position consistent with this approach. In a strategy he labels "Offshore Control," he calls for a US force structure and war plan that is simultaneously capable of both a long-distance blockade of Chinese seaborne imports and of attacking targets in the seas and airspace near China.[22] He explicitly advocates foregoing strikes on the Chinese mainland in the belief that "the concept of decisive victory against a nation with a major nuclear arsenal is fraught with risks."[23] Wayne Hughes and Jeffrey Kline of the Naval Postgraduate School have developed a "war at sea" strategy that provides military options short of strikes on the Chinese mainland. Their proposal includes capitalizing on American strengths in undersea warfare and the development of small missile-armed surface combatants.[24] Eric Heginbotham and Jacob Heim propose an "active denial strategy" that emphasizes "combat against offensive maneuver forces instead of strikes against home territories."[25] Their description of capabilities to support this strategy includes American submarines, anti-ship missiles, and mines.[26] Sam Tangredi urges the US military to keep "war confined to the seas"

Mainland Strikes and US Military Strategy

and advocates for a navy capable of sea denial, armed with adequate long-range munitions, and air forces equipped for long-range interdiction.[27]

Another strain of strategic thought that can be grouped under maritime denial strategies includes operational concepts that focus on the US or its partner deploying ground-based anti-ship missile forces in East Asia.[28] These strategies, broadly speaking, call for forces that find and destroy offensive Chinese forces without strikes on the Chinese mainland. Though a consensus on what forces can best accomplish this mission does not exist, analyses associated with this approach tend to emphasize American undersea warfare capabilities and the platforms and munitions to support long-range stand-off naval strikes.

The final strategic camp supports a naval blockade. This strategy calls for deterring or compelling Chinese leaders by implementing a blockade of Chinese seaborne commercial traffic.[29] Whether implemented relatively near Chinese coasts (a close-in blockade) or at faraway maritime chokepoints (a distant blockade), this strategy takes advantage of Chinese reliance on ship-borne trade, especially its oil imports. Whereas past analysis tends to assume that the US Navy already possesses sufficient capabilities for a naval blockade against China (especially a distant blockade), there are likely niche capabilities, such as offensive mine-laying, that this strategy would require above and beyond those currently planned by American forces.[30] Proponents of this option argue that its de-emphasis of conventional strikes on the Chinese mainland makes it less escalatory.

These three approaches encompass a broad range of American military strategies toward China.[31] And, of course, any strategy implemented by the US will likely combine elements of the poles described earlier. That said, given limited resources and the competing demands of other strategic challenges, American leaders, both in and out of uniform, will have to make tough choices about strategies toward China and will likely be reluctant to embrace all force structure and war planning recommendations made by the strategists described earlier. Therefore, American defense policymakers will need to assess and compare these strategies. Fortunately, this assessment process has begun in earnest.[32] This book attempts to contribute further to this process of policy analysis by focusing on the willingness of an American president and the presidential advisors to authorize or recommend mainland strikes—conventional strikes on the Chinese mainland—during a possible future US-China war.

THE MAINLAND STRIKES DEBATE

The US military strategies described earlier can be differentiated by their attitude toward mainland strikes. This disagreement is a mostly unexamined and certainly unresolved issue in the broader debate.[33]

One of the earliest references to the issue that mainland strikes pose for American military strategy toward China can be found in a 1999 RAND report. Zalmay Khalizad and his coauthors wrote:

> It is difficult to imagine that the United States would wage a largely unconstrained strategic air campaign as in Operation Desert Storm against an opponent that could wreak devastation on the American homeland, both because the United States would be concerned about crossing a threshold that might trigger Chinese nuclear retaliation and because the United States might not want to break all communications links between the Chinese leadership and its nuclear forces.[34]

In contrast to Khalizad's notes of trepidation, CSBA's 2010 report emphasized the likelihood of mainland strikes by way of noting their military necessity. Jan van Tol and his fellow writers warned, "according these targets ["high-leverage" targets inside China] sanctuary status would severely undermine US attempts to maintain a stable military balance in the Western Pacific."[35] Strategists David Ochmanek and Elbridge Colby have embraced a similar line of argument, though they have also noted that a US administration would likely (and should) only strike targets in the geographic areas near the site of conflict.[36]

Another camp argues that mainland strikes are dangerous and are much less likely to be authorized than some past CSBA writings imply. Chinese possession of nuclear weapons, according to T. X. Hammes, the analyst most closely associated with this camp, will loom too large in elite decision-making, preventing authorization of conventional strikes due to fear of escalation to nuclear war.[37] Similarly, Jeffrey Kline and Wayne Hughes have classified mainland strikes as "potentially escalatory," and Eric Heginbotham and Jacob Heim have suggested that mainland strikes "may well be inadvisable when confronting a nuclear-armed great power."[38] Michael Beckley has written that a doctrine that emphasizes mainland strikes "risks turning conventional wars into nuclear wars."[39] Joshua Rovner has also highlighted the dangers of mainland strikes, though he argues that there is a dilemma for American policymakers between the twin perils of nuclear escalation and protracted conventional war.[40]

Both camps rely mostly on intuitive logic and brief references to history to support their case. Neither marshals a systematic, empirical approach to examine the conditions under which a future US administration in a war with China would or would not authorize conventional strikes on the Chinese mainland. Nor has any other researcher attempted this task. That said, Caitlin Talmadge has published on a closely related topic: whether China would use nuclear weapons during a conventional conflict with the United States. She analyzes the technical and strategic reasons China might turn a conflict nuclear. But her research does not deal directly with what US decision-makers would do in a conflict.[41]

THE POLICY IMPLICATIONS OF THIS DEBATE

Military planners would benefit greatly from a more accurate and empirical understanding of the conditions under which mainland strikes will or will not be authorized in order to inform force planning and war planning. Generals and admirals at Indo-Pacific Command, officials in the Office of Secretary of Defense, and all concerned with American military strategy have an interest in understanding the likelihood and conditions under which mainland China will or will not be a sanctuary. The policy implications of this this research are threefold.

First, to the extent that this research suggests that current American military strategy toward China rests on unsound assumptions about the likelihood of mainland strikes, American strategists can devise new, alternative concepts of operations to counter the operational challenges posed by a strengthened Chinese military. This sort of new thinking can be seen in the work of David Gompert, T. X. Hammes, and the recent writings of CSBA.[42] These thinkers are searching for alternative strategies and concepts of operations because they believe that a president could be reluctant to authorize conventional strikes on the Chinese mainland.

Second, those charged with planning future military forces might design and procure different weapon systems based on different beliefs about the likelihood that conventional strikes on the Chinese mainland might or might not be authorized. For instance, Wayne Hughes has advocated that the navy purchase relatively small, cruise missile-equipped ships able to conduct a "war-at-sea" strategy that at least delays the decision to strike targets on the Chinese mainland.[43] Credible evidence on the likelihood of mainland strikes being authorized can help foster a salutary conversation on the benefits and disadvantages of different American force planning assumptions about potential conflict with China.

Third, this research can help the American national-security community develop a more accurate picture of a future US-China war, informing their assessment of the relative difficulty for US forces. Military commanders and civilian planners might then have a more refined understanding of potential casualty levels and equipment losses under different scenarios.

Perhaps most importantly, this book rests on the conviction that any changes in US military strategy toward China—including concepts of operations, procurement, and war planning—ought to rely on systematic, rigorous research that subjects the arguments of both sides of the mainland strikes debate to equally intense scrutiny.

To help an analyst grapple with the study of mainland strikes, the next chapters provide a series of theoretical lenses and methodological approaches.

Notes

1. Heginbotham, Nixon, Morgan, Heim, Hagen, Li, Engstrom, Libicki, DeLuca, Shlapak, Frelinger, Laird, Brady, and Morris, *The U.S-China Military Scorecard*, xxxii.
2. Shlapak, Orletsky, Reid, Tanner, and Wilson, *A Question of Balance*, xix.
3. Christensen, "Posing Problems without Catching Up,"; Cliff, Burles, Chase, Eaton, and Pollpeter, *Entering the Dragon's Lair*; Montgomery, "Contested Primacy in the Western Pacific."; Stillion and Orletsky, *Air Base Vulnerability to Conventional Cruise-Missile and Ballistic-Missile Attacks*.
4. Yoshihara and Holmes, *Red Star over the Pacific*; Cliff, *China's Military Power*; Fisher, *China's Military Modernization*.
5. Heginbotham et al., *The U.S-China Military Scorecard*, 45–70.
6. Heginbotham et al., 69; for an argument that that the RAND analysis is, in fact, optimistic, see Goldstein, "The US-China Naval Balance in the Asia-Pacific," 910–912.
7. Hagen, "Potential Effects of Chinese Aerospace Capabilities on US Air Force Operations."
8. Shugart and Gonzales, *First Strike*, 13.
9. Vick, "Air Base Attacks and Defensive Counters," 11–17.
10. The end of "sanctuary" for air bases is a concept borrowed from Vick, 19–37.
11. Mastro and Easton, *Risk and Resiliency*, 10–13.
12. Hendrix, *Retreat from Range*, 48, 51; Cropsey, McGrath, and Walton, *Sharpening the Spear*.
13. For an analysis that examined the limits of Chinese surveillance capabilities beyond its borders, see Biddle and Oelrich, "Future Warfare in the Western Pacific." For a debate on this topic, see Erickson, Montgomery, Neuman, Biddle, and Oelrich, "Correspondence: How Good Are China's Antiaccess/Area-Denial Capabilities?"
14. Beckley, "The Emerging Military Balance in East Asia"; for a counter-argument, see Sharp, Meyers and Beckley, "Correspondence: Will East Asia Balance Against Beijing?"
15. Chase, Engstrom, Cheung, Gunness, Harold, Puska, and Berkowitz, *China's Incomplete Military Transformation*.
16. Grossman and Meyers, "Minding the Gaps."

17. van Tol et al., *AirSea Battle*. For a shorter report less focused on the military-operational aspects of AirSea Battle, see Krepenevich, *Why AirSea Battle?*. For an analysis that labels this approach as all-aspects dominance, see Heginbotham and Heim, "Deterring without Dominance." Some analysts have argued that a mainland-strikes military strategy is not a strategy. Because it involves a problem framing (anti-access/area-denial capabilities) and a solution (mainland strikes), I argue it is.
18. My emphasis on a couple past CSBA reports should not be mistaken for a belief that these reports represent the sum total of views by CSBA analysts and researchers past and present on this topic.
19. For a discussion of anti-access/area-denial capabilities and "blinding strikes," see van Tol et al., "AirSea Battle," 17–47, 56–60.
20. van Tol et al., "AirSea Battle," 51.
21. Colby, "Don't Sweat AirSea Battle"; Colby, "The War over War with China"; Friedberg, *Beyond Air-Sea Battle*.
22. Hammes, *Offshore Control,* National Defense University, Strategic Forum; Hammes, "Offshore Control," *Military Strategy Magazine*. Hammes groups maritime denial and blockade together under the header of "offshore control." A future decision-maker could indeed combine these options. For analytical simplicity, I split these military strategies apart.
23. Hammes, "Offshore Control," National Defense University, Strategic Forum, 6.
24. Kline and Hughes, "Between Peace and the Air-Sea Battle." Some strategists call this the "feet wet" option.
25. Heginbotham and Heim, "Deterring without Dominance," 18.
26. Heginbotham and Heim, 193–194.
27. Tangredi, "Keep War Confined to the 'Seas.'"
28. Manhken, Sharp, Fabian, and Kouretsos, *Tightening the Chain*; Heim, *Missiles for Asia?*; Bonds, Predd, Heath, Chase et al., *What Role Can Land-Based, Multi-Doman Anti-Access/Area Denial Forces Play in Deterring or Defeating Aggression?*.
29. Mirski, "Stranglehold"; for a response to this article, see Montgomery, "Reconsidering a Naval Blockade"; see also Peifer, "China, the German Analogy and the New AirSea Operational Concept"; Collins and Murray, "No Oil for the Lamps of China?"; Collins, "A Maritime Oil Blockade Against China."
30. Mirski, "Stranglehold," 409; Cunningham, "The Maritime Rung on the Escalation Ladder."

31. It is worth noting that there is a broader debate about American grand strategy toward China. This book focuses on military strategy. For treatments of American grand strategy and China, see O'Hanlon and Steinberg, *A Glass Half Full?*; Christensen, *The China Challenge*; Goldstein, *Meeting China Halfway*; White, *The China Choice*.
32. Friedberg, *Beyond Air-Sea Battle*; Ochmanek, "Sustaining US Leadership in the Asia-Pacific Region"; Mahnken, "A Maritime Strategy to Deal with China."
33. An exception to the "unexamined" part of the claim is one research project based on a single case study. Meyers, "Will a President Approve Air-Sea Battle?"; Meyers, "The Real Problem with Strikes on Mainland China."
34. Khalizad, Shulsky, Byman, Cliff, Orletsky, Shlapak, and Tellis, *The United States and a Rising China*, 47.
35. van Tol et al., *AirSea Battle*.
36. Ochmanek, *Sustaining US Leadership in the Asia-Pacific Region*, 12; Colby, "The War over War with China."
37. See footnote 23 of this chapter for the main writings of T. X. Hammes on the topic.
38. Kline and Hughes, "Between Peace and the Air-Sea Battle," 35; Heim and Heginbotham, "Deterring without Dominance," 191.
39. Beckley, "The Emerging Military Balance in East Asia," 118.
40. Rovner, "Two Kinds of Catastrophe." See also Dougherty, *Why America Needs a New Way of War*, 20–21.
41. Talmadge, "Would China Go Nuclear?"
42. Gompert and Kelly, "Escalation Cause"; Gompert, "Sea Power and American Interests in the Western Pacific"; Gompert, Cevallos, and Garafola, "War with China"; Manhken, Sharp, Fabian, and Kouretsos, *Tightening the Chain*.
43. Kline and Hughes, "Between Peace and the Air-Sea Battle."

Chapter 2

The Theoretical Backdrop

The debate over mainland strikes—which can also be framed as a debate about the likelihood of conventional escalation during a war between nuclear-armed powers—has deep theoretical roots. In fact, past scholarship provides useful theories to understand the general conditions under which conventional strikes on the homeland of a nuclear power might or might not be authorized. Competing perspectives on nuclear weapons, scenarios, and the role of individuals all inform any judgment about the likelihood of conventional escalation in a US-China war.

The final portion of this chapter introduces the methodological approaches used to study the determinants of conventional escalation and mainland strikes. One section covers the use of historical case studies, another the interviews of American national-security elites, and a final section discusses the use of a scenario-based survey of American national-security elites.

Theories of Conventional Escalation and Mainland Strikes

Skeptics of mainland strikes believe that Chinese nuclear weapons reduce the probability of mainland strikes to nearly zero; for example, T. X. Hammes noted that "the United States must accept that China's nuclear arsenal imposes restrictions on the way American forces might attack Chinese assets."[1] An American president, this camp argues, would be loath to risk nuclear war by embracing so escalatory a tactic as strikes on the homeland of a nuclear adversary. CSBA's 2010 writings on *AirSea Battle*, the most forceful exposition of an operational concept relying primarily on mainland strikes, embraces an alternative perspective, though their argument is mostly implicit. Chinese and American nuclear weapons cancel each other out, creating mutual nuclear deterrence and thus freeing the American military to pursue escalatory tactics, such as conventional strikes, on the Chinese mainland[2]

Both camps are drawing on venerable traditions in the world of nuclear strategy. But there has been surprisingly little connection made to date between nuclear strategy and conventional escalation. The seminal work on conventional escalation, Richard Smoke's *War: Controlling Escalation*, devotes only a single, somewhat dismissive paragraph to nuclear weapons. It is worth quoting him in full to understand the motivation for this chapter's close attention to nuclear weapons and conventional escalation.

> The other piece is the assertion that in all recent military conflicts policy-makers have had in the back of their minds the possibility that sometime, somehow, the war might "go nuclear," and that this has made a difference in their decisions, even in low-level conventional conflicts. This is true, I think, yet I am uncertain how much difference it has made—and in what directions(s) the implications point. On the one hand, it can be argued that the nuclear possibility makes everyone more cautious; on the other, it can be argued that it makes the scope much greater for brinksmanship, for calculated efforts to make gains by appearing irrational ("playing chicken"), and for other ways of deliberately

manipulating a shared risk as part of one's strategy. Which is it? In my opinion, probably some of both.[3]

Smoke's choice to focus on pre-nuclear era cases perhaps contributed to his judgment. This chapter develops and extends Smoke's proto-theorizing.

Two terms require definition before the reader can be equipped with the necessary theoretical tools. First, conventional escalation refers to increases in the intensity or geographic scope of non-nuclear violence that cross significant thresholds according to the participants involved.[4] It should be emphasized that this definition of escalation relies on the subjective judgments of the participants. Conventional strikes on the homeland of a nuclear power, particularly the Chinese mainland, can be appropriately categorized as a form of conventional escalation given that many participants in this debate have viewed mainland strikes as escalatory.[5] Because the debate over mainland strikes has been in large part about wartime rules of engagement, the analysis in this book concerns itself with *intra-war* conventional escalation—that is, escalation after a crisis or war has started.

Nuclear symmetry is the second concept that requires an explanation. Nuclear symmetry exists when both states in a crisis or war possess nuclear weapons and delivery systems capable of striking relevant targets.[6] Some analysts could understandably prefer a definition that restricts nuclear symmetry to situations in which both sides possess secure second-strike arsenals, a nuclear posture invulnerable to an adversary's surprise attack. These analysts could argue that small nuclear arsenals, which lack protection from an enemy's first strike, should not count as nuclear symmetry. Although there is some theory and evidence to support this view, the line between secure second-strike and other arsenals is murky and worthy of a dedicated research project.[7] Given this blurriness, this project takes no definitive stand and instead pays attention to this concern in its empirical sections, especially the historical case studies.

Three models—caution, null, and emboldenment—predict different effects of nuclear symmetry on conventional escalation.

The Caution Model
This model suggests that nuclear symmetry introduces extreme caution into decision-making on conventional escalation. When conflict does occur between nuclear states, each side employs force with severe operational restraints to avoid the catastrophic prospect of nuclear war. The simplest formulation of this school of thought might be: nuclear symmetry creates extreme caution. Two mechanisms exist by which nuclear weapons generate caution. The high-costs logic emphasizes the tremendous costs of nuclear war. The accidental war logic argues that leaders fear that conventional escalation could result in accidental or inadvertent nuclear use. As a result, leaders restrain their actions and limit conventional escalation to minimize the possibility of accidental nuclear war. This thinking found expression in the Cold War period through "limited war" literature.[8]

Kenneth Waltz, in a 1981 monograph, made the argument that more nuclear weapons mean more peace and a reduced chance of conventional escalation. On the importance of nuclear weapons as a force for peace, he wrote, "they [nuclear weapons] make the cost of war seem frighteningly high."[9] He further explained that "the presence of nuclear weapons makes states exceedingly cautious."[10] The consequence of nuclear weapons for conventional conflict between nuclear rivals is that "war has been confined geographically and limited militarily."[11]

Robert Jervis also predicted that the high cost of mutual nuclear destruction will create tremendous caution during encounters between nuclear powers. Nuclear weapons, Jervis argued, are distinct from even massive uses of conventional force because nuclear devastation would be "unimaginably enormous," mutual, and potentially swift.[12] After noting the "unusual...caution with which each superpower has treated the other," he then offered a concise explanation of the total-destruction logic.[13] He wrote, "nuclear weapons can explain superpower caution: when the cost of seeking excessive gains is an increased probability of total destruction, moderation makes sense."[14]

Other prominent international relations scholars have made a similar argument, pinning the pacifying effects of nuclear weapons on the high-costs logic.[15] This mechanism reduces the probability that nuclear states will engage in conflict and reduces conventional escalation should war occur.

A second logic by which nuclear weapons induce caution and reduce the incentives for conventional escalation is the fear of accidental nuclear war.[16] As a result, leaders and advisors might avoid tactics that have battlefield utility but which could increase the probability of accidental nuclear use.

The term "accidental" is intentionally broad and subsumes not only accidental but also inadvertent nuclear use.[17] Fear of accidental nuclear use includes fear that the enemy's nuclear forces might be used even though the adversary's leadership did not wish to use them. This pathway to nuclear war has been explored by scholars including Paul Bracken, Bruce Blair, Scott Sagan, and Eric Schlosser and includes proximate causes like mechanical failures and failures of command and control.[18] For this research, accidental use also includes what has been termed "inadvertent" nuclear use. Inadvertent nuclear use occurs when a combatant's actions are unintentionally escalatory, crossing a threshold of one party that the other party failed to realize was a redline. A reluctance to use conventional escalation could therefore arise from an uncertainty over adversary red lines related to nuclear use.

A relatively new pathway to accidental nuclear war arises from nuclear-conventional entanglement, systems that have both "conventional" warfighting roles and roles related to nuclear warfare.[19] Recent scholarship has speculated in particular about the precise ways that Chinese nuclear systems are entangled and the implications of this entanglement for American military strategy and the possibility of a US-China conventional war becoming a nuclear war.[20] Scholars have worried that if the United States employs mainland strike—conventional strikes on targets located on the Chinese mainland—Chinese leaders could misperceive these strikes as part of a disarming, counterforce campaign. This risk of misperception, these writers theorize, could increase the probability that China actually uses nuclear weapons in a future US-China war.

To buttress their claim, scholars argue that great-power politics before the atomic bomb was a deadly affair that twice in the twentieth century resulted in world war. Only NATO and Soviet possession of nuclear weapons prevented inevitable Cold War crises from spiraling out of control.[21] When crisis did occur, notably during the Cuban Missile Crisis, both sides restrained their use of conventional force, limiting the amount of force employed and restricting the geography of conflict, in order to reduce the possibility of nuclear war.[22] The caution model also predicts reduced conventional escalation in India-Pakistan crises because "states approaching nuclear conflict invariably retreat from confrontation."[23] Scholars cite other historical cases too.[24]

This school of thought can also point to statistical evidence in favor of its argument, though these articles tend to focus on the occurrence of war rather than the extent of conventional escalation. Victor Asal and Kyle Beardsley have published two quantitative articles whose key findings support the caution model.[25] Robert Rauchhaus, employing Correlates of War data, also found that nuclear weapons significantly and dramatically reduced the occurrence of major war.[26] Other scholars, using increasingly advanced statistical techniques, have come to similar conclusions.[27]

The caution model therefore expects that an adversary's possession of nuclear weapons will cause leaders to exercise restraint when using force, that is, to dampen conventional escalation. The caution model, in the historical case studies presented later, predicts that US leaders did not strike some targets for fear of nuclear escalation. Similarly, for the interview and survey portion of this book, this theory suggests that elites will be fearful of potential Chinese nuclear use despite US

The Theoretical Backdrop

possession of nuclear weapons. For a modern war between the United States and a nuclear-armed power, this theory predicts that an American president will exercise extreme caution in authorizing conventional strikes on the adversary's homeland. A president and their advisors will foresee pathways that lead to nuclear war and restrict American rules of engagement and the level of force used in order to minimize nuclear danger.

The Null Model

According to the null model, mutual nuclear possession produces no discernible effect on conventional escalation compared to a world free of nuclear weapons. Nuclear powers treat other nuclear powers as if the nuclear revolution never occurred. War between nuclear powers remains possible and crises between nuclear adversaries are just as likely to spin out of control as crises between non-nuclear states. When leaders consider using force against a nuclear-armed adversary, they do not act particularly cautiously and do not restrain their decisions on conventional escalation for fear of nuclear war. Instead, leaders act much the way leaders have always acted, sometimes cautiously, sometimes incautiously. Nuclear weapons are only a minor part of the decision-making equation.

John Mueller's article "The Essential Irrelevance of Nuclear Weapons" captures the central propositions of scholars who argue that nuclear weapons are irrelevant in explaining patterns of conflict and escalation in international politics.[28] These scholars believe that the same forces that explain escalation in conflict between non-nuclear powers explain conflict between nuclear-armed adversaries. Mueller explained his logic with a metaphor:

> It is probably quite a bit more terrifying to think about a jump from the 50th floor than about a jump from the 5th floor, but anyone who finds life even minimally satisfying is extremely unlikely to do either.[29]

Mueller conceded that nuclear war is particularly horrific, but he postulated that major war, even absent nuclear weapons, has already become sufficiently costly such that it induces caution among leaders. Richard Ned Lebow similarly saw pre-nuclear and post-nuclear crisis and war behavior by statesmen as essentially the same. He wrote:

> If willingness to accept war as an outcome of crisis is measured along a continuum ranging from least to most, nuclear crises are certainly to be found clustered around the negative pole, but, as we have seen, some conventional crises are to be found there as well...Thus, the distinctions between conventional and nuclear crises may be more in degree than in kind.[30]

War and the results of higher levels of conventional escalation can be undesirable even in crises without nuclear weapons. Restraints on the use of force, according to the null model, are not the inevitable byproduct of nuclear weapons.

Robert McNamara advanced an alternative logic to explain the minimal role that nuclear weapons play in international politics. In a 1983 *Foreign Affairs* article, he wrote, "they [nuclear weapons] are totally useless—except to deter one's opponent from using them."[31] This logic suggests that two nuclear arsenals cancel each other out. The leaders of each state recognize that their opponent could retaliate with nuclear weapons in response to nuclear first use, and therefore nuclear weapons become useless, except, of course, to deter nuclear use by the adversary.

Vipin Narang's theorizing on nuclear postures has also endorsed this logic. He postulated a theory that suggests that an "assured retaliation" nuclear posture fails to deter even intense conventional attacks and escalatory conventional tactics.[32] His analysis of Pakistani and Indian foreign-policy behavior and a separate statistical analysis bolster his theorizing.[33] Nuclear weapons produce stalemate and therefore allow statesmen to conduct international politics as usual, using force as if nuclear weapons did not exist at all.

Null model advocates point to historical evidence in favor of their theory. Richard Ned Lebow analyzed twenty-six historical crises—including six from the post–World War II atomic era—and found that crisis behavior differed little before and after the advent of nuclear weapons.[34] Writing in 1981, Lebow stated, "the generic cause of crisis, the principles of strategic bargaining and the problems of crisis decision-making, appear to have changed very little during the last fifty or even seventy-five years."[35] John Mueller argued that nuclear weapons are unnecessary to explain the absence of direct conflict between the United States and the Soviet Union.[36] He wrote:

> nuclear weapons and the image of destruction they inspire were not necessary to induce the people who have been running world affairs since 1945 to be extremely wary of repeating the experience of World War II (or for that matter, of World War I).[37]

Research on the 1969 Sino-Soviet border war provides some support for the null model too; a close reading of secondary Soviet and Chinese sources finds that China's nascent nuclear arsenal did not explain the Soviet Union's decision to forego a wider attack on China.[38]

A range of statistical studies lend further support to the null model. Paul Huth and Bruce Russett found that possession of nuclear weapons fails to predict successful deterrence of attack on a third party ("extended deterrence") in a dataset of fifty-four post-1900 cases.[39] Erik Gartzke and Dong-Joon Jo used militarized interstate dispute data from 1945 to 2001 and found that nuclear weapons do not affect conflict propensity.[40] Similarly, Mark S. Bell and Nicholas L. Miller reevaluated the analysis of Robert Rauchhaus, mentioned in the caution model section, concluding that interactions between nuclear-armed states are not significantly less likely to result in war.[41] Other empirical quantitative studies have come to similar conclusions.[42]

The logic of the null model predicts that a leader will be willing to use force or escalatory measures against nuclear-armed adversaries. In the historical case studies presented later in the book, the null model, if correct, suggests that top decision-makers will select targets and write rules of engagement without regard for the enemy's nuclear capabilities. The model also suggests that the interviews and surveys of American national-security elites, the other methods employed in the book, will uncover that these professionals are either indifferent or unafraid of Chinese nuclear weapons when considering conventional strikes on the Chinese mainland. The implications of the null model for strikes on the homeland of a nuclear power are clear: an American administration would view adversary nuclear threats as incredible and therefore feel free to strike targets on an adversary's homeland as operational concerns dictate. For instance, an administration could believe that the American nuclear arsenal makes adversary nuclear use irrational, enabling the use of conventional forces as if nuclear forces did not exist at all.

Nuclear Emboldenment
A third school of thought views nuclear symmetry as potentially increasing the frequency and intensity of conflict and conventional escalation between nuclear-armed rivals. Nuclear arsenals neither induce caution nor simply produce stalemate. Instead, nuclear weapons and especially nuclear superiority can be used to bargain during crisis and war, enabling states to achieve outcomes more favorable than those in a non-nuclear world. In fact, leaders might use ever higher levels of conventional force against another nuclear power due to their belief that their rival fears nuclear escalation to a greater degree. In other words, nuclear weapons can be marshalled to use levels of conventional force that might otherwise be eschewed.

Matthew Kroenig explicated the chain of assumptions that connects nuclear superiority to behavior in crises between nuclear-armed states.[43] Possessing a larger nuclear arsenal compared to another nuclear adversary first convinces the leader of the state with superiority that it will incur less cost in the event of nuclear war than it otherwise would if it lacked nuclear superiority. This confidence leads to an increase in resolve.

Buoyed by this increase in resolve and willing to "push harder," the state with nuclear superiority can use riskier tactics, greater levels of force, and ultimately achieve victory.

Another logic, the stability-instability paradox, predicts that mutual nuclear possession leads to increases in the frequency and intensity in the use of conventional force between nuclear rivals. This logic claims that nuclear weapons enable both sides to engage in "low-level" uses of force with impunity. Glenn Snyder most famously formulated this theory: "the greater the stability of the 'strategic' balance, the lower the stability of the overall balance at lower levels of violence."[44] Robert Jervis has also contributed to this theory, characterizing it in this way: "to the extent that military balance is stable at the level of all-out nuclear war, it will become less stable at lower levels of violence."[45]

In plain language, the stability-instability paradox predicts that when both adversaries possess nuclear weapons, perhaps especially when both achieve secure second-strike status, then both states will engage in more provocative behavior at "lower" levels of conflict.[46] "Stability" in the nuclear realm, often defined as a state of mutually assured destruction, results in "instability," in the form of more use of conventional force and conventional escalation at all levels short of nuclear war.

Believers in emboldenment, especially the nuclear superiority logic, often point to the Cuban Missile Crisis as an example that lends credence to their argument. Marc Trachtenberg made a version of this argument when he claimed that in the Cuban Missile Crisis "the Soviets seem to have been profoundly affected by their 'strategic inferiority.'"[47] In this interpretation, the effect of American nuclear superiority was to "tie their [the Soviet's] hands, to limit their freedom of maneuver, and thus to increase their incentive to settle the crisis quickly."[48] Matthew Kroenig, the key modern proponent of theories of nuclear superiority, has also pointed to the Cuban Missile Crisis for evidence. He cites statements by several senior American officials—Chairman of the Joint Chiefs of Staff General Maxwell Taylor, Secretary of State Dean Rusk and other anonymous senior officials—that suggest that the favorable American nuclear balance increased the resolve of the American side.[49] Some scholars also point to India-Pakistan crisis behavior as similar evidence of nuclear emboldenment.[50]

The emboldenment school also relies on statistical evidence. Kroenig defines this line of research; using a dataset of twenty post–World War II crises, he argues that nuclear superiority leads to victory in crisis.[51] Rauchhaus's statistical research, mentioned earlier in the caution-school section, also bears on the emboldenment school. His statistical results conform with the predictions of the stability-instability paradox: the statistical analysis suggests that disputes, disputes with fatalities, and uses of force all increase under conditions of nuclear symmetry.[52] Nuclear weapons might therefore provide a shield from behind which nuclear-armed states are even more willing (compared to a nuclear-free world) to challenge even nuclear-armed adversaries.

The emboldenment model sees leaders employing more and greater conventional escalation in situations of mutual nuclear possession compared to a nuclear-free world. Due either to nuclear superiority or the freeing effects of the stability-instability paradox, this school of thought sees more conflict, potentially waged at greater intensity, among nuclear-armed states. In the historical case studies, the emboldenment model suggests that decision-makers may opt for escalatory uses of conventional force against nuclear opponents. The model further suggests the interviewees and survey takers will be willing to authorize mainland strikes to the extent that they perceive America to be in a position of nuclear superiority or that they believe America's nuclear arsenal shields it from Chinese counteractions.

The emboldenment model implies that American decision-makers will be willing to authorize conventional strikes on the homeland of a nuclear power, if decisionmakers perceive American nuclear superiority or there is a belief that nuclear weapons provide protection from escalatory Chinese responses.

SCENARIO CHARACTERISTICS

The characteristics of a scenario also potentially explain levels of conventional escalation. The scenario includes, for instance, the actions and preferences of an ally, enemy actions, military-operational aspects, and the availability of other foreign-policy tools. Scenario characteristics lack systematic treatment in international relations scholarship. Individual pieces of scholarship sometimes emphasize scenario-related variables, but there is no theoretical category for these variables with the same status as Kenneth Waltz's three images: individuals, states, and the international system.[53] Readers who wonder if this lack of focus on scenarios is the result of a disciplinary focus on system-level outcomes in international relations might be surprised that even *Foreign Policy Analysis*, the journal devoted to studying a state's foreign policy, has an explicitly "actor-specific" focus.[54] Scenario characteristics and their effects on phenomena within international relations is an under-theorized and under-explored aspect of international relations. This section describes several salient features of a scenario that potentially bear on a decision-maker's or advisor's willingness to authorize (or recommend) conventional escalation, particularly mainland strikes.

This theoretical perspective is also motivated by the observation that participants in the early mainland strikes debate often stressed different and sometimes contrasting scenario characteristics when analyzing the likelihood of mainland strikes. Past analysis from CSBA often highlights the likelihood of Chinese conventional strikes on American forces in the Pacific during a future US-China conflict; T. X. Hammes' writings do not accentuate this scenario factor to the same degree.[55] These divergent views of a future war could partially explain their different attitudes toward mainland strikes. Similarly, CSBA's 2010 analyses often emphasized relatively comprehensive conventional strikes on the Chinese mainland as part of a "blinding" campaign whereas Elbridge Colby's analyses tend to note the possibility of relatively limited strikes on the Chinese mainland. This potential difference in scenarios could also be salient in a future conflict.

Ally Actions and Preferences
Alexander George and Richard Smoke originally identified the important role of allies in defining the likelihood and nature of American conventional escalation.[56] American foreign policy is often executed on behalf of its allies and partners, and American conduct in East Asia is no exception. Any conflict with China would likely involve an American ally or partner: Japan, South Korea, the Philippines, or, most importantly for this research, Taiwan. The conflict could even be fought explicitly to protect these countries from Chinese aggression. The actions and preferences of these allies could therefore be important in shaping American elite and public attitudes toward conventional escalation.

If an ally acts recklessly or otherwise provokes an attack upon itself, American decision-makers could be less inclined to intervene, and even if they did intervene, decision-makers might be less inclined to cross conventional escalation thresholds. In the case of Taiwan, past American strategy has emphasized that strong American support is predicated upon a moderate Taiwanese policy toward China and cross-strait relations.[57] Additionally, should an ally prefer to be left out of a conflict and therefore potentially shielded from the harm of war or the harm of a particular action, it might object to American use of bases for the purposes of the conflict. Moreover, allied leaders could threaten to reduce their military contributions in future conflicts. For instance, Japan could object to the use of its bases for mainland strikes. American decision-makers might heed Japanese objections in order to protect the alliance relationship.

Enemy Actions
Because the enemy can influence how a war will play out, their actions must be a central part of a framework for scenario characteristics. Enemy decision-makers play a part in controlling the pace and geography of war, influencing the pace of escalation in the process. Their actions can

create American casualties and attrition, cross American redlines, and play a role in defining the situation American policymakers face. These actions can also indicate how aggressive they are, shaping American perceptions of future adversary behavior and the appropriateness of a given American response.[58] More escalatory enemy actions will likely lead to a greater willingness on the behalf of American leaders and advisors to recommend conventional escalation and mainland strikes.

Operational Aspects
A host of factors related to a proposed military operation can also influence the likelihood of an American president embracing a particular action. The geographic location of a target can be important; its location near international borders, across an international border, or near diplomatically sensitive sites, for instance, could all affect whether a particular conventional escalation threshold will be crossed.

Two factors are especially worth highlighting. First, the early stages of a scenario could differ greatly from later stages. The first days, weeks, or even months of a conflict can be filled with uncertainty about potential enemy actions, the possibility of peaceful resolution, and other considerations. Decision-makers might be reluctant to use greater levels of force before the situation becomes clearer. Second, the probability of operational failure and the possibility of failing to accomplish key political and military objectives will surely be an important part of any calculation to use mainland strikes. All things equal, the worse the prospects for political and operational victory, the greater the need and likelihood of mainland strikes.

Availability of Other Foreign-Policy Tools
A final formal category of scenario-related characteristics concerns the availability of alternative foreign-policy tools in a given situation.[59] Decision-makers and advisors considering a particular form of conventional escalation, such as the possible initiation and extent of mainland strikes, must weigh that option against relevant alternatives. Diplomatic,

economic, and even other military alternatives might all outperform some form of conventional escalation, leading the president and his advisors to shelve a particular action. The implication is that decision-makers with more appealing alternatives to some form of conventional escalation will, all things equal, be less likely to endorse conventional escalation. In this sense, conventional escalation will only be considered by its *relative* merits and not on an absolute scale.

INDIVIDUALS

That different individuals might make different foreign-policy decisions is both appealing to common sense and backed—to varying degrees—by a long research tradition in political science. A theoretical emphasis and investigation of leaders (so-called first-image theorizing) has been an important, though sometimes criticized, part of international-relations theorizing since Kenneth Waltz's *Man, the State, and War*.[60] And although the mainland-strikes debate in its written form has largely omitted discussion of the role of individual leaders and administrations, analysts have often voiced to me their perceptions that the beliefs and attributes of the future American president and the president's advisors surely matter in determining the likelihood and scope of mainland strikes.

This section therefore articulates several attributes and beliefs of individuals that are potentially linked to a willingness to endorse higher levels of conventional escalation in general and mainland strikes in particular.

Military Background

This study pays particular attention to the effect of current or prior military service on the willingness of a leader or advisor to authorize conventional escalation during war. A focus on military service as a determinant of foreign-policy attitudes and behavior has a long history in strategic-studies scholarship. Samuel Huntington's *The Soldier and the*

State first articulated the idea of a distinct military mindset that "rarely favors war" compared to the preferences of his civilian counterparts.[61] Richard Betts built on this idea, arguing that military officers have distinct pre-war and intra-war attitudes toward the use of force.[62] Drawing on early Cold War historical cases, including the Korean War and Vietnam War, he argued prewar caution transforms into a preference for intra-war escalation. In a reference to the attitudes of military officers after a war starts, he writes, "generals prefer using force quickly, massively, and decisively."[63] Betts also found that air force generals, navy admirals, and field commanders most exemplified this tendency.[64] Two statistical articles, one by Christopher Gelpi and Peter Feaver and another by Michael Horowitz and Allan Stam, find evidence that corroborates the theory advanced by Betts.[65]

Military advisors, according to Huntington's depiction of military officers as cautious realists, will eschew conventional escalation. Military officers will be less likely than their civilian peers to recommend strikes on the mainland. Bett's image of military advisors suggest the opposite once the war has begun. Military leaders will embrace conventional escalation mid-war, reflecting their preference for decisive force. Military officers might therefore have more favorable attitudes toward mainland strikes.

A vein of scholarship that explores the exact content of the so-called military mindset blossomed after the early civil-military relation texts of Huntington and Betts. In separate lines of research published in the 1980s, Barry Posen, Jack Snyder, and Stephen van Evera all developed this theoretical perspective.[66]

Political Party

Conventional wisdom among commentators on American foreign policy holds that Republicans tend to hold more "hawkish" views than Democrats. Survey evidence supports this assertion.[67] There is some recent, though tentative, evidence that Republican hawkishness also extends to views on China. In a 2017 Chicago Council of Global Affairs survey, for instance, 46 percent of Republicans and 47 percent of core supporters of President Trump backed the use of US troops if China initiated a military conflict with Japan about disputed islands. Only 35 percent of Democrats supported the use of US troops in this situation.[68] There also exists a moderately sized statistical literature that finds leaders from right-wing parties tend to use force abroad more often than their left-wing counterparts.[69] Furthermore, experimental evidence from simulated international crises buttresses the conventional wisdom.[70] Whether this relationship results from ideology, personal values, or some other connection is unclear, but the strong positive relationship between holding conservative values (or being a Republican) and holding hawkish views is clear. The implication for crisis scenarios involving mainland strikes is that conservative, Republican leaders and advisors are more likely, on average, to authorize mainland strikes.

Gender

This research also considers whether gender affects the willingness of an individual to recommend mainland strikes. Previous scholarship between gender and foreign-policy attitudes among the general public has demonstrated that "on average, women are less supportive of the use of military force for any purpose."[71] Richard Eichenberg, a scholar of public opinion and foreign policy, analyzed nearly five-hundred separate questions on American surveys between 1990 and 2003 to arrive at this conclusion.[72] A survey experiment on American adults by Deborah Jordan Brooks and Benjamin Valentino amends this finding, however; the researchers discovered that women are actually more supportive of humanitarian war than men.[73] Because this research focuses on war for strategic purposes and because Brooks and Valentino find that men are more supportive of war for strategic reasons, their research actually buttresses this study's focus on gender. Rose McDermott has also pioneered a research agenda that employs techniques from experimental psychology to examine the effects of gender on foreign-policy attitudes and decision-making. The cumulative findings, in large part based on laboratory setting crisis simulation experiments, strongly suggest that men are more likely to employ aggressive behavior during crises and conflicts.[74]

There are two caveats related to this research. The first concerns the differences between women in the general public and female foreign-policy professionals. Women who rise to leadership positions, either as an elected leader or advisor, could differ from women in the general public. One perspective holds that women in leadership positions are likely to hold attitudes similar to male foreign-policy professionals and are therefore unlikely to exhibit behavioral differences from their male peers. A second caveat relates to the extant research's focus on behavior in crisis simulations. Skeptics could wonder if female leaders behave differently than male leaders while discharging their foreign-policy duty. Perhaps the imperatives of statecraft nullify any possible gender-based differences. A nascent research agenda has broached this topic.[75] In fact, one study has even suggested that female heads of government in democracies are more likely than their male counterparts to initiate conflict.[76] Regardless, the bulk of existing evidence leads to the tentative hypothesis that female leaders and advisors would be less willing than their male counterparts to authorize strikes on the Chinese mainland.

Age
Another potential correlate of views on mainland strikes could be an individual's age. Research at RAND and the Chicago Council on Global Affairs has focused on the effect of age on foreign-policy beliefs with an emphasis on whether younger Americans possess different attitudes on national security in comparison to older Americans. The RAND researchers found that millennials (those born between 1982 and 1996) were less worried about national-security issues than people from older generations.[77] A CATO institute report, done in collaboration with the Charles Koch Institute, found that "each generation from the Silent Generation onward entered adulthood somewhat less supportive of expansive American internationalism, with more recent generations

expressing lower support for militarized approaches to achieve foreign policy goals."[78] Finally, an empirical investigation of the relationship between age and the outbreak of militarized dispute finds that older leaders are more likely to initiate and escalate disputes.[79] A simple hypothesis emerges from this literature: older leaders will be more likely to employ conventional escalation and to endorse mainland strikes.

Foreign-Policy Beliefs

One more important variable is an individual's foreign-policy beliefs. Although harder to observe than variables like military background, party, gender, and age, foreign-policy beliefs are relevant because of their logical proximity to foreign-policy behavior. For instance, leaders and advisors who believe that their enemy is unremittingly hostile are more likely to embrace more aggressive tactics than leaders and advisors who view an enemy as only semi-hostile.

Investigating beliefs and belief systems has been a staple of international-relations scholarship for the past fifty years.[80] Scholars have attempted to first identify coherent beliefs, assemble them into an internally consistent worldview, and examine their ability to predict other beliefs or even behavior.

One grouping of beliefs is how elites define and measure the national interest. Specifying the "national interest" is an important and difficult step for leaders and advisors dealing with a given foreign-policy scenario.[81] The "national interest" is often a matter of debate. Moreover, the resolution of that debate within a given individual's mind often reveals important policy preferences and potentially predicts the actions that actor will endorse. When it comes to conventional escalation, individuals who ascribe relatively more importance to the national interest at stake in a given scenario are, all things being equal, more likely to endorse higher levels of force.

Beliefs about the use of military force form the second grouping. Scholars have long identified beliefs related to the use of force as salient

The Theoretical Backdrop

and meaningful for understanding the foreign-policy attitudes of citizens and elites alike.[82] Beliefs about the use of military force can be further subdivided. Civilian-versus-military questions concern whether military officers or civilians should exert more control over the course of war and whether the goals of top military officers or the civilians should be important while prosecuting a war.[83] Another subdivision is beliefs about how force should be applied, especially whether limited uses of force are ever justified and the relative importance of defensive versus offensive operations.[84]

Finally, this project's focus on the prospect of nuclear escalation during a conventional war also calls for paying attention to the beliefs of leaders and advisors with regard to nuclear war and nuclear weapons. Will mainland strikes lead to Chinese nuclear use? Will American elites fear that Chinese leaders will misperceive mainland strikes as part of a counterforce campaign? Presumably, decision-makers who answer affirmatively to these questions will be less willing to recommend mainland strikes. Analysts could also potentially group these beliefs under a broader category of beliefs related to strategic empathy, that is, attentiveness to and awareness of the assumptions of adversary decision-makers.[85] This project will therefore focus on these nuclear-related beliefs and their connection to mainland strikes.

FINAL THOUGHTS ON THE THREE THEORETICAL PERSPECTIVES

The three perspectives presented here—the role of nuclear weapons, scenario characteristics, and individuals—are used to focus the analytical attention of the remainder of this research. Other perspectives such as structural factors like unipolarity versus bipolarity or regime characteristics (democracy versus autocracy) might also matter in a future mainland-strikes decision, but pursuing all of these analytical angles is beyond the scope of any one research project. Duly noted is the important implication that these theoretical perspectives have had on the course of this research project. Their selection derived in part from the content of the mainland-strikes debate that transpired in the early 2010s and in part from my own reading of international-relations scholarship. Other researchers would doubtless emphasize or deemphasize other conceptual factors.

Methods for Studying the Mainland Strikes Decision

My selection of methodologies for studying the willingness of a future American president and their advisors to authorize or recommend conventional strikes on the Chinese mainland starts with the project's central methodological problem. As more than a few persons have pointed out and have done their best to convince me, researchers cannot study the future. Scholars lack a crystal ball to study an event that has never happened. The so-called mainland-strikes decision, if one embraces this research logic, can therefore not be studied. It is an event that has thankfully never occurred. But I must respectfully disagree, at least partially. This initial section thus explains my use of traditional historical methods and also of an approach I term "synthetic history." Later sections then broadly explain method-by-method my use of historical case studies, interviews with American national-security elites, and scenario-based surveys of American national-security elites.

Historical Methodologies: Traditional and Synthetic

Although it is true that conventional strikes on the Chinese mainland are the stuff of a hypothetical and hopefully unlikely potential future war, traditional and synthetic historical approaches exist that allow an analyst to shed light on this phenomenon.

Readers will be more familiar with the traditional historical approach. Historians, political scientists, and others have developed a rich literature on using history in the pursuit of knowledge about the future. The applied history school, exemplified in the work of Richard Neustadt and Ernest

May, has done an admirable job of probing the uses and abuses of history in service of policymaking, a domain that must ultimately be future-oriented.[86] Political scientists use similar historical methods, though they often focus on a relatively greater number of cases, less often do archival research, more often explicitly use social-science theory, and pay greater attention to methodological issues related to causal inference.[87] Policy analysts more broadly also often turn to history to understand emergent phenomena.[88] Because there are often historical precedents and analogues for any given phenomenon, including mainland strikes, traditional historical approaches offer one promising method for studying a future that has never occurred. In other words, one can study the past to understand, albeit imperfectly, the future.

Readers will likely be less acquainted with an approach I term "synthetic history." Scholars within security studies have embraced synthetic-history methods, although few, if any, scholars would currently identify their research with this label. Synthetic history refers to any method that creates an artificial decision-making environment and populates it with decision-making agents in order to make inferences about how similar real-world events will transpire. Researchers often turn to this approach given that actual history is far from a perfect laboratory, sometimes offering no examples of a phenomenon of interest and often precluding the researcher's control over the decision-making environment or the decision-makers. For instance, Erik Lin-Greenberg's dissertation examined how groups of American military officers participating in a crisis simulation responded when a remotely piloted aircraft (a "drone") versus a manned aircraft was shot down.[89] Reid Pauly used records from declassified political-military wargames to investigate why nuclear weapons have not been used since 1945.[90] Elizabeth Bartels and her coauthors researched the effects of different analytical products on Department of Defense decision-making by placing former officials in wargames with different analytical inputs.[91] Andrew Reddie and his coauthors have devised a "next-generation wargame," an online game that simulates international politics in the hope of studying nuclear deterrence and conflict escalation.[92] Jacqueline Schneider has used Naval War College wargames to study the influence of cyber operations on crisis and escalation.[93] Lest the reader think that this use of synthetic history is recent, it is worth pointing to a now-declassified RAND report by Marc Dean Millot and his colleagues also falls in the synthetic-history category. That report surveyed senior American military and civilian officials to understand their willingness to implement different readiness actions during a nuclear crisis scenario involving the Soviet Union.[94] Synthetic history offers the exciting prospect of studying a phenomenon that has never occurred or one that has occurred but over which a researcher had little control. Practitioners of this new method will still face problems, but this broad school of approaches does seem to offer a means for studying the future at least partially free of the constraints of the traditional historical methodology.

These approaches qualify the earlier injunction that no researcher can study the future. Analogous previous historical episodes can sometimes provide grist for a curious researcher interested in a phenomenon that has not yet and may never occur. And synthetic-historical methods can conjure up a situation similar to the one imagined. The next sections elaborate on the exact traditional and synthetic historical methods employed to study the topic of mainland strikes.

Historical Case Studies

The first analytical approach employed is that of traditional historical research. Two major case studies focus on the geographic restraints on conventional bombing during the Korean and Vietnam Wars. Based on archival research at the Harry S. Truman and Lyndon B. Johnson presidential libraries, in combination with a broader reading of secondary historical material, these two chapters examine whether nuclear weapons can account for the restraints on American bombing present in those wars and also the role of other political and military factors.

These cases were selected based on a number of criteria. Most importantly, both of these cases involve the United States engaged in a major war in which there was intense debate over the proper dimensions of the American bombing campaign. China was also a member of the adversary coalition in both wars. The crude outlines of a historical analogy to a mainland strikes decision are obvious. Also importantly, Soviet nuclear weapons, tested in 1949 a year before the start of the Korean War, could have influenced American decisions about the dimensions of its conventional bombing campaign in Korea. Chinese and Soviet nuclear weapons both could have influenced American bombing decisions in the Vietnam War. Important prior historical interpretations of these bombing campaigns have sometimes even emphasized Communist nuclear weapons as one reason for American restraint. These cases therefore provide a test bed for whether Chinese nuclear weapons will decrease the willingness of future American leaders and advisors to authorize or recommend conventional strikes on the Chinese mainland. There is also ample historical, unclassified data in English to study these wars.

Additionally, there are four minor historical case studies that provide supplementary evidence: the 1958 Taiwan Strait Crisis, the Cuban Missile Crisis, the Sino-Soviet border war, and the Kargil War. Although these case studies, taken individually, each have important limitations, their similarities to a potential future US-China war merited their inclusion.

These analytic cases do not explore the individual determinants of attitudes on conventional escalation. Though there is a literature on the causes of differing attitudes toward force among American elites during the Vietnam War, there was simply too much conceptual ground to cover within these cases to also pursue this analytical perspective. The individual perspective receives more attention in the synthetic historical methods discussed next. Finally, these cases are not perfect analogies; their limits will be explained in the appropriate chapters. But the resemblance to a future US mainland-strikes decision is close enough that analytical scrutiny yields analytic insights. Importantly, the other methods, including interviews and a survey of contemporary national-security elites, compensate for many of the weaknesses of historical case studies, and any reader who believes that a modern US-China conventional war is without precedent can still find ample relevant evidence in the other chapters.

Interviews with American National Security Elites
The second method of this project can be viewed as a first step into the methodological universe of synthetic history. This stage of the project involved interviewing twenty American national-security elites about their views toward mainland strikes during a potential future war between China and the United States. Interviewees were selected based on their long careers in national security and foreign policy. The sample was also chosen with an eye toward political diversity and to ensure representation from the Defense Department, State Department, and the intelligence agencies. The majority of interviewees had served in senior levels of responsibility within the American government, either in uniform or as a civilian. The goal was to examine the range of views on mainland strikes and to elicit the decision-making logic these elites would use in order to gauge their willingness to recommend mainland strikes. After recording and transcribing the interviews, the analysis used qualitative thematic analysis to answer two research questions. First, what role, if any, do Chinese nuclear weapons play in the decision-making about mainland strikes among these elites? Second, what scenario factors do these elites emphasize?

A Scenario-Based Survey of American National-Security Elites
The scenario-based survey of American national-security elites fully embraces the synthetic-history approach. This method entailed providing an online scenario-based survey experiment to American national-security and foreign-policy professionals working at a diverse group of American foreign-policy research institutions. The final survey sample

The Theoretical Backdrop 41

included eighty-five national-security elites. The four scenarios in each survey explored how changing scenario conditions affected respondent willingness to recommend conventional strikes on the Chinese mainland in a potential US-China war. The survey instrument also included questions about the background and foreign-policy beliefs of each respondent. The analysis largely relies on descriptive statistics, data visualization, and linear regression to understand the effects of different scenarios and respondent characteristics on the willingness of elites to recommend mainland strikes.

A Diverse Methodological Approach
These methods offer three different approaches to studying the topic of mainland strikes. The traditional historical method is retrospective. It probes the fit of the debate over geographic restrictions on conventional bombing campaigns in the Korean and Vietnam Wars (and in several minor case studies) to a potential debate over conventional strikes on the Chinese mainland in a future US-China war. These major case studies offer the advantage of providing insight into how an actual American president thinks in a relevant wartime situation and how the machinery of the American national-security bureaucracy operates in real time. The interview and survey methods are prospective and invoke what might be termed synthetic history. These approaches ask experienced national-security professionals to envision a future US-China war and to describe or reveal their decision-making logic. The interviews are a relatively rich source, but their lack of structure precludes easy comparison. The survey provides data well-suited to comparison and statistical analysis, though the survey scenarios are, of course, artificial compared to a real-world war.

Admittedly, the three methods do not answer precisely the same research questions. Instead, these methods provide three overlapping streams of evidence about the willingness of a future American president and their advisors to authorize or recommend mainland strikes in a future US-China war. Another merit of multiple streams of evidence is that readers who find the historical evidence uncompelling can focus on the evidence generated by the prospective methods and vice versa. Additionally, the streams of evidence are meant to be cross-referenced and, especially when it comes to the historical case studies, are meant to provide mutual analytical support.

This project uses the combination of three theoretical lenses and three distinct methods to study the mainland strikes issue. These lenses and methods should not be misconstrued as the definitive word on mainland strikes. Other lenses and methods are feasible and potentially worthwhile. This research does, however, attempt to be the most thorough analysis to date on the willingness of a future American president and their advisors to authorize or recommend mainland strikes. It also attempts to use relatively formal methodological approaches, borrowed from history and social science, to analyze this issue. Whether this research has succeeded or not can be measured by whether strategists, planners, and researchers who consider this question find that it illuminates the mainland strikes issue more than past analysis and intuitive logic already do.

Notes

1. Hammes, *Offshore Control*, 4; see also Hammes, "Strategy and AirSea Battle" and Hammes, "Sorry, AirSea Battle is No Strategy."
2. See the paragraph-long "critical assumption" the report authors make that "mutual nuclear deterrence holds." van Tol, Gunzinger, Krepinevich, and Thomas, *AirSea Battle*, 50.
3. Smoke, *War*, 41–42.
4. Morgan, Mueller, Medeiros, Pollpeter, and Cliff, *Dangerous Thresholds*, xi, 5.
5. See the debate between Elbridge Colby and T. X. Hammes cited in chapter 1 footnotes 22 and 23.
6. There is a large body of literature on nuclear asymmetry, or crises and wars in which one side possesses nuclear weapons and the other does not. This chapter excludes that research given that this project's focus is on the interaction between the United States and China, two nuclear-armed powers.
7. Goldstein, "Do Nascent WMD Arsenals Deter?"; Basrur objects to the evidence in Goldstein's article, however. Basrur, "Correspondence: Do Small Arsenals Deter?"
8. Osgood, *Limited War*; Halperin, "Nuclear Weapons and Limited War"; Halperin, *Limited War in the Nuclear Age*; Smoke, *War*; Osgood, *Limited War Revisited*.
9. Waltz, *The Spread of Nuclear Weapons*, 3. See also Waltz, "More May Be Better" in Sagan and Waltz, *The Spread of Nuclear Weapons*, 3–45.
10. Waltz, *The Spread of Nuclear Weapons*, 5.
11. Waltz, 2, 24–25.
12. Jervis, "The Political Effects of Nuclear Weapons," 83.
13. Jervis, 80.
14. Jervis, 81; see also Jervis, *The Illogic of American Nuclear Strategy*, 24–25.
15. Snyder and Diesling, *Conflict Among Nations*, 450.
16. Schelling, *Strategy of Conflict*, 188; Jervis, *The Illogic of American Nuclear Strategy*, 12–13, 20–21, 137–140, 168, 170; Jervis, *The Meaning of the Nuclear Revolution*, 21–22, 238.
17. These definitions come from the work of Forrest Morgan and other RAND researchers. Morgan et al., *Dangerous Thresholds*, 23–28.

18. Bracken, *The Command and Control of Nuclear Forces*; Blair, *Strategic Command and Control*; Sagan, *The Limits of Safety*; Schlosser, *Command and Control*.
19. Acton, "Escalation through Entanglement," 58.
20. Talmadge, "Will China Go Nuclear"; Rovner, "Two Kinds of Catastrophe"; Christensen, "The Meaning of the Nuclear Evolution"; Riqiang, "Assessing China-US Inadvertent Nuclear Escalation."
21. Gaddis, "The Long Peace," 99, 120–123; Jervis, "The Political Effects of Nuclear Weapons"; Waltz, *The Spread of Nuclear Weapons*, 30; for a recent essay premised on the pacifying effect of American nuclear weapons, strategic and tactical, during the Cold War, see Colby, "If You Want Peace, Prepare for Nuclear War."
22. Allison and Zelikow, *Essence of Decision*, 115, 118, 229; Dobbs, *One Minute to Midnight*, 21–23, 229, 271, 324.
23. Basrur, "Correspondence: Do Small Arsenals Deter?" 203; van Creveld, *Nuclear Proliferation and the Future of Conflict*, 77–96.
24. For case research based on China, India, Pakistan, Israel, and the Arab states, see Van Creveld, *Nuclear Proliferation and the Future of Conflict*, 65–121.
25. Asal and Beardsley, "Proliferation and International Crisis Behavior"; Beardsley and Asal, "Winning with the Bomb."
26. Rauchhaus, "Evaluating the Nuclear Peace Hypothesis"; for a rebuttal, see Bell and Miller, "Questioning the Effect of Nuclear Weapons on Conflict."
27. Narang, "What Does It Take to Deter?"; Suzuki, "Is More Better or Worse?"
28. Mueller, "The Essential Irrelevance of Nuclear Weapons"; Mueller, *Retreat from Doomsday*, 94, 110–116; Mueller, "Nuclear Weapons Don't Matter."
29. Mueller, "The Essential Irrelevance of Nuclear Weapons," 66–67.
30. Lebow, *Between Peace and War*, 15–17.
31. McNamara, "The Military Role of Nuclear Weapons."
32. Narang, "Posturing for Peace?" 43–44.
33. Narang, See also Narang, "What Does It Take to Deter?"
34. Lebow, *Between Peace and War*, 13, 15–17.
35. Lebow, 14–15.
36. Mueller, *The Remnants of War*; see also Mueller, "The Essential Irrelevance of Nuclear Weapons," 56; for another thinker who agrees with this logic, see Wilson, *Five Myths about Nuclear Weapons*, 87–103.

37. Mueller, *The Remnants of War*, 164–165.
38. Goldstein, "Do Nascent WMD Arsenals Deter?"
39. This finding is weak for two reasons: 1) The results approached statistical significance (p = .12), and 2) the results hinged on the decision to include or exclude Vietnam from the dataset. See pages 517–518. A later study by the same authors using an expanded dataset is stronger and comes to the same conclusion, finding that the "defender's possession of nuclear weapons makes little difference." Huth and Russett, "What Makes Deterrence Work?"; Huth and Russett, "Deterrence Failure and Crisis Escalation." The authors again caution against excessive faith in their results, emphasizing that they only have "limited confidence" in their statistical analysis.
40. Gartzke and Jo, "Bargaining, Nuclear Proliferation, and Interstate Disputes." Importantly, the theory and empirical testing in this article suggests that opponents accommodate nuclear powers during disputes. The authors theorize that this accommodation accounts for the null effect. This causal mechanism is in tension with the other predictions of the null model, but this article is included in the null section given the statistical evidence in favor of no effect of nuclear weapons on conflict.
41. Bell and Miller, "Questioning the Effect of Nuclear Weapons on Conflict."
42. Blechman and Kaplan, *Force without War*, 127–129; Organski and Kugler, *The War Ledger*, 147–179; Kugler, "Terror without Deterrence."
43. Kroenig, *The Logic of American Nuclear Strategy*, 15–26; see also Kroenig, "Nuclear Superiority and the Balance of Resolve," 146–152.
44. Snyder in Seabury, *Balance of Power*, 198–199.
45. Jervis, *The Illogic of American Nuclear Strategy*, 31.
46. The precise definition of "lower" levels of violence is contested. Snyder's essay mentioned earlier includes "initiating conventional war...[and] the limited use of nuclear weapons" in his definition of lower levels of violence. Snyder, *Balance of Power*, 199. Others believes that "lower" levels of violence should be confined to insurgency and terrorism. For the purposes of this study, I use the wider definition originally employed by Snyder.
47. Trachtenberg, "The Influence of Nuclear Weapons in the Cuban Missile Crisis," 163.
48. Trachtenberg, 163. Strangely, Trachtenberg also reports that the nuclear balance "did not have an important direct influence on American policy." Nuclear superiority seems to have mattered less to the American side

than nuclear inferiority to the Soviets. See his summary of the results on pages 162–163.
49. Kroenig, "Nuclear Superiority and the Balance of Resolve," 150–151. For a critique and cross-examination, see Logan, "The Nuclear Balance is What States Make of It."
50. Kapur, "India and Pakistan's Unstable Peace," 142; Kroenig also cites this case in Kroenig, "Nuclear Superiority and the Balance of Resolve," 151; see also Tellis, Fair, and Medby, *Limited Conflicts Under the Nuclear Umbrella*, 77, 79.
51. Kroenig, "Nuclear Superiority and the Balance of Resolve," 154. This article has generated controversy. For one exchange between Kroenig's main critics, see Fuhrmann Sechser, and Kroenig, "Debating the Benefits of Nuclear Superiority for Crisis Bargaining."
52. Rauchhaus, "Evaluating the Nuclear Peace Hypothesis," 270.
53. Waltz, *Man, the State, and War*.
54. "About the Journal," *Foreign Policy Analysis*.
55. van Tol et al, *AirSea Battle*, xiii-xv, 12, 19–21, 24; see the T. X. Hammes articles cited in chapter 1, footnote 23.
56. George and Smoke, *Deterrence in American Foreign Policy*, 50.
57. Christensen, "A Strong and Moderate Taiwan."
58. Snyder, *Deterrence and Defense*, 32.
59. Oakes, *Diversionary War*.
60. Horowitz and Fuhrmann, "Studying Leaders and Military Conflict"; Byman and Pollack, "Let Us Now Praise Great Men"; Saunders, *Leaders at War*; Dafoe and Caughey, "Honor and War"; Macdonald and Schneider, "Presidential Risk Orientation and Force Employment Decisions"; Whitlark, "Nuclear Beliefs."
61. Huntington, *The Soldier and the State*, 69.
62. Betts, *Soldiers, Statesmen, and Cold War Crises*, 4–5.
63. Betts, 5.
64. Betts, 117, 119–122, 142.
65. Gelpi and Feaver, "Speak Softly and Carry a Big Stick?"; Horowitz and Stam, "How Prior Military Experience Influences the Future Militarized Behavior of Leaders."
66. Posen, *The Sources of Military Doctrine*; Snyder, "Civil-Military Relations and the Cult of the Offensive, 1914 and 1984"; van Evera, "The Cult of the Offensive and the Origins of the First World War."

67. Smeltz, Daalder, Friedhoff, and Kafura, "What Americans Think about America First," 9, 32, 34; Smeltz, Daalder, Friedhoff, and Kafura, "America Divided," 11–12, 26; Gries, *The Politics of American Foreign Policy*.
68. Smeltz et al., "What Americans Think about America First," 34.
69. Bertoli, Dafoe, and Trager, "Is There a War Party?"; Arena and Palmer, "Politics or the Economy?"; Palmer, London, and Regan, "What's Stopping You?"
70. Johnson, McDermott, Cowden, and Tingley, "Dead Certain."
71. Eichenberg, "Gender Differences in Public Attitudes toward the Use of Force by the United States, 1990–2003," 112.
72. Eichenberg, 112.
73. Brooks and Valentino, "A War of One's Own."
74. McDermott and Hatemi, "The Relationship Between Physical Aggression, Foreign Policy, and Moral Choices"; H. McIntyre, Barret, McDermott, Johnson, Cowden, and Rosen, "Finger Length Ratio (2D:4D) and Sex Difference in Aggression During a Simulated War Game"; McDermott, Johnson, Cowden, and Rosen, "Testosterone and Aggression in a Simulated Crisis Game"; Johnson, McDermott, Barrett, Cowden, Wrangham, McIntyre, and Rosen, "Overconfidence in Wargames: Experimental Evidence on Expectations, Aggression, Gender and Testosterone"; McDermott and Cowden, "The Effects of Uncertainty and Sex in a Crisis Simulation Game."
75. Imamverdiyeva and Shea, "Female Leaders and Interstate Conflict"; Dube and Harish, "Queens."
76. Schramm and Stark, "Peacemakers or Iron Ladies?"
77. Posard, Kavanagh, Edwards, and Efron, *Millennial Perceptions of Security*, 1.
78. Thrall, Smeltz, Goepner, Ruger, Kafura, "The Clash of Generations?" 2.
79. Horowitz, McDermott, and Stam, "Leader Age, Regime Type, and Violent International Relations."
80. Jervis, *Perception and Misperception in International Politics*; Holsti and Rosenau, *American Leadership in World Affairs*; Mead, *Special Providence*.
81. Early awareness of the difficulty of pinning down the national interest can be found in Wolfers, "'National Security' as an Ambiguous Symbol."
82. Holsti and Rosenau, *American Leadership in World Affairs*; Gacek, *The Logic of Force*.
83. Huntington, *The Soldier and the State*; van Evera, "The Cult of the Offensive and the Origins of the First World War"; Snyder, "Civil-Military Relations and the Cult of the Offensive, 1914 and 1984"; Posen,

The Sources of Military Doctrine; Desch, *Civilian Control of the Military;* Cohen, *Supreme Command;* Feaver, *Armed Servants.*

84. Van Evera, "The Cult of the Offensive and the Origins of the First World War"; Snyder, "Civil-Military Relations and the Cult of the Offensive, 1914 and 1984"; Gacek, *The Logic of Force.*
85. Smoke, *War,* 252–253; Jervis, *The Meaning of the Nuclear Revolution,* 152–153.
86. Neustadt and May, *Thinking in Time;* Gaddis, *Strategies of Containment;* Kennedy, *The Rise and Fall of Great Powers.* For more recent scholars and scholarship in this applied history vein, see Gavin, *Nuclear Statecraft;* Inboden, "Statecraft, Decision-Making, and the Varieties of Historical Experience"; Brands and Inboden, "Wisdom without Tears."
87. For the canonical literature that addresses case study research design for scholars of international relations, see Van Evera, *Guide to Methods for Students of Political Science;* King, Keohane, and Verba, *Designing Social Inquiry.*
88. Examples of analysts turning to history for understanding the future include Healey, ed., *A Fierce Domain;* Boot, *War Made New.*
89. Lin-Greenberg, "Wargame of Drones: Remotely Piloted Aircraft and Conflict Escalation."
90. Pauly, "Would US Leaders Push the Button?"
91. Bartels, Mikolic-Torreira, Popper, and Predd, *Do Differing Analyses Change the Decision?*
92. Reddie, Goldblum, Lakkaraju, Reinhardt, Nacht, and Epifanovskaya, "Next-Generation Wargames." This article has caused a stir. See Oberholtzer, Doll, Frelinger, Mueller, and Pettyjohn, "Applying Wargames to Real-World Policies"; Reddie, Goldblum, Reinhardt, Lakkaraju, Epifanovskaya, and Nacht, "Applying Wargames to Real-World Policies—Response."
93. Schneider, *The Information Revolution and International Stability: A Multi-Article Exploration of Computing, Cyber, and Incentives for Conflict.*
94. Millot, Perry, Niblack, Lachman, Replogle, and Van Winkle, *Response to Warning.* This report was declassified by the US air force on March 30, 2017.

CHAPTER 3

SANCTUARY AND THE KOREAN WAR

Arguably the most puzzling aspect of the Korean War is the same feature that should most intrigue modern analysts: the Truman administration's decision to limit the Korean War from expanding to Chinese territory. The Chinese military poured over the Yalu River and into North Korea in November 1950, dealing massive defeats to United Nations (UN) forces. Striking Chinese air bases, masses of army forces, or supply lines on Chinese territory could have at least slowed down the rout of UN forces.[1] Instead, President Harry S. Truman and his advisors chose, as a matter of high policy, to refrain from attacking any targets in China proper, with nuclear or non-nuclear weapons.[2] As a result, the US air force operated under tight restrictions. Not only could American pilots not bomb the ample targets in China, targets crucial to the Chinese war effort, but American pilots could neither fly over Chinese territory nor engage in hot pursuit, that is, counter-attacking Chinese MIGs based in China.[3] General Douglas MacArthur, the commander of UN Command and therefore the field commander for US and allied forces in the Korean

War, criticized these restrictions as constituting an "enormous handicap, without precedent in military history."[4]

Explaining this limit on the conduct of American operations in the Korean War has become important to the modern debate over US military strategy toward China. In an extended debate in the *National Interest*, T. X. Hammes asks, "given that Truman and Johnson refused to strike China when hundreds of thousands of US troops were in combat, are we sure a future President will authorize an extensive strike campaign into China?"[5] Elsewhere, he poses a similar question: "we need to ask if the President is likely to allow strikes into China. President Truman in Korea and President Johnson in Vietnam did not think it was a good idea."[6] Even noted correspondent James Fallows has used this historical analogy. In reference to the new US air force bomber program designed with the ability to penetrate Chinese airspace, he claims that "bombing runs deep in to China" is a "step so wildly reckless that the US didn't consider it even when fighting Chinese troops during the Korean War."[7] This interpretation of the Korean War analogy suggests that a future administration might similarly deny permission for strikes on the mainland, instituting tight rules of engagement for US forces and providing China a sanctuary.

The Korean War is an important case study in any debate about the willingness of an American president during a future US-China war to strike targets on the Chinese mainland. First, it is the only time that the United States and China have engaged in open combat. Second, that there was an extensive American debate in late 1950 and early 1951 about whether to bomb targets in China makes this case excellent for the purposes of the study. Once Chinese intervention occurred in the fall of 1950, there was active consideration of bombing China, though a policy of "no strikes" crystallized by early 1951, after which there was no more discussion of this policy option. Third, the Soviet Union had acquired nuclear weapons in 1949, which potentially cast a shadow over President Truman's decision-making given the Sino-Soviet alliance.[8] This development permits the case to test models of the relationship between nuclear weapons and conventional escalation.

NUCLEAR WEAPONS AND THE ESCALATION DEBATE

The single most striking fact that emerged from the majority of historical analysis of this case is that Soviet possession of nuclear weapons did not figure into the decision to limit the geography of American bombing. Contrasting this, however, the caution model strongly implies that the close alliance between China and the Soviet Union should prompt American leaders to fear nuclear war. There is even some scholarship that implies this was the case.[9] Historian H. W. Brands in his 2016 book *The General vs. the President: MacArthur and Truman at the Brink of Nuclear War* explains Truman's decision not to expand the war to China by informing the reader that Truman "couldn't go forward without risking a nuclear World War III."[10] Military historian Russell Weigley argued that "the atomic bomb had raised expectations about the next war" and that the "very apocalyptic nature of those expectations now held back the Korean contestants and persuaded them to limit their warfare."[11] Late RAND researcher Carl Builder argued that restrictions against expanding the Korean War to Chinese territory resulted "not because of the range of airplanes but the political limitations imposed by the threat of an expanded war in a world of atomic bombs."[12] Still, these claims are inconsistent with the most thorough secondary historical research on this decision and also archival records.

Korean War Scholarship and the Role of Soviet Nuclear Weapons

The claim that Soviet nuclear weapons explain President Truman's decision not to expand the war to China finds no support in arguably the three key texts on this decision. Rosemary Foot's 1985 *The Wrong War: American Policy and the Dimensions of the Korean Conflict, 1950–1953* explicitly focuses on "American policy discussions during the Truman and Eisenhower administrations concerning the objectives and likely consequences of any expansions of the Korean conflict into China."[13] She finds that the debate on expanding the war to China to have been "extensive, rich" and "one of the most important and all-consuming questions of the period."[14] Yet nowhere does she find evidence—despite her own archival digging in the United States and the United Kingdom—that Soviet nuclear weapons produced the limitations on bombing China. Instead, she places weight on a variety of factors including an American decision-making process dominated by the State Department early in the war and a related emphasis on allied unity over military expediency.[15]

Military historian Conrad Crane provides a remarkably detailed chronology and interpretation of the US air force's role in the Korean War in his book *American Airpower Strategy in Korea, 1950–1953*.[16] Through detailed archival work in air force and navy archives in addition to combing through the personal papers of key figures including Secretary of Defense George C. Marshall and UN Commander Douglas MacArthur, he provides an account of the contributions and limits of airpower to the Korean War. He gives extensive attention to the decision to forbid expanding the war to China but never mentions Soviet nuclear weapons.[17] Instead, he attributes this policy decision to fear of Soviet intervention and American accommodation of allied reservations about expanding the war.[18] Once again, a historian's inductive spadework turns up no evidence that Soviet nuclear weapons explains Truman White House decision-making.

Finally, Robert Frank Futrell wrote the definitive United States Air Force history of the Korean War titled *The United States Air Force in Korea, 1950–1953*.[19] This seven-hundred-page text deals with nearly every aspect of the air war in Korea, including the geographic limitations placed on the air force. In fact, Futrell extensively treats the decision to restrict operations against China.[20] Nowhere does his comprehensive explanation mention fear of Soviet nuclear weapons. Instead, Futrell gives weight to American concern for allied and UN preferences.[21]

Sanctuary and the Korean War

These three key scholarly sources on the American air war over Korea, all of which address the American decision to bar strikes on China, fail to mention Soviet nuclear weapons as a factor in American decision-making. Other scholarly sources come to a similar conclusion.[22] Nevertheless, perhaps the most compelling method for assuaging any critics can be found, however, in an examination of the archival records of the Truman administration, especially National Security Council (NSC) meeting records and memos.

Archival Documents from NSC Meetings and the Role of Soviet Nuclear Weapons

From November 1, 1950, to February 28, 1951, there were fifteen National Security Council meetings.[23] Each of these meetings occurred after the October 1950 Chinese intervention in the Korean War, but crucially all the meetings also transpired before a policy of not striking Manchuria had crystallized and become the policy status quo.[24] The Chinese military had already intervened on behalf of the North Korean army and begun dealing massive defeats to UN forces.[25] This military pressure on the United States created obvious incentives for President Truman to expand the war to China by striking airfields, troop concentrations, and supply lines.[26] As a result, these fifteen meetings are an ideal venue to examine the Truman cabinet discussion on the policy of striking targets in China. National Security Council documents from this period also provide a useful window into the views of top policymakers and advisors and will be referenced later.

Meeting 71 on November 10, 1950, is the first high-level policy discussion in which President Truman and his advisors grapple with how to respond to Chinese intervention.[27] Several participants, including Central Intelligence Agency (CIA) Director Walter Bedell Smith, Secretary of Defense George C. Marshall, and Secretary of State Dean Acheson, directly mentioned attacks on Manchuria by the US air force as an option, though none advocate it.[28] Yet there was not a single mention of Soviet nuclear weapons as a consideration in expanding the war despite concerned talk about the close relationship between China and the Soviet Union.

The potential of bombing targets in China resurfaced in the November 28th meeting (No. 73) of the National Security Council.[29] General Omar Bradley, Chairman of the Joint Chiefs of Staff, described the vulnerability of American airfields in Korea to strikes from Communist bombers based in Manchuria. He stated that the Joint Chiefs are "not recommending authority to violate the border at this time," but his characterization of the situation certainly impressed upon other attendees, including the president, the potential military benefits of attacking Chinese air bases and, conversely, the drawbacks of prohibiting strikes on targets in China.[30] Secretary Acheson later in the meeting cautioned, "very careful thought should be given before authorizing air operations over Manchuria...such an authorization would extend our commitment and might even cause the Russians to come in under their pact with China."[31] But he doesn't explain further. No participant in this meeting mentions Soviet nuclear weapons despite the concern expressed about a possible Soviet intervention.

The 74th meeting, which took place on December 12, 1950, again returned to the discussion about US policy on whether to bomb targets on Chinese territory.[32] Secretary Marshall, General Bradley, and President Truman discussed the matter, which had come up in a meeting with British Prime Minister Clement Atlee earlier in the month. The notes read:

> The President:...He noted that it has also been agreed that it would be terrible to get tied down in a war with the Chinese Communists.
>
> Secretary Marshall questioned whether it was not agreed that war with China should be avoided.
>
> General Bradley noted that we had reserved the right to take action against China, although we did not desire to be tied down there.

> Secretary Marshall thought that we had indicated we did not want to be restrained from bombing Chinese bases, although we would not do it for other than the protection of our units...
>
> The Vice President asked if it wasn't agreed that we would not precipitate a general war with China.
>
> The President agreed, but said that we made it clear that we would not stand idly by.[33]

The participants were reluctant to authorize strikes on China for fear of getting "tied down," not due to Soviet nuclear weapons. There is no mention of Soviet nuclear weapons in the notes.

Discussion of American attacks on Manchuria does not occur again until the January 18th 80th meeting of the National Security Council.[34] Secretary of State Dean Acheson raised "the question of removing present restrictions on aerial reconnaissance over Communist China" and voiced his objection to this step. General Bradley supported the policy, noting that the proposal does not "involve penetration into the interior of China." Bradley also openly pondered whether the United States should "take off on a unilateral course of action in Korea," obliquely referring to action like bombing targets in Manchuria.[35] The meeting is notable because even reconnaissance over China generated bureaucratic disagreement. Consideration of bombing Manchuria doesn't even emerge as a point of discussion. A Joint Chiefs of Staff memo associated with this meeting, NSC report 101, does directly discuss "naval and air attacks on objectives in Communist China" but only recommends this action "at such time as the Chinese Communists attack any of our forces outside of Korea."[36] The memo, which does not mention Soviet nuclear weapons, appears to accept that attacks on targets in China were not under consideration unless China expanded the war first.

The 81st meeting, held on January 25, 1951, largely concerned the reactions of top leaders to a paper prepared by the National Security

Resources Board, an organization then led by Stuart Symington. The paper advocated attacks on lines of communication in China and "aggression-support-industries" in Manchuria.[37] Secretary Acheson, the meeting notes record, "stated his belief that if the United States followed certain of the courses recommended in this paper, it would probably bring on a third world war."[38] But neither he nor any other members present mentioned a specific fear of Soviet nuclear weapons.

At the next three meetings of the National Security Council, there was no discussion about the possibility of striking targets in Manchuria.[39] The status quo of no attacks on targets in China appears to have crystallized by late February 1951. Foot's *The Wrong War* also identifies this time period as one in which the United States "settled" for a "limited conflict" rather than expanded the war to China.[40] UN forces recovered from their rout, and the forward line of battle stabilized. In addition, talks related to an armistice began. In other words, striking targets in China lost salience as a policy option as the war entered a new phase.

Nuclear Weapons and Conventional Escalation in the Korean War

The review of secondary texts and primary research reveals that the caution model is inconsistent with Truman White House decision-making after Chinese intervention. Despite extensive discussion about this topic among President Truman and his top advisors as well as some cabinet members' belief that the Soviets might intervene on China's behalf should the United States expand the war, no participant in the fifteen National Security Council meetings after Chinese intervention mentioned a fear that American strikes on Manchuria could lead to Soviet nuclear use or nuclear war.

Nor does the emboldenment model accurately represent Truman administration decision-making during the debate over geographic limits of the bombing campaign. President Truman and his top advisors did not invoke American nuclear superiority as an aspect of the situation that increased their willingness to use greater levels of force.

The null model is most consistent with actual Truman White House decision-making. Soviet nuclear weapons did not weigh heavily on the president or the cabinet. In other words, the possibility of Soviet nuclear use did not constrain American decision-makers as some past scholars suggest or, equally importantly, as modern opponents of mainland strikes might theorize. One reason could be that American decision-makers simply thought that an American bombing campaign that impinged on Chinese territory would not trigger Soviet nuclear use. In other words, perhaps President Truman and his administration believed that the Soviets would not risk nuclear war over aiding an ally. Another reason could be that the Soviet nuclear arsenal at that point consisted of a mere handful of nuclear weapons that could be delivered only in theaters near the Soviet Union. Modern Chinese nuclear forces have greater ranges and are larger numerically. The analogy with a potential future US-China war is therefore imperfect.

But before proponents of mainland strikes see this case as simple confirmation of their side of argument or skeptics dismiss this case as too dissimilar, they should read the second component of this chapter. Although there were sound military reasons to strike air bases, troop concentrations, and supply lines in China, President Truman and his advisors decided against this course of action for a variety of political and strategic reasons related to the foreign-policy situation. The next section examines these reasons and assesses whether these factors could similarly create reluctance to strike mainland China in a future war.

Scenario Characteristics and the Escalation Debate

There are at least five distinct scenario-related explanations for President Truman's decision to not expand the war to Chinese territory. These explanations are presented in rough temporal order.

Uncertainty over Chinese Intentions Immediately after Chinese "Intervention"

The first impediment to striking Chinese territory can be found in the confusion and uncertainty about Chinese intentions in November 1950. Only limited numbers of Chinese troops initially appeared in North Korea, which fostered a belief among Americans that Chinese leaders were not committed to a full-scale intervention and that attacking China was an unnecessary and perhaps excessively escalatory step. The small-scale incursions by the Chinese could have been, according to one hypothesis popular at the time, an attempt to establish a cordon sanitaire, a buffer zone in between UN troops and Chinese territory.[41] Another possibility, advanced by the US Ambassador in Seoul John Muccio, was that the Chinese forces were fighting a "delaying action," buying time for the retreat of North Korean forces.[42] More generally, the chaos and uncertainty of the battlefield complicated any definitive judgement.[43] Faced with this basic uncertainty, American decision-makers preferred to probe Chinese intentions rather than expand the conflict.[44] Consequently, the rules of engagement, which barred strikes on China, were left unchanged for the fighting forces in Korea. It was only in the last week of November that a sufficiently large Chinese offensive convinced American decision-makers that China intended something more than a small-scale intervention.[45] A similar uncertainty over Chinese intentions in a future war might also delay a mainland-strikes decision.

Fear of a New World War

President Truman and his senior advisors were also generally wary of any prospect of reigniting a world war. A broader conflict with the Soviet Union was considered all too likely if the United States expanded the war to Chinese territory.[46] Secretary of State Dean Acheson worried, "to do so would, we believe, increase—and materially increase—the risk of general war in the Far East and general war throughout the world."[47] Even the Joint Chiefs of Staff expressed worries that actions against forces in Manchuria could potentially lead the Soviets to join the fight.[48]

Importance of Defending Western European Allies

Once Chinese intentions became clear, another set of reasons for delaying or avoiding strikes on China emerged: the beliefs that American military strength should be reserved for the defense of Europe and that strikes on China would damage American relations with its UN allies.

Though General MacArthur, the UN commander, saw Asia and Korea as the critical theater in the emerging Cold War and supported an escalation of the war in Asia to accomplish American objectives, most other senior leaders thought differently.[49] Led by Secretary of State Dean Acheson, this group of advisors, which arguably included the president himself, thought that the "real enemy is the Soviet Union" and that a larger fight in Asia would divert resources from Europe.[50] Military leaders especially worried that a serious attempt to bomb important sites in China could sap the American military strength that deterred the Soviet Union from starting a war in Europe.[51] A related worry was that the Soviets were actually attempting to ensnare the United States in a war in Asia and intentionally dilute American strength before a Soviet attack on Europe.[52] These concerns were exacerbated by the widespread belief that American military forces were weak and required rapid rebuilding.[53] President Truman's advisors could not support an expansion of the war in Asia when they viewed Europe as the true prize of the Cold War struggle.

Concern with unity among the UN allies, especially those governments contributing forces to oppose North Korean and Chinese troops, also partially explains the Truman administration's reluctance to strike targets in China.[54] Other UN member governments, particularly the British, were strongly opposed to expanding the geography of the war to China.[55] The British even opposed "hot pursuit," the practice of pursuing Communist aircraft into Chinese airspace.[56] Bombing Manchuria, at least from the perspective of America's allies, was out of the question. For President Truman and his advisors, maintaining allied cohesion helped ensure these nations would keep providing forces in Korea and cooperating in case of further Communist aggression around the world, especially in Europe.

The influence of these kinds of dynamics on a future decision to authorize mainland strikes is ambiguous. Should allies such as Japan call for restraint, this could weigh heavily on American decision-makers. Alternatively, should American allies push for mainland strikes, allied concerns could tip the scales in that direction.

Mutual UN-Communist Restraint and Fear of UN Vulnerability

Restraint was also a mutual phenomenon.[57] President Truman and his advisors seem to have barred strikes on China partially because the Soviets and Chinese had limited their fighting geographically too.[58] The Communist side did not attack American targets and supply lines outside of the Korean peninsula or American air bases in South Korea.

A decision to expand the war to China became premised on whether the Chinese and Soviets attacked UN forces outside of Korea. January 1951 NSC documents call for "initiat[ing] damaging naval and air attack on objectives in Communist China at such time as the Chinese Communists attack any of our forces outside of Korea."[59] Chief of Naval Operations Forrest Sherman and Vice Chief of Staff of the Air Force Nathan Twining supported this reasoning; Admiral Sherman noted "the advantage of keeping our air on our side of the frontier" as long as China reciprocally restrained its air forces.[60] Chief of Staff of the Air Force Hoyt Vandenberg also endorsed this logic. He reasoned, "the sanctuary business...is operating on both sides."[61]

The Korean War analogy therefore requires caution in an application to a modern US-China war. If one assumes Chinese restraint in attacking American air bases and aircraft carriers, there might indeed be a mutual restraint logic operating, constraining American operations. If China attacks American air bases, though, and Chinese doctrine indicates that such an attack is plausible, the Korean War analogy breaks down.[62] A modern American president might be more disposed to attacks on mainland China in this case than President Truman was.

Armistice Negotiations

A disgruntled officer best summarized the effect of the pursuit of an armistice on the geographic rules of engagement during the Korean War: "don't employ air power so the enemy will get mad and won't sign the armistice."[63] The desire to sign an armistice and the necessity of maintaining a congenial negotiating environment complicated any decision to strike targets in China.

The policy of seeking an armistice began in December 1950, when President Truman's military and civilian advisors agreed that a ceasefire agreement and an end to fighting represented the best exit from the war.[64] Secretary Acheson appears to have been the strongest supporter of this position and therefore also an opponent of actions that threatened the success of the armistice talks, like bombing air bases in Manchuria.[65] Military historian Conrad Crane documents the tension between pursuing military advantage and attempting to achieve armistice negotiations, and writes about how that tradeoff created a "crisis" for senior air force leaders.[66] The pursuit of armistice so constrained American escalation that an expansion of war to China eventually became premised on China breaking off negotiations first.

The pursuit of an armistice gathered a momentum of its own during the Korean War and provides yet another explanation of why China remained off-limits to American bombing. American commanders in a future US-China war could be subject to a similar diplomatic pressure. Pursuing peace talks could constrain the tempo or type of military operations directed against the Chinese mainland, though it is also possible that strikes on the mainland could be used as part of coercive diplomacy to induce China to initiate or conclude a negotiation.[67]

Summary of Scenario Factors and Conventional Escalation in the Korean War

A number of scenario factors overrode the military imperative of expanding the Korean War to Chinese territory through conventional bombing. American military planners ought to consider a similar possibility that a range of political and strategic factors could similarly constrain a contemporary decision about mainland strikes. Initial uncertainty over Chinese intentions, allied demands to avoid mainland strikes, or even Chinese restraint could also constrain American decision-makers. There could also be other idiosyncratic factors that reduce American willingness to employ mainland strikes.

Some scenario factors could also increase American willingness to recommend mainland strikes. For instance, this analysis of the Korean War experience suggests Chinese and Soviet restraint partially explains American restraint in the Korean War. If the Communist side had attacked American forces outside of Korea, the American side might have been more willing to expand the war to China. It stands to reason that if in a future US-China war Chinese forces strike American air bases or aircraft carriers in East Asia, then an American president might be relatively willing to authorize mainland strikes.

Assessing the ultimate import of this analysis therefore also requires a judgment about the likelihood of each scenario factor in a future US-China conflict, which is beyond the scope of this empirical analysis. Suffice it to say that a range of scenario-related factors constrained American escalation against China in the Korean War. It is therefore possible to imagine a future major conventional war against China operating, at least initially, with similar restraints.

The Korean War and Implications for Mainland Strikes

The beginning of the chapter described how some analysts have invoked the restraints in the bombing campaign from the Korean War to cast doubt on the likelihood that a future president would authorize conventional strikes on the Chinese mainland. The analogy is fruitful, though not as straightforward as past analysis suggested.

Sanctuary and the Korean War 63

On the one hand, the evidence on Soviet nuclear weapons shows that the Truman administration had a relatively free hand to consider strikes on China. The nuclear caution model did not seem to operate in this case. The shadow of nuclear weapons did not loom over American decision-making on conventional escalation. Instead, the null model best explains American decision-making; Soviet nuclear weapons, despite the Sino-Soviet alliance, hardly factored in President Truman and his advisor's decision-making on whether to expand the war into China. To be sure, the Chinese lacked their own nuclear arsenal, and the Soviet nuclear arsenal was nascent and limited in range at this time. Additionally, because China lacked its own nuclear forces, there were no fears of conventional-nuclear entanglement that may have come about with a future possible US decision to employ mainland strikes against China. In any case, this chapter therefore puts a dent in the belief that the presence of nuclear weapons is so strong as to smother intra-war conventional escalation.

On the other hand, the analysis of scenario factors and their relationship to conventional strikes on the Chinese mainland suggests that a range of political and strategic factors could delay, constrain, or preclude mainland strikes. Just as uncertainty over Chinese intentions, alliance concerns, and Communist restraint reduced the Truman administration's willingness to expand the Korean War to China, similar situational factors could reduce the willingness of a future administration to authorize conventional strikes on the Chinese mainland. The perspective of mainland strikes skeptics therefore receives some backing too in this chapter.

The Korean War case, while not definitive, is suggestive. Adversary nuclear weapons, at least in this case, did not preclude American conventional escalation; contemporary Chinese nuclear possession, it seems possible, might not preclude mainland strikes. Some aspects of the foreign-policy situation also militated against the expansion of the war to China. Political and strategic concerns in a modern US-China war could also trump the military imperative for mainland strikes.

Notes

1. The adverse impact of granting sanctuary to Chinese forces in Manchuria, the northern part of China adjacent to North Korea, was severe. Futrell, *The United States Air Force in Korea 1950-1953*, 183, 195, 222, 240–241, 246, 253, 313, 315, 701; Foot, *The Wrong War*, 23–24, 89–90, 117; Crane, *American Airpower Strategy in Korea*, 50, 83–84, 157–159.
2. Brodie, *Strategy in the Missile Age*, 328–329; Halperin, "The Limiting Process in the Korean War," 13, 30; DeWeerd, *The Triumph of the Limiters*, 12–13; Smoke, *National Security and the Nuclear Dilemma*, Second Edition, 77–78.
3. Futrell, *The United States Air Force in Korea 1950–1953*, 222.
4. Harry S. Truman Library, SMOF: Selected Records...Relating to the Korean War, Box 1, Department of State: Chronology File Subseries, June-November 1950, Chronology of Principal Events Relating to the Korean Conflict, December 1950, undated. All archival references will note the library, collection, box, folder, and document date. The Harry S. Truman Library will be abbreviated HSTL.
5. Hammes, "Sorry, AirSea Battle is No Strategy"; Colby, "Don't Sweat AirSea Battle"; Colby, "The War over War with China."
6. Hammes, "Hammes: Strategy and AirSea Battle."
7. Fallows, "The Tragedy of the American Military."
8. The Soviets had one nuclear weapon in 1949, five in 1950 and twenty-five in 1951. Kristensen and Norris, "Global Nuclear Weapons Inventories, 1945–2013," 78. For delivery systems, the only "long range" Soviet bomber capable in the year 1950 of carrying a nuclear weapon was the Tu-4. The nuclear-capable version was the Tu-4A. The maximum range of a Tu-4 on a one-way mission is approximately 3,000 nautical miles. It could therefore only be used for strikes relatively close to Russia. For information on the Tu-4, see Podvig, ed,, *Russian Strategic Nuclear Forces*, 340. For range information on the Tu-4, see *Jane's All the World's Aircraft*, 1956. This Jane's information was provided by an analyst from Jane's. For another helpful resource on the early Soviet nuclear arsenal, see Geist, *Two Worlds of Civil Defense*.
9. Beyond the examples I list below, see Frank Gavin's claim that these limits were "necessary for the nuclear age" in Gavin, "What's in a Name? The Genius of Eisenhower."

Sanctuary and the Korean War 65

10. Brands, *The General vs. the President*.
11. Weigley, *History of the United States Army*, 506.
12. Builder, *The Icarus Syndrome*, 147.
13. Foot, *The Wrong War*, 9.
14. Foot, 23.
15. Foot, 34, 37, 90–91, 124–125, 128, 137.
16. Crane, *American Airpower Strategy in Korea, 1950–1953*.
17. Crane, 49–50, 56–57, 72, 85, 157
18. Crane, 56–57, 85.
19. Futrell, *The United States Air Force in Korea, 1950–1953*.
20. Futrell, 222, 230, 235, 240–243, 285.
21. Futrell, 241.
22. Halperin, "The Limiting Process in the Korean War"; Trachtenberg, "A 'Wasting Asset'"; Clodfelter, *The Limits of Airpower*; Gacek, *The Logic of Force*; Gaddis, *Strategies of Containment*.
23. A finding aid at the Truman Library for the Papers of Harry S. Truman provides a chronology of the National Security Council meetings. National Security Council meeting 70 occurred on November 2, 1950. National Security Council meeting 84 occurred on February 21, 1951.
24. Foot, *The Wrong War*, 89–90. Foot identifies November 6th as the day that Americans recognized "extensive Chinese involvement in Korea."
25. See HSTL, President's Secretary's Files, Box 188, Memorandum for the President, Summary of Discussion at 70th Meeting of the National Security Council, November 3, 1950. Hereafter, President's Secretary's File will be abbreviated PSF. National Security Council will be abbreviated NSC.
26. General MacArthur strongly desired to bomb (with conventional weapons) targets in China. And MacArthur was not alone. Futrell, *The United States Air Force in Korea, 1950–1953*, 240–241
27. Meeting 70 hardly mentions the war in Korea, likely because evidence of Chinese intervention was inconclusive at the time. See HSTL, PSF Box 188, Memorandum for the President, Summary of Discussion at 70th Meeting of the NSC, November 3, 1950.
28. HSTL, PSF, Box 188, Memorandum for the President, Summary of Discussion at 71st Meeting of the NSC, November 10, 1950. CIA Director Smith mentions an "attack on Manchuria by our planes." Secretary of Defense Bradley brings up the "increasing questions of how much pressure we could stand without attacking Manchurian bases." Secretary of State Acheson summarizes the outcome of the meeting by stating, "Gen-

eral MacArthur is free to do what he militarily can under his present directive without bombing Manchuria."
29. The 72nd meeting does not discuss operations in Korea. It is focused on the long-term military program. HSTL, PSF, Box 188, Memorandum for the President, Summary of Discussion at 72nd Meeting of the NSC, November 24, 1950.
30. HSTL, PSF, Box 188, Memorandum for the President, Summary of Discussion at 73rd Meeting of the NSC, November 28, 1950. The meeting notes record that General Bradley said, "The Chinese Communists therefore have the potential of striking a hard blow by air."
31. HSTL, PSF, Box 188, Memorandum for the President, Summary of Discussion at 73rd Meeting of the NSC, November 28, 1950.
32. HSTL, PSF, Box 188, Memorandum for the President, Summary of Discussion at 74th Meeting of the NSC, November 28, 1950.
33. HSTL, PSF, Box 188, Memorandum for the President, Summary of Discussion at 74th Meeting of the NSC, November 28, 1950.
34. There is no mention of this topic at the 75th, 76th, 77th, 78th, or 79th NSC meetings. HSTL, PSF, Box 188, Memorandum for the President, Summary of Discussion at 75th Meeting of the NSC, December 15, 1950. HSTL, PSF, Box 188, Memorandum for the President, Summary of Discussion at 76th Meeting of the NSC, December 26, 1950. HSTL, PSF, Box 188, Memorandum for the President, Summary of Discussion at 77th Meeting of the NSC, January 6, 1951. HSTL, PSF, Box 188, Memorandum for the President, Summary of Discussion at 78th Meeting of the NSC, January 11, 1951. HSTL, PSF, Box 188, Memorandum for the President, Summary of Discussion at 79th Meeting of the NSC, January 13, 1951.
35. HSTL, PSF, Box 188, Memorandum for the President, Summary of Discussion at 80th Meeting of the NSC, January 18, 1951.
36. HSTL, PSF, Meetings: 80: January 17, 1951, NSC 101 A Report to the National Security Council, January 12, 1951.
37. *Foreign Relations of the United States, 1951.* Volume I, National Security Affairs; Foreign Economic Policy, 7-18.
38. HSTL, PSF, Box 188, Memorandum for the President, Summary of Discussion at 81st Meeting of the NSC, January 25, 1951.
39. HSTL, PSF, Box 188, Memorandum for the President, Summary of Discussion at 82nd Meeting of the NSC, February 2, 1951. HSTL, PSF, Box 188, Memorandum for the President, Summary of Discussion at 83rd Meeting of the NSC, February 14, 1951. HSTL, PSF, Box 188, Memoran-

dum for the President, Summary of Discussion at 84th Meeting of the NSC, February 23, 1951.
40. Foot, *The Wrong War*, 120.
41. HSTL, National Security Council File (hereafter NSC file), Box 3, Memoranda for the President, Korean Situation & Daily Korean Summary/Bulletin, September 1, 1950–March 30, 1951 [Folder 1 of 2], CIA Memorandum for the President on Chinese Communist Intervention in Korea, November 1, 1950.
42. HSTL, NSC File, Box 3, Memoranda for the President, Korean Situation & Daily Korean Summary/Bulletin, September 1, 1950–March 30, 1951 [Folder 1 of 2], Daily Korean Summary, November 20, 1950.
43. Foot quotes a late November 1950 CIA report claiming that intelligence on Chinese intentions was "not conclusive." Foot, *The Wrong War*, 99.
44. Foot, 99.
45. HSTL, NSC File, Box 3, Memoranda for the President, Korean Situation & Daily Korean Summary/Bulletin, September 1, 1950–March 30, 1951 [Folder 1 of 2], Daily Korean Summary, November 28, 1950.
46. Brodie, *Strategy in the Missile Age*, 317–318.
47. Futrell, *The United States Air Force in Korea 1950–1953*, 241–242; see also HSTL, PSF, Box 188, Memoranda for the President: Meeting Discussions: 1950, Memorandum for the President, November 28, 1950.
48. Crane, *American Airpower Strategy in Korea, 1950–1953*, 56.
49. Gaddis, *Strategies of Containment*, 116; Millett and Maslowski, *For the Common Defense*, 487.
50. Foot, *The Wrong War*, 124–125; Gacek, *The Logic of Force*, 57; DeWeerd, "The Triumph of the Limiters: Korea," 15.
51. Futrell, *United States Air Force in Korea 1950–953*, 241–242.
52. Foot, *The Wrong War*, 123; Brodie, *Strategy in the Missile Age*, 317–318; HSTL, PSF, Box 188, Memoranda for the President: Meeting Discussions: 1950, Memorandum for the President, November 10, 1950.
53. Foot, 23.
54. Clodfelter, *The Limits of Airpower*, 13.
55. Crane, *American Airpower Strategy in Korea 1950–1953*, 85.
56. Foot, *The Wrong War*, 90–91.
57. Halperin observed this phenomenon over fifty years ago, though he lacked archival documentation from both sides to corroborate this theory. Halperin, "The Limiting Process in the Korean War," 36. Foot emphasizes this aspect of the narrative in explaining American restraint. She wrote about the period, "at this point it seemed that the absence of

a Chinese air attack was all that kept the administration from an expansion of the war." Foot, *The Wrong War*, 143–144.
58. There were, in fact, a host of restrictions on Communist jets flying from Manchuria. Zhang, *Red Wings over the Yalu*, 139.
59. HSTL, PSF, Box 182, Meetings: 80: January 17, 1951, NSC 101 A Report to the National Security Council, January 12, 1951. NSC 101/1 has similar language. See, in the same folder, NSC 101/1 dated January 15, 1951.
60. Gacek, *The Logic of Force*, 57–58. See also Foot, *The Wrong War*, 118–119.
61. Foot, *The Wrong War*, 138.
62. Cliff et al., *Entering the Dragon's Lair*, 62–64.
63. Clodfelter, *The Limits of Airpower*, 20.
64. Futrell, *The United States Air Force in Korea 1950–1953*, 373.
65. Futrell, 373. See also a December 1950 meeting in which Secretary Acheson appears to oppose blockade of China partly because of his pursuit of an armistice. HSTL, PSF, Box 188, Memorandum for the President: Meeting Discussions: 1950, Memorandum for the President, December 15, 1950.
66. Crane, *American Airpower Strategy in Korea, 1950–1953*, 75.
67. Manzo, "After the First Shorts: Managing Escalation in Northeast Asia," 95–96.

CHAPTER 4

OPERATION ROLLING THUNDER AND THE VIETNAM WAR

Operation Rolling Thunder, the codename for US air operations over North Vietnam, was fought, in a metaphor that pervades the historical record, with "one hand tied behind our back."[1] For some stretches of the air campaign over North Vietnam from 1965 to 1968, all of North Vietnam was off limits.[2] During these times, the entire air campaign would grind to a halt on presidential orders, and Communist troops could resupply without the threat of air attack. At other times, only particular geographic sections of North Vietnam were deemed open for bombing. Especially at the beginning of Operation Rolling Thunder, only targets relatively close to the 17th parallel were allowed.[3] Targets farther north were barred. Most famously, targets in Hanoi and Haiphong, the capital of North Vietnam and the main port of North Vietnam, respectively, were often prohibited.[4] In fact, there were politically imposed rings, of varying diameters, centered on these zones in which bombing required presidential authorization.[5] The Chinese border also had a buffer zone, twenty-five or thirty miles depending on the particular part of the border, in which US planes were often denied access on political orders. This restriction was in force despite heavy Communist use of this area for transportation of war matériel from China to North Vietnam and eventually to the Communist-supported insurgents, the Viet Cong, in South Vietnam.[6] Targets inside China, including Chinese air bases that harbored North Vietnamese planes, were emphatically placed beyond American attack.[7] Certain target types were also off limits. North Vietnamese air bases, which often housed fighters that posed a threat to American pilots and operations, were, for at least a time, inviolate from American attack.[8] Surface-to-air missile sites and North Vietnamese airfields, thought to be under construction by Soviet advisors, were also often shielded from attack by the rules of engagement.[9] Though many of these restrictions loosened in the later years of the war, their existence for months or years prior to their loosening reduced the effectiveness of the air campaign.[10]

Those interested in the modern debate over mainland strikes should devote their attention to the wrangling over target selection during Rolling Thunder for three reasons. First, debates over target selection defined the air war over North Vietnam. Different geographies and different targets in North Vietnam were often shielded from American air attack. Political restrictions led to the creation of "sanctuaries" above the seventeenth parallel in which the North Vietnamese could operate freely. Any researcher inquiring into debates over intra-war conventional escalation in American military history would be delinquent to exclude Operation Rolling Thunder. Second, the debates over target selection during Rolling Thunder were acrimonious.[11] As a result, this airing of bureaucratic grievances provides insight into the reasons why particular actors supported or opposed particular strikes.[12] Third, both Chinese and Russian possession of nuclear weapons enable this case study to analyze the extent to which adversary possession of nuclear weapons constrains American conventional escalation.

This chapter answers two questions about these restrictions. First, which of the models relating nuclear weapons to conventional explanations best explain these restrictions on conventional bombing during

Operation Rolling Thunder? Second, more broadly, what are the scenario-related factors that explained patterns of restraint in conventional bombing during Operation Rolling Thunder? A final section uses the analytical interpretations from earlier sections to engage the debate over mainland strikes.

COMMUNIST NUCLEAR WEAPONS AND CONVENTIONAL ESCALATION IN THE VIETNAM WAR

Despite the Soviet possession of nuclear weapons and the Chinese acquisition of nuclear weapons in late 1964, the historical record—many meetings and memos related to bombing over North Vietnam—is notably absent of concern by American policymakers of Chinese or Soviet nuclear use. An analyst should be especially surprised given the extent to which President Johnson and his advisors feared the possibility of Chinese and Soviet intervention on behalf of North Vietnam. This pattern of facts is most consistent with the null model: nuclear weapons, at least in this conflict, did not affect conventional escalation decisions. This section first documents the intense concerns of President Johnson and his advisors about Soviet and Chinese intervention and then systematically addresses the role of Soviet and Chinese nuclear weapons in explaining patterns of American escalation in Operation Rolling Thunder.

A Fear of Chinese and Soviet Intervention

The many, often conflicting historical accounts of President Johnson's decision-making agree on this point: preventing Soviet or Chinese entrance into the Vietnam War became a central consideration for the president and his advisors during deliberations over target selection in Rolling Thunder.[13] Neither President Johnson nor his advisors shied away from voicing their fear of this outcome.

Before Operation Rolling Thunder commenced, the president and his advisors spent the better part of a year considering different forms of airstrikes on North Vietnam. In one meeting, Central Intelligence Agency Director John McCone opposed a sustained air attack on North Vietnam because this action might "trigger major increases in Chinese communist participation."[14] Secretary of State Dean Rusk and William Bundy, the Assistant Secretary of State for East Asian and Pacific Affairs, also opposed more overt measures against the North in this early stage of the Vietnam War for fear of Chinese involvement.[15] Other advisors, throughout the war, expressed a similar fear. Clark Clifford, who replaced Robert McNamara as Secretary of Defense, opposed expansion of Operation Rolling Thunder in early 1968 because of the prospect of Russian or Chinese intervention.[16]

In the summer of 1966, during discussions about targeting petroleum, oil, and lubricants (POL) sites, General Earle Wheeler, the Chairman of the Joint Chiefs, and President Johnson exchanged acrimonious words about the possibility of Chinese and Soviet intervention. After General Wheeler proposed potentially mining Haiphong Harbor, a key port in Northern Vietnam through which the Soviets transported war matériel, President Johnson asked, "do you think this will involve the Chinese Communists and the Soviets?" When Wheeler replied, "no, sir," the president fired back, "are you more sure than MacArthur was?"[17]

Doris Kearns Goodwin's book *Lyndon Johnson and the American Dream* contains a collection of quotations from ex-President Johnson in which he discussed how he feared Chinese and Soviet intervention. In a conversation with Goodwin, he said:

> I never knew as I sat there in the afternoon, approving targets one, two, and three, whether one of those three might just be the one to set off the provisions of those secret treaties. In the dark at night, I would lay awake picturing my boys flying around North Vietnam, asking myself an endless series of questions. What if one of the targets you picked today triggers off Russia or China? What happens then? Or suppose one of my boys misses his mark when

he's flying around Haiphong? Suppose one of his bombs falls on one of those Russian ships in the harbor? What happens then?[18]

President Johnson clearly expressed fears that some targets in North Vietnam, if struck, might lead to a wider war with China or the Soviet Union.[19] Elsewhere in Goodwin's book, she quotes Johnson: "By keeping a lid on all designated targets, I knew I could keep the control of the war in my own hands. If China reacted to our slow escalation by threatening to retaliate, we'd have plenty of time to ease off the bombing."[20] Historical research by John Lewis Gaddis and Stanley Karnow corroborates that President Johnson genuinely feared Chinese and Soviet intervention—including direct intervention—and therefore restricted strikes on certain targets.[21]

The Shadow of Communist Nuclear Weapons?
The Soviet Union acquired nuclear weapons in 1949.[22] China developed nuclear weapons in October 1964, only months before the start of Operation Rolling Thunder.[23] Given that there is an abundance of evidence that President Johnson and his advisors feared Chinese and Soviet intervention and that so many restrictions on target selection existed, one might expect that communist possession of nuclear weapons led to constrained rules of engagement. One of the most prominent secondary sources on Rolling Thunder, Mark Clodfelter's *The Limits of Airpower*, even emphasizes Soviet and Chinese nuclear weapons as an explanation of President Johnson's strict rules of engagement.[24] This historical interpretation is similar to the argument advanced by skeptics of mainland strikes—that Chinese nuclear weapons reduce the probability of mainland strikes and constrain any decision to employ mainland strikes.[25]

According to the best available historical evidence, however, fear of nuclear war does not appear to underpin the caution that Johnson and his advisors displayed when restricting targets in North Vietnam. Instead, the null model best explains the pattern of conventional escalation decision-making in Operation Rolling Thunder. An examination of the historical records of the Johnson administration—especially meeting minutes and memos related to targeting decisions during Operation Rolling Thunder—does not reveal an American fear that Chinese and Soviet intervention would lead to nuclear war. The remainder of this section examines meetings and memos in which this fear, if it existed, would materialize, though no evidence of it appears.

At a July 1965 meeting, President Johnson and his advisors—most advisors at this particular meeting are connected to the military—extensively discussed the possibility of Chinese intervention. President Johnson repeatedly discussed the proper American response and the outcome should China intervene, but no advisor (nor the president himself) raised the possibility of nuclear escalation.[26] An absence of concern over nuclear war can also be seen in President Johnson's civilian advisors. A July 1965 meeting with significantly more civilian attendance also did not produce worries of nuclear conflagration if China intervenes. Notably, Undersecretary of State George Ball pointed out that "there remains a great danger of intrusion by Chicoms [Chinese communists]" but went on to discuss not the problem of nuclear war but the problem of casualties lowering US public support for the war and the difficulty for great powers of defeating guerillas.[27] The high cost of nuclear war or its possibility owing to inadvertent causes was not one of Undersecretary Ball's concerns when discussing Chinese Communist intervention.

In a June 1966 National Security Council meeting, President Johnson and his advisors discussed the potential advantages and disadvantages of striking North Vietnamese POL targets. Despite prodding by the president meant to elicit all the benefits and drawbacks of such a move and despite a clear worry of potential large-scale Chinese and Soviet intervention, no advisor mentioned nuclear war as a possible result. Even Ambassador to the United Nations Arthur Goldberg and Undersecretary Ball, both noted skeptics of the bombing, did not mention nuclear war despite their opposition to bombing POL targets.[28]

Operation Rolling Thunder and the Vietnam War   75

Meeting notes from the fall of 1967 reveal a similar absence of references to nuclear weapons. President Johnson and his advisors discussed strikes on Soviet fighter aircraft (MiG) air bases in North Vietnam, a target set that had long been restricted despite the threat that MiGs posed to US aircrew and aircraft. Because MiGs had been supplied to North Vietnam and were even operated by China and the Soviet Union, these air bases had been considered off-limits in order to minimize possible adverse reactions by the Communist superpowers. But the conversation about striking these targets never raised, even obliquely, worries about nuclear escalation.[29] A meeting from earlier on the same topic strengthens the confidence with which an analyst can say that nuclear fears were not important when the Johnson administration considered strikes on MiG air bases. Despite a warning from Secretary of Defense McNamara that these strikes put more "pressure on the Chinese and Soviets to react," neither McNamara nor other advisors raised the possibility of nuclear escalation.[30]

Some of the evidence suggesting that the Johnson administration did not factor in Communist nuclear weapons when making conventional escalation decisions comes from President Johnson himself. In an August 1967 meeting with news correspondents, he stated:

> We have many more targets authorized than have been hit. The ones which have not been authorized are delicate and dangerous. There are two reasons they are delicate and dangerous: hitting them might result in the possible involvement of China and the Soviet Union; there could be more loss of lives and aircraft involved than the destruction of targets would gain.[31]

But President Johnson does not elaborate further on the first reason. If nuclear fears were hanging over President Johnson's decision-making, such an elaboration would be reasonable and perhaps even expected. Later that fall, President Johnson again had an opportunity to demonstrate the fear that Chinese intervention could eventually lead to nuclear war, but his thinking and decisions do not reveal such a consideration. In a discussion between the president and Secretary McNamara about hitting targets that were previously restricted, including those in the Haiphong Harbor, Secretary McNamara noted that the "basic argument" against striking ships in Haiphong Harbor is "the fear of hitting Soviet ships."[32] But neither President Johnson nor Secretary McNamara directly mentioned any fear that accidentally striking a Soviet ship could lead eventually to a nuclear war. President Johnson again failed to mention a nuclear dimension to his political restrictions on some targets during a candid conversation with young sailors in February 1968. The president was on the *USS Constellation*, an aircraft carrier, and was fielding questions from young sailors. When one sailor suggested that the United States "hit them more," the president launched into a long explanation of why there are restrictions on some targets:

> We are trying to keep them (meaning Chinese and Russia) actively out of it. If you hit two or three ships in that harbor—it is like slapping and I would slap back. We don't want a wider war. They have a signed agreement that if they get into a war, the Russians and Chinese will come to their aid. They have two big brothers that have more weight and people than I have. They are very dangerous. If the whole family jumps on me—I have all I can say grace over now—this is the reason the Secretaries of Defense and State have to see that what damage we will do them will be in the end not so dangerous. We will do better tomorrow than yesterday, but if we provoke both of them and get them on us, if we have all three actively fighting us—we are not trying to make this a wider war.[33]

President Johnson clearly feared a "wider war" but his admittedly vague language never defined wider as "nuclear." If the President truly did fear nuclear war, one would expect that language to be used here, but it is not. A meeting between President Johnson and ex-President Dwight Eisenhower produces a similar finding; the two presidents exchanged frank remarks about the possibility of Chinese intervention—President Johnson even asks about what ex-President Eisenhower would recommend should Chinese forces "come South"—and instead of the two shuddering at the possibility of nuclear war, President Eisenhower urged military measures like ("hit them at once with air") and raised the possibility of American use of tactical nuclear weapons.[34] Chinese or Soviet nuclear use and the possibility of a nuclear exchange seems relegated to a lesser or nonexistent role in this conversation.

The strongest pieces of evidence can be found in a memo and an information paper prepared by Undersecretary of State George Ball and head of the Far Eastern Division of the Bureau of Intelligence and Research at the Department of State, Allen Whiting. Both officials were skeptics of bombing in North Vietnam and both worried about the possibility of a large-scale intervention by China reminiscent of China's previous entrance into the Korean War. Prior to the so-called Honolulu Conference, a major Vietnam War policy conference in early 1966, government officials and analysts debated many aspects of the war, including Rolling Thunder. Ball wrote a long, lawyerly memo (transmitted to national security advisor McGeorge Bundy and then placed into the president's nightly reading) laying out reasons why Rolling Thunder should be halted, but the central reason is captured in the memo's title: "The Resumption of Bombing Poses [a] Grave Danger of Precipitating a War with China."[35] He wrote, "sustained bombing of North Viet-Nam will more than likely lead us into war with Red China—probably in six to nine months." He warned that a "sustained bombing program acquires a life and dynamism of its own" and that this dynamic could lead to undesirable escalation. But the memo, despite laying out a forceful case against bombing premised on a likely massive Chinese intervention, never mentioned the possibility of nuclear war. Additionally, this memo is based on a piece of writing, somewhat unofficial, produced by Allen Whiting, a China scholar then working in the State Department's intelligence bureau. Whiting's memo is similarly thorough and also detailed the dangers of Chinese intervention—the memo has a series of rebuttals to common claims about why China will not intervene more directly in the Vietnam War.[36] Clearly attempting to marshal the strongest case possible about the perils of continuing to bomb North Vietnam, Whiting still never mentioned explicitly the possibility of nuclear war. At the very least, other reasons were sufficiently compelling that the logic of a conventional war transforming into a nuclear war never appears.

In sum, available unclassified records do not indicate that President Johnson and his advisors feared Chinese and Soviet nuclear use when making target selection decisions during Operation Rolling Thunder. As in the Korean War case study, the null model most easily accounts for this pattern. The caution and emboldenment models find no support. These findings cast some doubt on the beliefs of modern strategists who believe that Chinese possession of nuclear weapons will preclude mainland strikes.

Why do these findings contradict those of Mark Clodfelter's *The Limits of Airpower*, the seminal text on US airpower during the Vietnam War? Clodfelter relies on several pieces of relatively weak evidence to substantiate his point that adversary nuclear weapons constrained American air operations. For instance, Clodfelter places some weight on a line from the president's memoir *The Vantage Point* in which ex-President Johnson wrote, "above all else, I did not want to lead this nation and the world into nuclear war or even the risk of such a war."[37] This quotation does not, however, refer to specific targeting decisions, weakening this piece of evidence in comparison to the archival research presented earlier. Clodfelter also cites Secretary of State Dean Rusk's observation regarding the effect of nuclear weapons on the president. President Johnson's fear of nuclear war was, according to Rusk, "difficult to overestimate. That box [containing the command mechanisms needed to launch nuclear weapons] constantly followed the president and hung like a millstone around his neck."[38] This quotation, like the one above, is general and does not deal with specific targeting decisions. The other pieces of supporting evidence offered by Clodfelter have similar limitations.[39]

There are two significant caveats, however, to this chapter's nuclear-related claims. First, North Vietnam, the main belligerent fighting US

Operation Rolling Thunder and the Vietnam War 79

troops, did not possess nuclear weapons, so a future US-China conflict would differ in this regard. But the Chinese and Soviet governments provided direct support to North Vietnam, and the Johnson administration was sometimes fearful of direct intervention by the Soviets or Chinese, which should logically raise the possibility of Chinese or Soviet nuclear use. Second, China possessed only a rudimentary nuclear arsenal at the time and likely only had the capability, at most, to strike regional targets—US allies or military bases—in the East Asia region with nuclear weapons.[40] This regional capability is in contrast with the capability to target the US homeland with nuclear weapons. The Chinese inability to target the continental United States with nuclear weapons could explain why President Johnson and his advisors did not fear Chinese nuclear use. Nonetheless, China could have struck American allies in East Asia or American bases in East Asia. Additionally, the Soviet Union, also aiding North Vietnam and also a possible entrant into the Vietnam War, did possess the ability to target the American homeland.[41]

Scenario Factors and Conventional Escalation in Operation Rolling Thunder

There were nonetheless a variety of factors that did impinge upon the target selection process led by President Johnson and his advisors. Each of the following sections briefly comments on the relevance of that factor in a future US-China war for a mainland strikes decision. In aggregate, the large number of political and strategic reasons that inhibited conventional escalation during Operation Rolling Thunder should concern American strategists that see mainland strikes, especially mainland strikes early in a conflict, as important for American operational success in a potential US-China war.

Tit-For-Tat Retaliation

The proximate origins of Operation Rolling Thunder can be found in a series of decisions in 1964 and early 1965 in which aerial strikes on

North Vietnam were authorized in a tit-for-tat fashion. Only increasingly bold and brazen attacks on American forces triggered, albeit in many small steps, the massive bombing campaign in the North. The attacks associated with the Gulf of Tonkin incident, the raid at Pleiku on a US air base, and a bombing in Qui Nhon at a hotel housing American enlisted men precipitated limited, retaliatory strikes, though this circumscribed campaign eventually gave way to a much larger, sustained campaign of strikes on North Vietnam.

After an alleged attack in August 1964 by North Vietnamese patrol boats on US destroyers offshore of Vietnam in international waters, President Johnson authorized the first air attack against North Vietnam.[42] The air attacks, called Operation Pierce Arrow, were limited to targets directly related to the original attack: patrol boats, port facilities, and nearby oil storage facilities.[43] The Joint Chiefs of Staff had recommended a much larger campaign of strikes on ninety-four targets, but President Johnson and his advisors were willing to ratchet up American air attacks only in measured doses.[44] In a Joint Chiefs of Staff memo in September 1964, the chiefs even express their opposition to the term "tit for tat," which had been used in contingency planning for the air war in North Vietnam. The chiefs argue that the term "could be interpreted to limit too narrowly our response to an attack on US units."[45]

The tit-for-tat retaliation pattern continued in February 1965 despite the concerns of the top brass. Viet Cong attacks destroyed a score of aircraft and killed eight Americans on February 7. Operation Flaming Dart I began the next day. American and South Vietnamese planes then struck North Vietnamese barracks just across the demilitarized zone; retaliation was therefore limited and proportional. The then commander of Pacific Command, Admiral USG. Sharp, called this decision an example of an "unfortunate pattern throughout the war" in which the civilian policymaker chose the "weakest attack option available."[46] Notes from a post–Pleiku National Security Council meeting reveal that Secretary of Defense McNamara and US Ambassador at Large for Soviet Affairs Llewelyn

Thompson both viewed American actions as retaliatory. Thompson suggested, "the punishment should fit the crime. No additional air strikes should be made now."[47]

Another attack, this one on February 10 at an American quarters for enlisted men, produced another American retaliatory attack.[48] Operation Flaming Dart II included nearly thirty South Vietnamese planes and twenty American planes. These attacks were on targets previously struck a few days earlier or on sites near the demilitarized zone.[49]

These air operations quickly lost their tit-for-tat character. Operation Rolling Thunder commenced in March 1965 and was intended to be a sustained campaign of air strikes de-linked from any particular North Vietnamese provocation.[50]

This tit-for-tat dynamic constrained bombing operations over North Vietnam because the United State Air Force could only strike targets north of the 17th parallel after North Vietnam had committed sufficiently grave attacks. This phenomenon could foreshadow a future situation in which the US military only gains permissions for mainland strikes after sufficiently escalatory attacks by China—for example, missile attacks on an American air base or aircraft carrier. This sort of "defensive" authorization may contrast with the preferences of some strategists for early strikes on the Chinese mainland.

A Weak South Vietnamese Government
President Johnson expressed and demonstrated reluctance to bomb targets in North Vietnam when domestic politics in South Vietnam appeared in disarray. Especially in late 1964 and early 1965, President Johnson believed that "[there is] no point in hitting the North if the South [is] not together."[51] He therefore, in at least one instance after a bombing in Saigon, denied permission for attacks on targets in the North so that US reprisals did not spark further attacks while South Vietnam was "too shaky."[52] President Johnson had previously stated that he was loathe to "enter the patient [South Vietnam] in a 10-round bout, when he was in

no shape to hold out for one round. We should get him ready to face 3 or 4 rounds at least."[53] He also appears to have felt unwilling to authorize attacks that might be seen as condoning and supporting a regime with chaotic internal politics.[54]

Although this concern could be idiosyncratic, a future US administration might worry about supporting an ally or partner—for instance, Taiwan—that could be experiencing severe internal domestic turmoil during a future conflict with China. This is a concern not previously mentioned in the strategic debate over the likelihood of mainland strikes.

Bombing as a Tool of Coercive Diplomacy

The bombing in the North eventually morphed into a diplomatic tool. American leaders wielded it to inflict pain on the North Vietnamese leadership in the hope of inducing peace talks and repeatedly paused bombing in an attempt to signal American willingness to engage in talks. Early in Operation Rolling Thunder, senior officials began to view the operation as a means to "hurt" the North Vietnamese leadership.[55] More bombing meant greater damage, which theoretically produced more diplomatic leverage. This view was well-expressed through the words of retired General Curtis Lemay: "the military task confronting us is to make it so expensive for the North Vietnamese that they will stop their aggression against South Vietnam and Laos. If we make it too expensive for them, they will stop."[56]

The belief in bombing as a form of coercive diplomacy eventually transformed into a controversial argument in favor of periodic restrictions on bombing in North Vietnam. One bombing halt was in late December 1965, when all bombing operations over North Vietnam were stopped. President Johnson and his top civilian advisors hoped that a temporary halt might increase the chances for diplomacy to work; a Polish diplomat, sent by the Soviets, was negotiating in Hanoi, and the Americans did not want to sabotage the effort.[57] This instance was part of a larger pattern of "signaling," in which the United States leadership sought to convey to North Vietnam American willingness to halt bombing and, simultaneously, to hint at the threat of resumed bombing.[58] Critics have found fault in the attempt to use "studied restraint" in an attempt to send signals to Hanoi.[59] Whatever the merits of this approach, it is clear that these attempts to signal grew out of an earnest belief that American restraint might lead to a similar move by the North.[60] But to return to the late 1965 episode, American restraint did not produce the intended response from the adversary. Ho Chi Minh, the North Vietnam Communist leader, rejected the offer of peace talks presented by the Polish diplomat and criticized the bombing pause as a "sham peace trick."[61] This rejection led President Johnson and his advisors to resume bombing the North. There would be at least eight bombing pauses throughout the course of Operation Rolling Thunder.[62]

A future US decision about mainland strikes could be influenced by considerations about coercive diplomacy. For instance, one analyst has previously suggested that mainland strikes "could change their [China's] calculus and motivate them to seek a peaceful off-ramp" during a war.[63] And that coercive diplomacy via target selection featured so prominently during Operation Rolling Thunder does suggest that mainland strikes could become entangled in a high-stakes debate over American "signaling" to Chinese leaders.

Avoiding Civilian Casualties
Top decision-makers were also anxious to avoid civilian casualties during Operation Rolling Thunder. As a result, some targets, especially those in Hanoi and Haiphong, were restricted.[64] For instance, when discussing whether to bomb several bridges in the politically sensitive northeast quadrant of North Vietnam, Secretary of Defense Robert McNamara worried that these targets are "smack in the middle of Haiphong and Hanoi," and though he conceded that they may need to be struck "at some point," he asserted that this would be contingent on the "civilian casualties not being heavy."[65] This concern about bombing targets in Hanoi and the potential for civilian casualties resurfaces in a February

1968 meeting, when McNamara objects to shrinking the no-bomb circle around Hanoi with the observation that "the chance for civilian casualties is very high."[66] Secretary of State Dean Rusk shared McNamara's concern for civilian casualties when authorizing airstrikes in North Vietnam. In one targeting meeting, Secretary Rusk explicitly noted the "possibility of large civilian casualties" when expressing reservations about a request by the Joint Chiefs that bombing be permitted in areas close to the core of Hanoi and Haiphong.[67] Military exigencies did occasionally dampen concern for civilian casualties. The Tet offensive, during which Viet Cong forces staged major coordinated attacks through South Vietnam in early 1968, did lead Chairman of the Joint Chiefs General Earle Wheeler to shed his worries about civilian casualties. With the backdrop of a large, bloody attack by the Viet Cong, the chairman gained additional authority for more targets from Johnson.[68]

A future presidential advisor might similarly caution against targets—for instance, cyber units interspersed in major Chinese cities—that could entail civilian casualties.[69]

Public Opinion
Partially because of public aversion to civilian causalities but for other reasons as well, President Johnson and his advisors paid attention to American public opinion when making decisions about targets in Rolling Thunder. Mark Clodfelter emphasizes that restrictions on target selection owed their origins, in part, to President Johnson's desire to protect the Great Society (a package of domestic programs), maintain a favorable American image abroad, and keep the support of Western allies.[70] The eventual halting of Operation Rolling Thunder in March 1968 can similarly be partially attributed to the growing anti-war movement in the United States and President Johnson's reaction to it.[71]

But political concerns didn't always negate more aggressive targeting. During hearings in the fall of 1967 led by Senator John Stennis, military commanders used the publicity that came along with the hearings to gain approval for targets that were previously restricted. On the opening day of the hearing, a forum in which Johnson expected the chiefs to publicly express their frustration at bombing restrictions, the chiefs simultaneously requested authorization for seventy restricted targets. President Johnson quickly granted permission for sixteen of these strikes, likely to preempt criticism. In the following weeks, he authorized over twenty more.[72]

Meeting notes from the summer of 1966 corroborate the importance of domestic and international audiences in wartime decisions. In response to former Chairman of the Joint Chiefs and former Ambassador to South Vietnam Maxwell Taylor's urging to escalate the war, President Johnson demurs, saying, "I think that public approval is deteriorating, and that it will continue to go down." In that same National Security Council meeting, Ambassador to the United Nations Arthur Goldberg defends his opposition to an expansion of the war by noting his worry about "attrition of friends abroad and people at home." Similarly, once again at this summer 1966 meeting, Undersecretary of State George Ball worries that an expansion of bombing will "affect Europe," undermining allied support.[73]

American public opinion influenced targeting decisions during Operation Rolling Thunder. Public opinion and political jockeying could also determine the nature and timing of mainland strikes, or even whether mainland strikes are employed at all.

Operational Considerations
Top leaders, both military and civilian, also paid close attention to the military value of targets: the contribution of a target to operational goals and the military price in lives and aircraft paid to accomplish a mission. Secretary of Defense Robert McNamara laid out his formula for making targeting decisions during the Vietnam War: "the decision to hit or not hit is a function of an equation that has three primary elements: the value of the target, the risk of US pilot losses, and the risk of widening the war."[74]

Secretary McNamara, often implicated in charges of mismanagement of the air war because of a focus on political concerns, at least claimed to prioritize military considerations, especially the contribution to the war effort and the possibility of casualties. President Johnson shared this sentiment. At a June 1966 National Security Council meeting on the issue of potential strikes on POL targets in North Vietnam, President Johnson voiced a similar sentiment. He stated,

> We know that the North Vietnamese are dispersing their POL stocks in an effort to anticipate our bombing. The effect of not disrupting POL shipments to the North Vietnamese forces in the field is to pay a higher price in US casualties. The choice is one of military lives vs. escalation.[75]

Secretary Rusk framed the military value of targets during this meeting as a necessary consideration given the "elementary obligation to support our combat troops when they are carrying out an assignment."[76] Secretary McNamara also demonstrates that a changing military situation had altered his views on the worth of strikes on POL targets. During the meeting, he revealed,

> Strikes on POL targets have been opposed by me for months. The situation is now changing and the earlier bombing decision must be reconsidered. POL targets are military targets. The military utilization of these targets has been greatly increased. The North Vietnamese dispersion of their POL is lessening our chance of ever destroying their POL supplies. Military infiltration from the North is up sharply. Consequently, the pressure on their lines of communication has increased. Their POL imports have doubled. The military importance of their POL system is way up and will increase further.[77]

General Harold Keith Johnson, Chief of Staff of the Army, hammered home the importance of military considerations, emphasizing that the then ongoing dispersion of POL by North Vietnam meant that only strikes in the immediate future could ensure the complication of North Vietnamese supply routes.[78]

An American president and their advisors will naturally consider the military value of different targets when contemplating strikes. President Johnson and his administration did so when making target decisions during Operation Rolling Thunder. So too will a future president faced with the decision to authorize mainland strikes.

Tactical Cost Imposition

The secondary literature on Operation Rolling Thunder has generally overlooked a concern that motivated President Johnson in his decision to continue bombing targets in North Vietnam. President Johnson had a goal related to tactical cost imposition; he sought to use the bombing to "tie" down North Vietnamese manpower in a massive reconstruction process devoted to repairing the damage inflicted by Operation Rolling Thunder. President Johnson explained:

> Numerically, the North Vietnamese outnumber us 3 to 1. The difference is in the 400 US planes which tie down up to 700,000 of their people repairing their railroads, replacing their bridges, and rebuilding their highways. All of this would be freed to be used against us if we stopped the bombing.[79]

In another meeting with top foreign-policy advisors, President Johnson brought up this consideration in an effort to develop a justification for congressional audiences for continuing to bomb targets in North Vietnam. The meeting notes read:

> The President commented on the picture in today's *New York Times* showing about 20 North Vietnamese troops in water rebuilding a bridge. He suggested this picture be blown up along with another picture of North Vietnamese troops shooting American soldiers. He said the two pictures can be shown to Congressional

committees and you can ask, "Do you want their boys doing this (repairing bridges) or shooting your men?"[80]

President Johnson therefore saw tying down North Vietnamese manpower in the nonthreatening task of rebuilding as an important consideration in continuing to strike targets in North Vietnam.

This desire to occupy the enemy with a less threatening task could emerge during a future US-China war. Mainland strikes could conceivably play a tactical cost imposition role—by focusing Chinese forces on defending their homeland and forcing the Chinese to invest in air defense systems—and therefore lessen the pressure on US forces operating in the Pacific theater.

Managing Adversary Perceptions

Top American government officials also based their target selection calculations on the likely perceptions of Chinese, Soviet, and North Vietnamese officials. Clodfelter first mentioned this general tendency.[81] He writes, "to assure that the war remained limited, Johnson prohibited military actions that threatened, or that the Chinese or Soviets might perceive as threatening, the survival of North Vietnam."[82] A CIA assessment from May 1964 expresses a similar belief that US leaders ought to consider the perceptions of their Communist adversary. This draft special national intelligence estimate notes that "as the scale of GVN [South Vietnam] and US attacks mounted, however, especially if the US seemed adamant against entering negotiation, Hanoi would tend increasingly to doubt the limited character of US aims."[83] If Hanoi, that is, the leaders of North Vietnam, came to believe that the United States intended to overthrow the North Vietnamese state, then the United States would lose its ability to negotiate an end to the conflict.

Future American leaders could also incorporate Chinese perceptions into their decision-making, which could potentially constrain mainland strikes if American leaders feared that Chinese leaders might misperceive mainland strikes as an element of a nuclear counterforce campaign.

The Vietnam War and Implications for Mainland Strikes

The most striking implication is that Chinese nuclear weapons might not preclude or constrain mainland strikes to the extent suggested by mainland strike skeptics. Despite the Johnson administration's fear of Chinese and Soviet intervention, the president and his advisors did not exhibit a fear of conventional war turning into nuclear war. The caution model cannot explain this pattern of conventional escalation. This finding suggests a President could have a freer hand in employing mainland strikes against a nuclear-armed China than skeptics previously allowed. The null model, which does fit the facts of this case, predicts that American decision-makers will see Chinese nuclear weapons as not particularly relevant to their decisions to strike targets on the Chinese mainland—unless, of course, these nuclear weapons are used.

But before skeptics admit defeat, they should insist that one interpretation of the evidence does still benefit their case: the many, diverse, nonmilitary considerations that informed target selection could foreshadow an array of factors that could preclude, delay, or constrain mainland strikes. If the Johnson administration target selection decision-making process is any guide, then an adherence to tit-for-tat retaliation, an aversion to supporting an ally riven by domestic dissent, a belief in bombing as a coercive diplomatic tool, fear of civilian casualties, a need for US public support, operational considerations, tactical cost imposition, and a desire by American leadership to minimize adversary misperceptions could all influence the decision to wield mainland strikes. Some of these factors could favor the prompt use of mainland strikes; operational considerations and a desire to impose tactical costs could argue in favor of swift authorization. Several others, however, push in the opposite direction. For instance, an American leadership might fear that Chinese leaders could perceive American strikes as prelude or part of a decapitation strike aimed at Chinese nuclear weapons or leadership.[84] This might reduce the likelihood of mainland strikes, especially early in a conflict.

These interpretations are likely to irritate both camps. Skeptics of mainland strikes will argue that the historical context is too different to draw any inferences about the effect of Chinese nuclear weapons on the likelihood of mainland strikes. I have made my strongest argument possible why this is not the case and why skeptics should be surprised that Johnson did not fear conventional war turning into nuclear war. The caution model is not as powerful as some might expect. But proponents of mainland strikes will see the possible sources of restraint as idiosyncratic and isolated to Operation Rolling Thunder. They might be right. But that there were so many sources of restraints—so many reasons why the United States fought with "one hand tied behind its back"—should caution those who see mainland strikes as necessary for operational victory during a future US-China war.

The Lingering Question: What About Other Historical Cases?
Undoubtedly, some readers will wonder why this book doesn't focus on other potentially useful historical cases, especially the 1958 Taiwan Strait Crisis, the Cuban Missile Crisis, the Sino-Soviet Border War, the maritime strategy from late in the Cold War, or the India-Pakistan Kargil crisis. After reiterating the initial case selection criteria, this section will briefly address these additional cases and their relevance and implications for the research questions at hand.

This book has focused on the Korean War and Vietnam War because these historical episodes have many obvious similarities to the debate about mainland strikes in a potential future US-China war. Each case featured the United States fighting a hot war marked by a debate over the appropriate dimensions of the American bombing campaign. China was a member of the adversary coalition in both wars. These situations bear obvious similarities to a future US-China. Also importantly, Soviet nuclear weapons, debuted in 1949 before the Korean War, could have influenced American decisions about the dimensions of its conventional bombing campaign in Korea. Chinese and Soviet nuclear weapons could also have both influenced American bombing decisions in the Vietnam War.

Operation Rolling Thunder and the Vietnam War

Admittedly though, these wars were not direct contests between nuclear-armed adversaries, a key analytical limitation and hence a motivation for several of these alternative cases.

The 1958 Taiwan Strait Crisis featured an intense crisis between China, backed by the Soviet Union, and Taiwan, backed by the United States and the active consideration by the Eisenhower administration of strikes on Chinese mainland targets. The standoff involved over one-hundred-thousand Taiwanese troops located on Quemoy, an off-shore island near the Chinese coast, that were on the receiving end of Chinese shelling. The American objective was to ensure resupply of these troops without triggering a broader war.[85] On the one hand, this historical episode is markedly different from a potential future US-China war. Neither China nor Taiwan, the parties involved directly in the conflict, possessed nuclear weapons, and the war plans considered by the United States government actually involved strikes with "tactical"' nuclear weapons on the Chinese mainland. That said, the episode does highlight that strikes on the Chinese mainland received consideration at the highest levels of the US government, but despite this, these strikes were never authorized. Skeptics of mainland strikes will likely find support in this aspect of the case study. Nevertheless, it is worth noting that the war plans supporting mainland strikes persisted and received a hearing during this crisis in large part because of the inadequacy of other military alternatives. Ultimately, however, this crisis sheds relatively little light on wartime escalation given that the United States was able to resupply Taiwanese forces successfully. There was therefore never a wartime test of American willingness to authorize strikes on mainland China.

Next, many observers of twentieth-century politics immediately see parallels between a future US-China war and the Cuban Missile Crisis.[86] Most obviously, this crisis actually involved the potential for direct US-Soviet conflict and involved the possibility of nuclear war. Furthermore, the standard analytical narrative of the Cuban Missile Crisis suggests that both sides restrained their use of conventional force, limiting the amount of force employed and restricting the geography of conflict, in order to reduce the possibility of nuclear war. Skeptics of mainland strikes can therefore point to this case as a likely precedent that mainland strikes will receive a chilly reception in the situation room.

While this crisis did generate intense fears of nuclear war and has become the historical episode most associated with the role of nuclear weapons in international politics, it differs in critical ways from a future US-China war. First, as pointed out by Richard Smoke in *War*, his seminal study on conventional escalation, the Cuban Missile Crisis "was not, technically, a case of escalation in an ongoing war."[87] It was a crisis, a time of heightened tension, and never boiled over into combat. It is therefore conceptual stretching to include the Cuban Missile Crisis in a study of conventional escalation during war. Second, President John F. Kennedy and his advisors were considering conventional strikes on Soviet nuclear weapons stationed in Cuba, not simply Soviet or Cuban conventional forces. These strikes are different from the strikes a future US administration would consider in a US-China war. American leaders would likely target Chinese conventional forces and avoid deliberately targeting Chinese nuclear forces. In sum, it is unwise to rely heavily on this case for the analytical purposes of studying potential mainland strikes.

The Sino-Soviet border war in 1969 also has, according to more than one analyst, some bearing on nuclear weapons and conventional escalation in a future US-China war. A prolonged crisis punctuated by border clashes and war scares, the Sino-Soviet border war has mostly suggested to analysts the dampening effects of nuclear weapons on conventional escalation. T. X. Hammes notes that during the crisis the leadership of both countries "responded to the original crisis cautiously" and that "military moves were announced and essentially transparent."[88] Caitlin Talmadge also offers an analysis of the crisis that emphasizes Chinese paranoia of Soviet nuclear use and that "China's fear...eventually led it to de-escalate the crisis."[89] One interpretation of these findings for a

Operation Rolling Thunder and the Vietnam War

modern US-China conflict might be that the nuclear weapons of both sides will dampen conventional escalation.

But it is hard to make the case that key features of the Sino-Soviet border war are similar to those of a US-China conventional war, as Talmadge notes. The stakes in this border war involved remote geographic territory, and neither side mounted large scale conventional military operations. A Chinese war with Taiwan in which the United States intervened would involve politically and militarily more important stakes and would feature much larger military movements and levels of violence. This case is also therefore of dubious value for the purposes of research on mainland strikes, conventional escalation, and nuclear weapons.

The US maritime strategy in the 1980s also contains notable parallels to US military strategies that emphasize mainland strikes. The Reagan-era "maritime strategy" capitalized on intelligence about Soviet naval doctrine and called for, in the event of war, attacking "bastions" in which the Soviet navy hoped to protect Russian submarine-based ballistic missile forces.[90] Whereas proponents defended this strategy as helping to deter Soviet aggression, skeptics criticized the strategy as creating excessive risk of nuclear war.[91] The emphasis on large-scale offensive action against a nuclear-armed adversary understandably leads to comparisons with modern strategies that involve mainland strikes.

The maritime strategy case study does suggest that leaders are willing to adopt, at least in peacetime, offensive strategies against nuclear-armed powers. But the guidance that this case can provide related to wartime behavior is limited. The US navy and its chain of command never found itself faced with the wartime decision about whether to actually employ attacks on Soviet ballistic missile submarine bastions. Without such a decision, it is hard for an analyst to use this case to weigh in on conventional escalation during war and US military strategy towards China.

At least in comparison to these other potential case studies, the Kargil War, a conflict between Pakistan and India in 1999, bears the closest resemblance to a potential future war involving the United States and China. This conflict was indeed a war, involving the actual employment of violent force and not simply threats of force, and both sides possessed nuclear weapons.[92] The conflict also involved Pakistani military forces seizing Indian territory across an international boundary. Perhaps most importantly, the conflict remained "limited" in that the two sides, especially India, restricted military operations to a relatively proximate geography, choosing not to expand the conflict.

Before explaining the differing interpretations of this conflict and the implications of these interpretations, it is worth reminding the reader that this Kargil War was not chosen for intensive study because the conflict did not involve China and the United States as belligerents (unlike the Korean and Vietnam Wars) and did not involve debate about the geographic dimensions of an American bombing campaign (again, unlike the Korean and Vietnam Wars.) The Korean and Vietnam War cases, for the narrow purposes of a book on US conventional escalation and military strategy towards China, assume priority. But it is understandable that readers will demand to know about other cases, even if inference is harder.

One vein of scholarship argues that nuclear weapons played a key role in the conflict, either in Pakistan's decision to initiate the conflict or India's decision to not attack Pakistan in other theaters or the supply lines of Pakistani troops still in Pakistani territory.[93] In this interpretation of the war, India chose a second-best military strategy (direct ground force attacks on fortified Pakistani positions in inhospitable, mountainous terrain) because Pakistan's nuclear weapons deterred Indian leaders from choosing other, potentially more effective but more escalatory options. The implication of this for US military strategy toward China is that Chinese nuclear weapons could similarly deter US decision-makers from escalatory actions like mainland strikes. The nuclear shadow, in other words, will lead to caution and restraint.

But there is another view, which has received more recent scholarly support: that nuclear weapons mattered little in the Kargil War and that conventional military considerations are adequate for explaining restrained Indian military operations.[94] In this alternative rendering, the threat that Pakistani troops posed was actually relatively minimal, the more escalatory options wouldn't have helped India eject Pakistani troops, and, in fact, India used restraint to increase the chances that US leaders would lean on Pakistan to end the conflict. For scholars of this persuasion, the Kargil War suggests that Chinese nuclear weapons might not be particularly influential in determining American military strategy during a potential conflict.

Analysts interested in US military strategy and conventional escalation should continue to pay attention to the debate over the Kargil War. But, for now, researchers will have to content themselves with the fact that large-scale bombing operations and debate over their geographic limits are relatively rare; still, the Korean and Vietnam Wars have obvious parallels, which is why this book focused its attention on the bombing campaigns within those wars. The next two chapters, which use interview and survey evidence, try to compensate for the inadequacies of using historical cases to study a potential future war.

Notes

1. For an example of this imagery, see Sharp, *Strategy for Defeat,* book jacket. President Lyndon B. Johnson also used this imagery. Lyndon Baines Johnson Presidential Library, Meeting Notes File, Box 1, July 25, 1967–6:10 p.m. Senate Committee Chairmen, Meeting of the President on July 25, 1967, at 6:00 p.m., with the Senate Committee Chairmen, July 25, 1967. All references to archival materials include, in this order, the library, collection, folder, document name, and document date. I also abbreviate Lyndon Baines Johnson Presidential Library as LBJPL and Meeting Notes File as MNF.
2. Clodfelter, *The Limits of Airpower,* 91–92, 119. In fact, President Johnson stopped Rolling Thunder eight times between March 1965 and March 1968.
3. Clodfelter, 63–64, 83, 85; Tilford, *Crosswinds,* 71.
4. Lewy, *American in Vietnam,* 379; Clodfelter, *The Limits of Airpower,* 89.
5. Tilford, *Crosswinds,* 73.
6. Kreis, *Air Warfare and Air Base Air Defense 1914–1973,* 281.
7. Kreis, 297.
8. Air bases Kien An, Cat Bai, Gia Lam, Phuc Yen, and Kep were kept off the target list for much of Operation Rolling Thunder. Kreis, 281; Lambeth, *The Transformation of American Air Power,* 18.
9. Clodfelter, *The Limits of Airpower,* 85.
10. Lewy, *America in Vietnam,* 378–379, 383; Karnow, *Vietnam,* 510; Clodfelter, *The Limits of Airpower,* 92, 95–96, 106; Tilford, *Crosswinds,* 95–96.
11. Sharp, *Strategy for Defeat,* 2–3; Herring, *America's Longest War,* 149, 172–173.
12. Betts first analyzed Vietnam, along with many other cases, to test for the existence of differences between civilian and military attitudes on the use of force before and during war. Betts, *Soldiers, Statesmen, and Cold War Crises.*
13. Clodfelter, *The Limits of* Airpower, 113; Goodwin, *Lyndon Johnson and the American Dream,* 277, 283; Sharp, *Strategy for Defeat,* 4, 33; Barrett, ""Doing Tuesday Lunch" at Lyndon Johnson's White House," 678; Herring, *America's Longest War,* 164, 166; Karnow, *Vietnam: A* History, 504; Tilford, *Crosswinds,* 82, 91, 196; Lambeth, *The Transformation of American Air Power,* 19.

14. LBJPL, MNF, Box 1, September 9, 1964–11:00 a.m. Meeting with Foreign Policy Advisors on Vietnam, Memorandum for the Record, September 9, 1964.
15. Clodfelter, *The Limits of Airpower*, 113.
16. Clodfelter, 113.
17. Clodfelter, 97.
18. Goodwin, *Lyndon Johnson and the American Dream*, 283.
19. One caveat: these conversations happened after the war. A skeptical reader could understandably worry that the ex-President was rationalizing and trying to explain his behavior, behavior that led to a divisive and unpopular war. Perhaps, this reader might worry, ex-President Johnson thought that this worry exculpated him and therefore expressed it in order to deflect blame. He might therefore have never actually had this worry. To assuage this concern, I use statements from other sources too. But because this admission to Kearns is so vivid—and because it jibes with other historical evidence—it clearly demonstrates the analytical point and therefore merits inclusion.
20. Goodwin, *Lyndon Johnson and the American Dream*, 277.
21. Gaddis, *Strategies of Containment*, 245, 248–249; Karnow, *Vietnam*, 426, 481, 499–501.
22. Holloway, *Stalin and the Bomb*.
23. The landmark work on Chinese nuclear weapons, especially their development, is Lewis and Litai, *China Builds the Bomb*. For a widely respected source documenting the start and growth of nuclear weapon inventories country-by-country, including China, see Kristensen and Norris, "Global Nuclear Weapons Inventories, 1945–2013." Kristensen and Norris estimate that China possessed one nuclear warhead in 1964, five in 1965, twenty in 1966, twenty-five in 1967, and thirty-five in 1968. See page twenty-five. Another source, also written by Robert Norris but with different coauthors also provides data on China's limited nuclear weapon delivery capabilities from 1964 to 1968. Chinese nuclear-capable bombers, including the Tu-4 (~3000 nautical mile one-way maximum range), H-6 (~3,500 nautical mile one-way maximum range), and H-5 (~1,500 nautical mile one-way maximum range), grew from a combined inventory of fourteen in 1964 to an inventory of nineteen in 1968. China's DF-2A (NATO codename CSS-1) missile (~1,250 kilometer range) inventory increased from five in 1966 to fifteen in 1968. See table 7-1, "Chinese Nuclear Forces, 1964–1993," from Norris, Burrows, and Fieldhouse, *Nuclear Weapons Databook*, 359. A link to this table can be

found at Burr, "The Chinese Nuclear Weapons Program: Problems of Intelligence Collection and Analysis: 1964-1972," The National Security Archive, George Washington University, http://nsarchive2.gwu.edu//NSAEBB/NSAEBB26/ index.html. The data for the ranges of the bombers are from: *Jane's All the World's Aircraft* editions 1956, 1966, and 1965, respectively. This is an annual aviation publication published by Jane's Information Group. An analyst from Jane's with access to these old editions provided this information; my intent was to use range estimates from that time period, estimates that are more likely to be salient to American policymakers then in comparison to retrospective estimates. The DF-2A range is from *Jane's Strategic Weapon Systems,* "Jane's by IHS Markit" Online Portal, posted 10/13/2011.
24. Clodfelter, *The Limits of Airpower,* 142, 209–210.
25. Joshua Rovner has argued that Chinese nuclear weapons could lead to restrictive rules of engagement and therefore to a protracted US-China war. Rovner, "Two Kinds of Catastrophe"; Michael Beckley also makes a similar argument. Beckley, "The Emerging Military Balance in East Asia," 118–119.
26. The advisers present were Secretary of Defense Robert McNamara, Deputy Secretary of Defense Cyrus Vance, Chairman of the Joint Chiefs General Earle Wheeler, Chief of Staff of the Army General Harold Johnson, Undersecretary of the Army Stanley Resor, Chief of Staff of the Air Force General John McConnell, Commandant of the Marine Corps General Wallace Greene, Chief of Naval Operations Admiral David McDonald, unofficial White House counsel Clark Clifford, Secretary of the Navy Paul Nitze, Secretary of the Air Force Eugene Zuckert, Secretary of the Air Force Harold Brown, and National Security Advisor McGeorge Bundy. These were predominantly military advisers, which could explain this finding. Other meetings and memos, however, contain more civilian representatives and similarly lack discussion of nuclear war. LBJPL, MNF, Box 1, July 21–27, 1965–Meetings on Vietnam, Untitled [Meeting on Vietnam], July 22, 1965.
27. LBJPL, MNF, Box 1, July 21–27, 1965–Meetings on Vietnam, Untitled [Meeting on Vietnam], July 21, 1965.
28. LBJPL, MNF, Box 1, June 22, 1966 National Security Council Meeting, Notes of the President's Meeting the National Security Council, June 22, 1966.

29. LBJPL, MNF, Box 2, October 11, 1967–Prior to Regular Weekly Luncheon Meeting with Foreign Policy Advisors, Private Meeting in the President's Office, October 11, 1967.
30. LBJPL, Tom Johnson Meeting Notes, Box 1, August 24, 1967–5:33 p.m. Rusk, McNamara, Gen. Johnson, Gen. McConnell, Nitze, Notes of the President's Meeting with Secretary Rusk, Secretary McNamara, General Harold Johnson, General John P. McConnell, Under Secretary Paul Nitze, August 24, 1967. I will abbreviate all references to the Tom Johnson Meeting Notes as TJMN.
31. LBJPL, TJMN, Box 1, July 1967–May 1968, Meeting with Correspondents, Notes of the President's Meeting with Bob Lucas, August 14, 1967.
32. LBJPL, TJMN, Box 1, October 4, 1967–7:02 p.m. McNamara, Rusk, Rostow, Notes of the President's Meeting with Secretary McNamara, Secretary Rusk, Walt Rostow, and George Christian, October 4, 1967.
33. LBJPL, TJMN, Box 2, February 18, 1968–8 a.m. President's breakfast with boys on Aircraft Carrier Constellation, Summary of President' Breakfast with Boys on Carrier Constellation, February 18, 1968.
34. LBJPL, TJMN, Box 1, February 17, 1965–10:00 a.m. Meeting with General Eisenhower and Others, Memorandum of Meeting with the President, February 17, 1965.
35. Foreign Relations of the United States, Volume IV, Vietnam, 1966, Document 41, "Memorandum from the Under Secretary of State (Ball) to President Johnson," January 25, 1966, available at https://history.state.gov/historicaldocuments/frus1964-68v04/d41, accessed June 3, 2019.; LBJPL, National Security File, National Security Council History, Honolulu Conference, Box 44, Honolulu Conference, February 6–8, 1966, Vol. 1, Tabs 11–31, Tab 18, Memorandum from McGeorge Bundy, 25 January 25, 1966. I will abbreviate all references to the National Security File, National Security Council History as NSF, NSCH.
36. LBJPL, NSF, NSCH, Box 44, Honolulu Conference, The Resumption of Bombing and Chinese Communist Involvement, January 24, 1966.
37. Clodfelter, *The Limits of Airpower*, 42.
38. Clodfelter, 43.
39. Clodfelter also wrote, "Johnson thought that North Vietnam had entered into secret treaties with the Chinese and Soviets, under which increasing force beyond a certain level would trigger communist…involvement. That involvement could in turn lead to nuclear conflict." But Clodfelter does not provide support for this claim. Elsewhere, he wrote, "by influencing the Soviets to support Hanoi, Rolling Thunder intensified the

President's fear that Vietnam might trigger a nuclear holocaust." This claim rests on two citations, neither of which provide supporting evidence that President Johnson feared Vietnam might trigger a nuclear holocaust. Clodfelter, 42–43, 142.

40. See footnote 226 for a full description of the Chinese nuclear arsenal and its nuclear weapon delivery platforms from 1965 to 1968, the years of Operation Rolling Thunder.
41. The Soviet Union nuclear stockpile increased from approximately 6,100 warheads to 9,500 warheads in the years 1965–1968. And the Soviet Union had developed intercontinental ballistic missiles that could carry nuclear warheads to the continental United States by this time. For stockpile figures, see Kristensen and Norris, "Global Nuclear Weapons Inventories, 1945–2013." For a thorough scholarly work on Soviet nuclear forces, see Podvig (editor), *Russian Strategic Nuclear Forces*.
42. Lambeth, *The Transformation of American Air Power*, 15; For the landmark study of the Gulf of Tonkin Resolution, see Moise, *Tonkin Gulf and the Escalation of the Vietnam War*.
43. Herring, *America's Longest War*, 144.
44. Lambeth, *The Transformation of American Air Power*, 15.
45. LBJPL, MNF, Box 1, September 9, 1964–11:00 a.m. Meeting with Foreign Policy Advisors on Vietnam, Memorandum for the Secretary of Defense, Courses of Action for South Vietnam, September 9, 1964.
46. Tilford, *Crosswinds*, 68.
47. LBJPL, MNF, Box 1, February 7, 1965–8:00 a.m. National Security Council Meeting, Summary Notes of 546th NSC Meeting, February 7, 1965.
48. Herring, *America's Longest War: The United States and Vietnam*, 153.
49. Tilford, *Crosswinds*, 68.
50. Lambeth, *The Transformation of American Air Power*, 16.
51. Clodfelter, *The Limits of Airpower*, 56, 95–96.
52. Herring, *America's Longest War: The United States and Vietnam*, 151.
53. LBJPL, MNF, Box 1, September 9, 1964–11:00 a.m. Meeting with Foreign Policy Advisors on Vietnam, Memorandum for the Record, Meeting on South Vietnam, 9 September, 1964, 11:00 a.m., Cabinet Room, September 9, 1964.
54. Herring, *America's Longest War*, 151.
55. Lambeth, *The Transformation of American Air Power*, 20. For instance, director of the CIA John McCone wrote in April 1965 that the bombing had not yet been "sufficiently heavy and damaging really to hurt the North Vietnamese."

56. LeMay and Kantor, *Mission with LeMay*, 564.
57. Clodfelter, *The Limits of Airpower*, 91–92.
58. Rosen, "Vietnam and the American Theory of Limited War."
59. Lambeth, *The Transformation of American Air Power*, 19.
60. Another example of this belief can be seen in May 1965. The United States had halted bombing for six days. In a meeting with his advisers discussing the pause, President Johnson remarks, "For six days we have held off bombing. Nothing happened. We had no illusions that anything would happen. But we were willing to be surprised. We are anxious to pursue every diplomatic adventure, to get peace. But we can't throw our gun away." LBJPL, MNF, Box 1, May 16, 1965 6:45 p.m. Meeting with Foreign Policy Advisors on Vietnam, Untitled Document, May 16, 1965. Similarly, President Johnson tells his advisers in late 1967 that he will only halt bombing in the North in return for "prompt" and "productive" negotiations." LBJPL, TJMN, Box 1, October 5, 1967–6:55 p.m. McNamara, Rusk, Rostow, Notes of the President's Meeting with Secretary McNamara, Secretary Rusk, Walt Rostow, October 5, 1967.
61. Clodfelter, *The Limits of Airpower*, 91–92.
62. LBJPL, TJMN, Box 1, September 26, 1967–5:46 p.m. Educators from Cambridge, Mass. Small Colleges and Universities, Notes of the President's Meeting with Educators from Cambridge, Massachusetts Colleges and Universities, September 26, 1967.
63. Manzo, "After the First Shots: Managing Escalation in Northeast Asia," 96.
64. Russett, "Vietnam and Restraints on Aerial Warfare," 12.
65. LBJPL, MNF, Box 2, September 5, 1967–1:05 p.m. Tuesday Luncheon, Untitled Document, September, 1967. Another target selection meeting from this time period also contains several references to civilian casualties as an important criterion in target selection. LBJPL, MNF, Box 1, August 18, 1967–8:35 p.m. Meeting with Foreign Policy Advisors on Vietnam, Untitled Document, August 18, 1967. President Johnson in a 1967 interview also implies that "populated areas" (Hanoi in this document) are sometimes off-limits, ostensibly because of the chance of civilian casualties. LBJPL, TJMN, Box 1, July 1967–May 1968, Meeting with Correspondents, Notes of the President's Meeting with Bob Lucas, August 14, 1967.
66. LBJPL, TJMN, Box 2, February 13, 1968–1:12 p.m. Tuesday luncheon group–Rusk, McNamara, Helms, Clifford, Wheeler, Rostow, Notes of the President's Luncheon Meeting, February 13, 1968.

67. Humphrey, "Tuesday Lunch at the Johnson White House: A Preliminary Assessment," 91.
68. Clodfelter, *The Limits of Airpower*, 113. Secretary Rusk's civilian casualty concerns also seem to weaken in the aftermath of Tet. During a discussion of targeting a Hanoi radio headquarters and in response to a question from the president about Rusk's views, he reveals, "it will get a lot of civilians but I feel less strong about the matter now." LBJPL, TJMN, Box 2, February 20, 1968–1:05 p.m. Tuesday luncheon with Rusk, McNamara, Wheeler, Helms, Rostow, Clifford, Notes of the President's Luncheon Meeting with Foreign Policy Advisers, February 20, 1968.
69. Sanger, Barboza, and Perlroth, "Chinese Army Unit Is Seen as Tied to Hacking Against US," *The New York Times*, February 18, 2013.
70. Clodfelter, *The Limits of Airpower*, 118; Stanley Karnow argues that Johnson took moderate steps partly to "reassure the American people." Karnow, *Vietnam: A History*, 426.
71. Clodfelter, *The Limits of Airpower*, 4.
72. Clodfelter, 109.
73. LBJPL, MNF, Box 1, June 22, 1966 National Security Council Meeting, Notes of the President's Meeting the National Security Council, June 22, 1966.
74. Russett, "Vietnam and Restraints on Aerial Warfare," 12.
75. LBJPL, MNF, Box 1, June 17, 1966–6:05 p.m. National Security Council Meeting, Summary Notes of the 559th NSC Meeting, June 17, 1966.
76. LBJPL, MNF, Box 1, June 17, 1966–6:05 p.m. National Security Council Meeting, Summary Notes of the 559th NSC Meeting, June 17, 1966.
77. LBJPL, MNF, Box 1, June 17, 1966–6:05 p.m. National Security Council Meeting, Summary Notes of the 559th NSC Meeting, June 17, 1966.
78. LBJPL, MNF, Box 1, June 17, 1966–6:05 p.m. National Security Council Meeting, Summary Notes of the 559th NSC Meeting, June 17, 1966.
79. LBJPL, TJMN, Box 1, September 26, 1967–5:46 p.m. Educators from Cambridge, Mass. Small colleges and Universities, Notes of the President's Meeting with Educators from Cambridge, Massachusetts Colleges and Universities, September 26, 1967.
80. LBJPL, MNF Box 1, August 18, 1967–8:35 p.m. Meeting with Foreign Policy Advisors on Vietnam, Untitled Document, Meeting with Secretaries Rusk and McNamara, General Earl Wheeler, and Walt Rostow, August 18, 1967.
81. Clodfelter, *The Limits of Airpower*, 43.
82. Clodfelter, 43.

83. National Security File, Country File, Vietnam, Box 201, Vietnam, Special Meeting on Southeast Asia, Vol. I, Draft SNIE 50-2-64: Probable Consequences of Certain US Actions with Respect to Vietnam and Laos, May 23, 1964.
84. Talmadge, "Would China Go Nuclear?"
85. Meyers, "Will a President Approve Air-Sea Battle?"; Halperin, "The 1958 Taiwan Strait Crisis"; Zhang, *Deterrence and Strategic Culture*.
86. Allison and Zelikow, *Essence of Decision*; Dobbs, *One Minute to Midnight*.
87. Smoke, *War*, 44.
88. Hammes, "Offshore Control."
89. Talmadge, "Would China Go Nuclear?" 90.
90. Ford and Rosenberg, "The Naval Intelligence Underpinnings of Reagan's Maritime Strategy"; Swartz and Connell, "Understanding an Adversary's Strategic Calculus"; Hanley, "Creating the 1980s Maritime Strategy and Implications for Today."
91. Posen, "US Maritime Strategy."
92. Tellis, Fair, and Medby, "Limited Conflicts Under the Nuclear Umbrella."
93. Ganguly and Hagerty, *Fearful Symmetry*; Kapur, *Dangerous Deterrent*; Ganguly and Kapur, *India, Pakistan, and the Bomb*.
94. Pegahi, "Pakistan's Nuclear Weapons and the Kargil Conflict."

Chapter 5

Peering into the Future, Part I

Interviews

To complement the historical analysis in the previous chapters, the next two chapters employ "synthetic-historical" methods, probing how American national-security professionals with extensive experience would make decisions in potential conflict scenarios involving mainland strikes. This chapter specifically uses interviews to understand the range of views on mainland strikes across a diverse set of elites and to elicit the decision-making logic they would use in such a situation. Interviewees had both civilian and military credentials and a range of national-security and foreign-policy professional backgrounds that include the State Department, the Defense Department, and the intelligence agencies. They also had a variety of political leanings.

This chapter seeks to answer two research questions. First, what role, if any, do Chinese nuclear weapons play in decision-making about mainland strikes among these elites? Second, which scenario factors do these elites emphasize?

The remainder of this chapter is divided into four sections. The first section describes the interview methodology. Sections two and three address each research question. The final section summarizes the findings.

METHODOLOGY

This chapter's interview methodology comprises a sample of twenty national-security elites, an interview protocol, and a thematic analysis.[1]

Interview Sample

The first step in defining the project's sample involved conceptualizing the universe of American national-security elites. This broad term refers to persons with extensive professional experience in American defense and foreign policy. For the purposes of this research, potential interviewees had to have gained this experience through sustained professional service in the military or as a civilian in the Defense Department, intelligence agencies, the Department of State, Congress, or on the national-security staff. Unfortunately, there is no single list that enumerates American national-security elites.

Turning my broad conceptualization of national-security elites as persons with extensive experience in defense policy and foreign policy into reality therefore required that I contact persons with the requisite professional backgrounds.[2] Approximately thirty emails, many with an introduction from a trusted colleague, turned into twenty interviews.[3] This sample was chosen with an eye to ensuring diversity in several dimensions. First, the interviewees included both military officers and civilians. There were five senior (generals or admirals) and two mid-level military officers (O4-O6) in the sample. The thirteen other interviewees were civilian. Second, the sample included persons with service at a range of organizations: the Defense Department, including US Pacific Command, the Joint Chiefs of Staff, and the Office of the Secretary of Defense; the Department of State, including the Bureau of East Asian and

Pacific Affairs; the national-security staff; and intelligence agencies. Third, interviewees came from both sides of the aisle; there were (excluding the senior military officers) eight Democrats, four Republicans, and three without an obvious partisan affiliation.[4]

A final note about the sample is that approximately half the interviewees have served at the highest levels of the American government. These persons have direct experience with advising presidents and can credibly channel the types of considerations that a president might encounter when deliberating over mainland strikes. The remainder of the sample was far from junior, however, perhaps with the exception of one, though even he had unusually close access to senior levels of decision-making and therefore merits inclusion. All interviewees had significant and relevant professional experience. Additionally, none of the persons had views on mainland strikes that were previously known to me and none were close professional associates to me before the interview.

Interview Protocol
All interviews were semi-structured; that is, while the interview followed a loose script, probing questions sometimes led down unexplored and previously unconsidered avenues. The questionnaires I present in this section should therefore not be taken too literally. They demonstrate the general categories of questions that I asked, but the exact order in which I asked questions varied and there were as many idiosyncratic probes in these interviews as there were planned questions.

The interview questionnaire also evolved over the course of its implementation. The first ten interviews, beginning in September of 2017, were relatively open-ended. Appendix A contains the questionnaire I employed. These questions were intended to identify concepts and language related to mainland strikes that were meaningful to these elites. Additionally, these interviews tried to enumerate considerations related to the decision to recommend mainland strikes. Finally, these interviews were also essential in providing the grist for the initial draft of my survey instrument. The second round of ten interviews, which concluded in August 2018, used relatively specific questions and sometimes even modified versions of the survey instrument presented as vignettes. I often sent these vignettes to the interviewee before the interview so that the interviewee had a chance to read them beforehand or could read them during the interview process. I sometimes read language from these vignettes to the interviewee to elicit their views on specific aspects of a scenario. See appendix B for the interview vignettes.

Seventeen interviews were audio recorded. One interviewee declined to be recorded, and the interview process with two others precluded recording. I kept interview notes for the three interviews that were not recorded. All others were transcribed in full. The interviews lasted anywhere from twenty minutes to an hour and the majority were conducted over the phone. I interviewed three individuals multiple times, so the total number of interviews actually exceeds twenty. To ensure interviewees were candid, I identify them only by their former professional role and the date of their interview.

Finally, it is worth adding some more detail about the questions I asked. One grouping of questions concerned the interviewee's view of Chinese nuclear weapons:

- Do Chinese nuclear weapons make you reluctant to strike targets on the Chinese mainland? Why or why not?
- Do you worry about inadvertent or accidental nuclear war?
- Do you worry about nuclear-conventional entanglement?
- Do you worry about intentional Chinese nuclear use?
- Does the fact that America also possesses nuclear weapons affect your decision-making?

Second, I attempted to discover the potentially wide range of situational factors that would affect the interviewee's decision-making process. I often vaguely described a potential war between China and the United

States and then filled in details as the interviewee asked for context. The questions included but were not limited to:

- If you were in a presidential advisor role, what would be your strategic and tactical considerations? How would you prioritize these considerations?
- How does the scenario matter to you?

These interviews led to ten hours of audio recording and nearly one-hundred pages of transcripts.

Thematic Analysis

The next step was the identification of recurring themes present in the interviews. Before formal analysis began, I drafted a code tree, an a priori series of themes and subthemes. Appendix C contains the code tree. Emergent themes were also created and placed in the tree as they became apparent. In total, the analysis discovered 233 quotations associated with key themes, which focused on Chinese nuclear weapons and on scenario-specific factors.

Chinese Nuclear Weapons

These interviews provide intriguing evidence on the three competing theoretical perspectives on the relationship between nuclear weapons and conventional escalation. To briefly remind the reader, the theoretical chapter outlined the existence of the caution model (mutual nuclear possession leads to less conventional escalation), the null model (no difference in escalation), and the emboldenment model (more conventional escalation). These models compare the level of conventional escalation in conflicts in which both sides possess nuclear weapons to conflicts in which neither side possesses nuclear weapons. The caution model expects interviewees to fear Chinese nuclear escalation either because of the high costs of nuclear war or the possibility of accidental or inadvertent nuclear use, potentially exacerbated by the fear of Chinese conventional-nuclear entanglement. The null model predicts that the interviewees will evince indifference about Chinese nuclear weapons when considering conventional strikes on the Chinese mainland. This theoretical variant argues that adversary nuclear weapons are made irrelevant by other policy considerations or that leaders believe mutual nuclear arsenals lead to nuclear stalemate. Finally, the emboldenment model holds that interviewees and survey takers will be willing to authorize mainland strikes to the extent that they perceive America nuclear superiority or believe the stability-instability paradox operates.

The findings are twofold. First, the caution and null models perform similarly well despite their contrasting predictions. A number of national-security elites express views consistent with one of these two positions. In short, Chinese nuclear weapons do induce fear among some, though not all, interviewed national-security elites when considering mainland strikes. Second, the emboldenment model finds no support from the interviewees. American nuclear superiority did not figure in the decision model of these nationa-security elites when they were considering mainland strikes. The remainder of this subsection explains these findings.

The Caution Model
Eleven of the twenty interviewees made statements that expressed at least some caution about conventional strikes on the Chinese mainland and the danger of nuclear war. A handful of these interviewees demonstrated extreme skepticism toward the use of mainland strikes and a heightened sense of fear, whereas the rest of the eleven exhibited minimal to moderate levels of reservation. Some interviewees expressed worries about nuclear-conventional entanglement and the possibility of Chinese misperception. The caution school therefore finds moderate, though not overwhelming, evidence in its favor. Some elites do express the intensity of caution that this theoretical perspective predicts. The rest of this section provides notable quotations and a more fine-grained analysis.

Peering into the Future, Part I 111

A few national-security elites voiced intense concerns about the potential for conventional strikes on the Chinese mainland to lead to Chinese nuclear escalation. For instance, one former senior officer with experience at Pacific Command told me:

> Doing mainland strikes on somebody's country is 1960's thinking, 1950's thinking...It's just not realistic. Like some superpower is just going to stand by and let you just plink away on their homeland. We wouldn't do it. We wouldn't stand by.[5]

The same individual mentioned the opposite perspective—that "we'll just go in and attack the mainland, we'll just drop three or four thousand precision weapons on top of another country that is emerging as a nuclear superpower"—and stated, "that's probably not something you would like to do." He also worried that mainland strikes would "probably" lead to a nuclear conflagration. And although he did concede that an American president might be willing to take this step in some circumstances, he warned:

> I think you've got superpowers out there that think they can win a nuclear war with the United States, they can survive it...They've said it already back to Mao and I think it has been repeated in the Chinese approach...This is something that if you're the president of the United States you've got to consider as you think about actions you take against a nuclear power.[6]

Another interviewee, this one a former senior Department of Defense civilian official, cautioned that mainland strikes would be "escalatory" and that "launching thousands of strikes into Beijing or mainland China elsewhere doesn't seem like the smartest way to keep things constrained and below the nuclear threshold."[7] The interviewee added, "I think you would take significant pause at the fact that the Chinese had nuclear ICBMs," and further clarified that this worry would hold even though Chinese leaders would know the United States "would hit back." Another senior civilian official repeated the fear that American nuclear weapons might not preclude Chinese nuclear use. The interviewee explained, "you can't convince ourselves that just because the theory says they should be deterred....It may not work that way."[8] China's possession of nuclear weapons was salient to this interviewee and motivated the interviewee's search for "asymmetric" options (the interviewee's term) other than mainland strikes.

Other national-security elites expressed moderate concern about Chinese nuclear weapons when considering mainland strikes. A formerly high-level civilian at the Defense Department described nuclear weapons as "hanging over" the situation. He said, "there's no way it can't hang over and can't be a consideration. And any presidential advisor would have to have that be a consideration."[9] Another interviewee argued that China's nuclear weapons "changes how you are going to fight them." He elaborated, "the possession of nuclear weapons by China puts us into something where we have to be more judicious in our connection of the ends of what we are trying to pursue with the ways and the means."[10] Others also expressed concern, though their language suggested that Chinese nuclear weapons were simply one important concern among many when considering mainland strikes.[11]

Several interviewees did worry out loud about the potential for Chinese nuclear-conventional entanglement in combination with mainland strikes to lead to Chinese fears of an American counterforce or leadership decapitation campaign. A civilian with experience at Pacific Command wondered if the United States can "demonstrate to China or guarantee to China that our strikes are not meant to limit their first strike stability and are purely focused on conventional?"[12] He feared that mainland strikes could be interpreted as aimed at eliminating China's secure second-strike capability. Another interviewee expressed general concern about "blinding" Chinese decision-makers, that is, striking systems that provide Chinese leadership with early warning of American nuclear attacks and general situational awareness.[13] Several national-security elites singled out Chinese nuclear command and control systems, the technical capabilities to direct Chinese nuclear forces, as particularly dangerous when it came to mainland strikes.[14] One interviewee specifically mentioned the possibility that the Chinese leadership could perceive the United States as engaged in a leadership decapitation strategy and another worried about Chinese fears of losing "integrity" in their command and control systems.[15]

In sum, slightly more than half of the national-security elites that I interviewed demonstrated thinking consistent with the predictions of the caution school. Mainland strikes, at least under some circumstances, could generate the possibility of Chinese nuclear use. Much of the evidence did not directly bear on the exact logic at play, high costs or inadvertent nuclear use, but there were a handful of interviewees who did express concern about Chinese nuclear-conventional entanglement and the possibility that Chinese leaders might misperceive mainland strikes as part of a counterforce campaign. Although some scholars have argued that American leaders ought not to fear Chinese perceptions of a "use it or lose it" situation, this evidence suggests that at least some American decision-makers do exhibit such strategic empathy.[16]

The Null Model
The null model and its prediction that American national-security elites will believe Chinese nuclear weapons to be irrelevant or stalemated by American nuclear weapons were also consistent with the thinking of some interviewees. A number of the elites expressed outright skepticism about a potential connection between mainland strikes and Chinese nuclear use. Others seriously qualified the circumstances under which mainland strikes, in their opinion, could lead to Chinese nuclear use.

One former national-security staff member summed up the logic of nuclear stalemate by stating that China knows "what is coming second," an allusion to America's possession of nuclear weapons.[17] Another interviewee, an experienced diplomat, described his belief that "in general I think the calculation would be that nuclear capabilities cancel each other out and you would proceed on the assumption that neither side would initiate a nuclear conflict."[18] Other comments suggested that Chinese nuclear weapons were not necessarily a central consideration among some elites. One interviewee revealed that Chinese nuclear possession only "very slightly" reduces his willingness to recommend mainland strikes.[19] Another emphasized that the threshold for Chinese nuclear use was high and expressed skepticism that "any conflict with a nuclear armed state necessarily and inevitably becomes a nuclear conflict."[20] Another interviewee, when asked about his views on the claim that mainland strikes could lead to Chinese nuclear use, responded, "I think it [this worry] is overdrawn. My sense would be that [the] Chinese would be cautious, not just any strike on the mainland [would lead to Chinese nuclear use]."[21]

Several interviewees also stated their beliefs about the conditions under which mainland strikes would not lead to Chinese nuclear escalation. For instance, one said, "China won't go nuclear if we hit their coast line," referring to targets located geographically near China's coastline.[22] Another referred to strikes on "peripheral targets" in a "tactical move" and said that the Chinese are not "going to commit suicide" in response to these strikes.[23] One interviewee also implied that Chinese nuclear use would become virtually a moot concern for him if the Chinese should strike American forces in East Asia.[24]

More broadly, a number of interviewees refused to take a strong position, either determining that intelligence was insufficient on the likely Chinese response to mainland strikes or this was a decision for the US president alone to ponder.[25]

The null model therefore receives some evidentiary support too. Either because of their belief in nuclear stalemate or the importance of additional concerns, Chinese nuclear weapons do not preclude some elites from recommending at least some forms of mainland strikes.

The Emboldenment Model

A third and final model predicts that interviewees will be willing to authorize mainland strikes due to perceived American nuclear superiority or the logic of the stability-instability paradox. If this model accurately describes the relationship between nuclear weapons and conventional escalation, then America's nuclear arsenal, roughly an order of magnitude larger than China's, should free American leaders to use force with fewer operational constraints.[26]

Yet not a single interviewee made reference to either logic. Put another way, among the nearly sixty interview passages (i.e., excerpts of interviews) that this analysis identified as relevant to nuclear weapons, none were consistent with the logic of the emboldenment model. American nuclear superiority was not a salient factor to any of the interviewees when considering mainland strikes. The logic of the stability-instability model similarly never materialized during interviews.

Advocates of nuclear superiority will likely apply extra scrutiny to this finding. They might therefore view a shortcoming of my interview questionnaire as responsible for this finding: none of my questions directly asked interviewees about their views on American nuclear superiority. An absence of evidence, in these critic's eyes, should therefore not be confused with evidence of absence. And although the inclusion of this question would certainly be preferable in retrospect, this view goes too far. Interviewees repeatedly had a chance to answer open-ended questions about their considerations when thinking about mainland strikes. Interviewees voiced dozens of different approaches, many nuclear-related. None mentioned American nuclear superiority. This is, at least, strongly suggestive evidence of absence. Why was American nuclear superiority not salient then to these interviewees? Perhaps because the fact of American nuclear superiority provides cold comfort to American national-security elites when considering mainland strikes.[27]

Interview Evidence on the Competing Nuclear Models

Both the caution model and the null model received support from the interview evidence. A slight majority of the interviewees did express reluctance to recommend mainland strikes. Some truly do fear Chinese nuclear use as a result of mainland strikes, citing concerns such as Chinese conventional-nuclear entanglement. But some of those interviewees and others who didn't express concern also voiced a willingness to authorize mainland strikes. Both proponents and skeptics of mainland strikes can find support for their original debating points in the content of the interviews. Chinese nuclear weapons, despite American superiority, do dampen American national-security elites' attitudes toward conventional escalation and mainland strikes in particular, but this fear does not preclude all forms of mainland strikes.

The emboldenment model was inconsistent with the interview evidence. The interviews turned up no supporting evidence for the view that American nuclear superiority might actually make American national-security elites more willing to recommend mainland strikes.

Supporters and skeptics of mainland strikes may both have reservations. Skeptics could charge that interviewees were hiding their nuclear fears strategically. Because these national-security elites may have feared that Chinese leaders will come to believe that Americans are reluctant to authorize mainland strikes, these skeptics might allege that some American national-security elites will overplay their willingness to authorize mainland strikes in order to deceive Chinese leaders. This concern is a legitimate one. One interviewee even warned about this possibility.[28] But the interview evidence is inconsistent with a strong form of this worry. Many interviewees did express a worry about mainland strikes. Perhaps more would have except for this strategic motivation to deceive. It is hard to know. But given the willingness of many interviewees to recommend mainland strikes in certain situations, the potential fears of skeptics seem overblown.

Peering into the Future, Part I 117

SCENARIO FACTORS

The interviewees also discussed aspects of potential scenarios and their relationship to mainland strikes. Perhaps unsurprisingly, scenario factors appear to exert a strong influence on the interviewees and their decision-making.

South China Sea Scenario versus Taiwan Scenario

Arguably the two most-discussed potential flashpoints for the United States and China are the South China Sea and Taiwan. In the South China Sea there has been a simmering territorial dispute between China and a number of southeast Asian countries, including the Philippines, a US ally.[29] The Taiwan Strait has been a potential flashpoint between China and the United States for nearly seventy years. This historic tension, in combination with China's unwillingness to renounce the use of force in dealing with Taiwan and America's adherence to the Taiwan Relations Act, means that the US involvement in a China-Taiwan war is a real possibility.[30] Asking interviewees about their willingness to consider mainland strikes in these two scenarios was an important component of the interviews.

Many respondents conveyed a relative unwillingness to consider mainland strikes in a South China Sea scenario and a relative willingness to recommend mainland strikes in a Taiwan scenario. These national-security elites repeatedly emphasized the relatively low stakes for the United States in any potential South China Sea confrontation. One interviewee said, "I think the South China Sea stakes are clearly of less importance," dismissing the possibility that the United States would "escalate...over rocks in the South China Sea," though he did leave open the possibility of defensive retaliation.[31] The most forceful dismissal of the possibility of mainland strikes came from another interviewee. He argued:

> Let's say you're the President...somebody walks into [the Oval Office], says...I want to start a war in the South China Sea over rocks and fish that will include doing strikes on mainland China

that takes you right up to the nuclear threshold, possibly. If you were President, what would you say? He'd say, "You've got to be kidding me." If you ask the average American, "Do they care about rocks and fish on the South China Sea?" No.[32]

One interviewee reasoned that mainland strikes are "hard to imagine" in a South China Sea scenario.[33] Another wondered whether mainland strikes would even "come into play" during a South China Sea scenario.[34] Other interviewees questioned the general likelihood of a potential conflict in the South China Sea and the willingness of China to use force in the South China Sea.[35]

Not all respondents believed American stakes were minimal in a South China Sea conflict. One did mention the "credibility" of American treaty commitments, and another emphasized Chinese actions in the South China Sea as a "signal of China's maritime ambitions."[36] But even these elites appeared to agree that the likelihood of mainland strikes was lower in a South China Sea scenario.

Mainland strikes were considered more appropriate for a Taiwan scenario by many of the participants. One national-security elite noted, "I do think it's probably more likely to be on the table in the Taiwan scenario."[37] Another implicitly recognized the possibility of mainland strikes in a Taiwan scenario when he dismissed the South China Sea scenario as "not a Taiwan strait scenario, it's not all-out war."[38]

The interview evidence suggests that the interviewed national-security elites see mainland strikes as relatively more plausible in a Taiwan scenario than in a South China Sea scenario. This evidence is consistent with results of a South China Sea wargame exercise conducted by Peter Wilson of RAND in 2018. He found participants in a South China Sea scenario exercise to be similarly cautious about US conventional strikes against the Chinese mainland.[39] This strong finding influenced the later methodological decision in the survey chapter to focus all survey vignettes on a Taiwan scenario.

Allied Actions and Preferences
The interviewed elites also identified American perceptions of ally[40] behavior and the preferences of allies as key considerations related to mainland strikes. If elites believed that ally behavior provoked a conflict, their willingness to recommend mainland strikes decreased markedly. Similarly, allied objections or an ally perceived as unwilling to fight could also dampen the willingness of elites to recommend mainland strikes. These concerns are grouped together given that an American ally's actions or beliefs is the key determinant of this scenario aspect.

Perceptions of Blame for Conflict Onset
Six of the interviewees believed that the extent to which China or the ally was at fault was a fundamental node in their decision-making logic. Their language was unambiguous. One asked, "did Taiwan cause this?" in reference to a potential China-Taiwan-US conflict.[41] The same interviewee further suggested that should Taiwan "start the war," American support might be "tentative." Another elite also placed significant weight on, in his words, "who provoked the conflict and the degree to which the United States held Taiwan responsible for provoking the Chinese."[42] Several others expressed a similar sentiment.[43] Of course, this sentiment is nothing more than an expression of the status quo in American foreign policy toward China and Taiwan—that is, that American support of Taiwan is contingent upon a moderate Taiwanese foreign policy.[44]

Ally Preferences
Elites, especially ones with more foreign-policy experience rather than defense-policy experience, also incorporated the attitudes of America's Asian allies into their decision-making. If an ally should object to mainland strikes, or to mainland strikes conducted from bases on their territory, then this would, according to several interviewees, reduce their willingness to recommend mainland strikes.[45] These interviewees saw respecting ally wishes as sufficiently important to long-term alliance relationships to justify these operational constraints. In the South China Sea context,

several elites also mentioned that their views about mainland strikes would be partly conditional on the willingness of America's allies to fight and share the burden of conflict.[46] As one interviewee put it, "it's not a politically sustainable position for us [the United States] to go fight for something that belongs to another nation that they're not willing to fight for."[47]

Ally culpability, views, and perceived willingness to fight all appear to bear on mainland strike decision-making for at least some elites and could operate as sources of operational restraint. There is one caveat worth noting on the finding related to assigning fault to China versus Taiwan for conflict onset. The elites I interviewed could have been strategically using the interview to signal to Taiwanese leaders that American support for Taiwan is predicated upon a moderate Taiwanese foreign policy; this potential messaging means that these sentiments were potentially instrumental and not genuine (or both genuine and instrumental). It also could be a matter of habit because this position is reiterated in virtually all interactions between US and Taiwan government officials and even in interactions between academics and others who have no official responsibility to signal to Taiwan's representatives.

Chinese Actions
China's actions were a key determinant of how interviewees viewed mainland strikes. Scenarios in which Chinese forces attacked US forces in Japan or on American territory in Guam greatly increased the willingness of interviewees to consider and recommend at least some forms of mainland strikes.

One interviewee's remarks summarize the views of many: "if they attack Kadena [the US air base in Japan], they would be attacking the United States."[48] Consequently, conventional strikes on the Chinese mainland, especially on Chinese forces directly responsible for the attack, became a natural option to the interviewed elites. Interviewees suggested that Chinese strikes on US forces in Asia would "chang[e] the calculus" and that it would "trigger" serious consideration of mainland strikes.[49] One elite whose tone early in the interview suggested strong skepticism toward the use of mainland strikes became firm when queried about the effects of a Chinese attack on Guam in conjunction with a US-China-Taiwan scenario. He said, "would we then attack the mainland? Yes. Yes, we would, but it would be in response to a Chinese attack on the United States, not initiating it as our first attack on Chinese territory."[50] Another interviewee who had also expressed caution about mainland strikes similarly showed a different attitude when considering a Chinese attack on American forces. He offered this opinion: "I think to the extent that US assets are being struck from mainland China...one could easily envisage retaliatory or defensive strikes against airfields, for instance, that were launching attacks on US aircraft carriers or bases."[51]

Otherwise skeptical interviewees demonstrated increased willingness to consider mainland strikes in response to a Chinese attack on US forces in East Asia. Of course, as noted earlier, these elites may habitually use every opportunity (even research interviews) to signal to Chinese decision-makers this intent, thereby exaggerating their willingness to recommend mainland strikes to create a deterrent effect. It is also possible that their answer is both deterrent signaling as well as a sincerely held belief.

Comprehensive versus Limited Strikes
American national-security elites also divided mainland strikes into two categories depending upon target type: limited strikes and comprehensive strikes. Strikes on targets relatively close to the Chinese coast and directly associated with Chinese military operations against an ally or the United States were often deemed "limited," and interviewees expressed a relative willingness to consider these strikes. More "comprehensive" strikes on an inland target set and objectives not directly associated with the immediate tactical battle were the object of caution and trepidation. Some elites—though far from all—were especially worried about strikes that could impinge upon Chinese nuclear forces, even accidentally.

"All mainland strikes are not the same," one interviewee suggested.[52] Others agreed.[53] The distinction appeared to be based on at least three characteristics. First, targets located relatively close to the Chinese coast were considered different than strikes far inland: strikes on this second category were often referred to as "deep strikes." One elite described strikes "deep into mainland China" as a "different kettle of fish" in comparison to strikes on "coastal" targets.[54] Another specifically called out "coastal artillery" and rhetorically asked if this specific strike really refers to "mainland strikes" as the term is more commonly used.[55] Many of the interviewed elites expressed a much greater willingness to recommend strikes on coastal targets compared to deep inland targets. Similarly, these elites treated targets such as radars and anti-satellite weapon launch sites located deep inland as distinct and meriting greater caution. Second, targets associated with an immediate tactical battle were considered separate from targets only indirectly related to the operational fight. Interviewees repeatedly mentioned that any Chinese ports being used for staging amphibious operations would be considered directly related to combat.[56] Air fields from which the Chinese military was operating aircraft engaged in direct combat were also placed in this category.[57] The interviewees suggested a relative willingness to strike such targets. Third, some elites worried about target sets that impinged upon Chinese nuclear forces.[58] This "entanglement" concern caused some elites to be reluctant to recommend some mainland strikes that could sever the Chinese leadership command and control of nuclear forces or put in danger China's threat of assured nuclear retaliation.

Two caveats stand out. Some elites were reluctant to consider even limited mainland strikes; these same elites emphasized the perspectives of Chinese leadership and the panic among Chinese leadership any mainland strikes would generate.[59] In contrast, not all interviewed elites were concerned about conventional-nuclear entanglement. One interviewee, when asked whether he had any concerns about attacks on entangled Chinese forces, said, "it's too late for that…They [the Chinese] should have thought about that before they attacked the United States of America."[60]

Peering into the Future, Part I

Another thought fear of nuclear war arising from entanglement was a "marginal concern."[61]

In sum, the distinction between comprehensive and limited strikes was meaningful to the interview participants. Importantly, more limited strikes lead to greater support. More comprehensive strikes—especially ones that targeted inland targets, indirectly related military assets, and nuclear-conventional entangled Chinese forces—generated relatively more opposition.

Timing of Mainland Strikes
Debates about the conditions under which mainland strikes would occur often allude to whether decision-makers in the first few days or weeks of a US-China conflict would authorize mainland strikes. The interviews therefore included questions about whether the timing of mainland strikes during a conflict was a salient consideration. Several interviewees did resist the idea of prompt authorization of mainland strikes, lending some credence to those that suspect that restrictive rules of engagement will prevail in the opening days of a conflict.

One former national-security staff member with experience on Asia policy identified early authorization of mainland strikes as a "flaw" in some operational concepts that rely on mainland strikes. He thought that policymakers, presumably including himself, "will be loath to go to a war winning strategy by preemptively striking targets within China."[62] He appeared to believe that such, in his words, "early escalation" would be resisted, though his remarks do leave open the possibility that Chinese attacks on American forces could change his calculus. Another worried about employing mainland strikes "at the first chance we have" because of the "second and third order effects that could go wrong."[63] A former diplomat made similar comments: "I think that any escalation would be gradual and designed to test Chinese responses and see if the crisis could be de-escalated."[64] This gradual escalation philosophy conflicts with the demands of an operational plan that requires prompt authorization of mainland strikes. One former military interviewee, drawing on his professional expertise, thought that a prompt Chinese attack without a prolonged build-up was unlikely to result in prompt authorization of mainland strikes.[65] But not all interviewees were willing to contemplate delaying authorization of mainland strikes. One former senior military officer said, "you're going to want to create a strategic advantage...delays don't do that."[66]

The evidence on timing seems to indicate that at least some portion of elites would be reluctant to quickly employ mainland strikes early in a US-China conflict.

Summarizing the Scenario Factor Evidence

At the broadest level, the interviews indicate that the characteristics of a scenario exert a strong influence on the willingness of American national-security elites to recommend mainland strikes during a future US-China conflict. Both skeptics and proponents of mainland strikes will find evidence in these interviews to support their positions. Detractors will point to the implausibility of mainland strikes in a South China Sea scenario, the reluctance of elites to consider mainland strikes when elites perceive that an ally provoked the conflict, the unwillingness of elites to recommend mainland strikes on deep targets, and the reluctance to recommend prompt authorization of mainland strikes early in a conflict. Proponents will find succor in the mirror image of these arguments. Mainland strikes, the interview evidence reveals, are more thinkable in a Taiwan-related scenario, especially if the elites perceive China as culpable. Analysis of the interviews also suggests that if China should strike American forces in East Asia, American national-security elites become more willing to recommend mainland strikes. Additionally, elites are relatively willing to consider mainland strikes bounded by geography and target type.

CONCLUSION

This chapter used twenty interviews with American national-security elites to examine their views on conventional strikes on mainland China during a potential US-China war. These interviewees answered questions about their views on potential Chinese use of nuclear weapons during a US-China conflict and the influence of these nuclear weapons on their willingness to recommend mainland strikes during a potential war. The interviewees also addressed how particular scenario characteristics might influence their decision-making regarding mainland strikes.

The findings correspond to each section. Chinese nuclear weapons produced fear among many of the interviewees about the consequences of mainland strikes, but this fear was not so great as to preclude conventional strikes on the Chinese mainland. In fact, some skeptics of mainland strikes saw strikes limited by geography and target type as plausible even though Chinese nuclear use weighed on their decision-making. More generally, Chinese nuclear weapons did not produce uniform fear or indifference. Characteristics of the scenario appeared to matter greatly to the interviewed elites: when interviewees perceived China as at fault for a crisis, when the scenario involved Taiwan, when China attacked US forces in East Asia, and when mainland strikes were constrained by geography and type, interviewees became noticeably more willing to consider and potentially recommend mainland strikes.

The implications of this evidence for the mainland strikes debate are several. Chinese nuclear weapons, for the majority of interviewees, do not preclude their willingness to consider mainland strikes. Mainland strikes, in the context of a war, are not so "escalatory" to American national-security elites that they would avoid this tactic at all costs. That said, Chinese nuclear possession does induce caution among some interviewees. The caution model and null model of the relationship between adversary nuclear weapons and American conventional escalation therefore each receive partial support. The scenario characteristics also matter greatly. In other words, the actual course of a war would exert a strong influence on the willingness of American national-security elites and, by extension, the American president to recommend or authorize mainland strikes. Those who view these characteristics—such as a China attacking American forces first in East Asia—as likely to obtain in a potential US-China conflict will see this finding as evidence about the high likelihood of mainland strikes. Those who worry that the scenario factors mentioned are unlikely or unlikely until late in a conflict will find their sympathy leaning toward skeptics of mainland strikes occurring.

Notes

1. Broad methodological advice about interviewing elites for political science research can be found in the December 2002 issue of *PS: Political Science and Politics*. See Leech, "Asking Questions: Techniques for Semistructured Interviews"; Goldstein, "Getting in the Door"; Aberbach and Rockman, "Conducting and Coding Elite Interviews"; Woliver, "Ethical Dilemmas in Personal Interviewing"; Berry, "Validity and Reliability Issues in Elite Interviewing"; Rivera, Kozyreva, and Sarovskii, "Interviewing Political Elites."
2. All interviews were unpaid.
3. Twenty interviews became the target largely on the advice of a researcher with experience in large-scale qualitative interviewing. His broader advice was to ensure diversity of opinion and to stop when interviewees began repeating each other. I explain my attempt at diversity in the body of the text. On the point about interviewees repeating each other as a threshold for stopping, I can confidently say that I had no longer heard much that was new by the end of twenty interviews.
4. These categorizations were made based on the professional positions that these interviewees had held in the past. Military officers were not assigned a political affiliation given that most officers adhere to a nonpartisan ethic.
5. Interview with former senior officer with experience at Pacific Command, September 7, 2017.
6. Interview with former senior officer with experience at Pacific Command, September 7, 2017.
7. Interview with former Defense Department senior civilian, August 1, 2018.
8. Interview with former Defense Department senior civilian, June 7, 2018.
9. Interview with former Defense Department senior civilian, June 1, 2018.
10. Interview with a former senior officer with Pacific Command experience, May 7, 2018.
11. Interview with a former senior State Department official with East Asia experience, May 2, 2018; Interview with former national security staff member with Asia-related responsibility, September 6, 2017; Interview with former Defense Department senior civilian, May 24, 2018.
12. Interview with a former Pacific Command civilian, December 7, 2017.

13. Interview with former national security staff member with Asia-related responsibility, September 6, 2017
14. Interview with a former senior State Department official, December 14, 2017; Interview with a retired military officer and military strategist, May 2, 2018; Interview with a former intelligence official, May 28, 2018.
15. Interview with a former senior State Department official, December 14, 2017; Interview with a retired military officer and military strategist, May 2, 2018.
16. Kroenig and Massa, "Are Dual-Capable Weapon Systems Destabilizing?"
17. Interview with former member of the national security staff, September 29, 2017.
18. Interview with former diplomat, November 17, 2017.
19. Interview with former Defense Department senior civilian, May 24, 2018
20. Interview with former Defense Department senior civilian, June 1, 2018.
21. Interview with former diplomat, May 15, 2018.
22. Interview with former Defense Department senior civilian, May 24, 2018.
23. Interview with former diplomat, November 17, 2017.
24. Interview with former senior Defense Department official, April 16, 2018.
25. Interview with a former senior officer with experience at Pacific Command, October 29, 2017; Interview with a former senior military officer, September 15, 2017; Interview with a former senior military officer, September 15, 2017. The latter two interviews are separate.
26. The Federation of American Scientists reports that, in 2023, the US nuclear arsenal comprises 1,770 deployed nuclear warheads and a total of more than 5,200 warheads. The Chinese arsenal is 410 stockpiled nuclear weapons. Kristensen and Norris, "Status of World Nuclear Forces."
27. Alternatively, another interpretation might be that these elites do not perceive American nuclear superiority as measured by warhead count as equivalent to nuclear superiority as conceptualized by some strategists. Logan, "The Nuclear Balance is What States Make of It."
28. Interview with former Defense Department senior civilian, May 24, 2018.
29. For background, see Fravel, "Threading the Needle."
30. For background, see Garver, *Face Off*.
31. Interview with former diplomat, November 17, 2017.
32. Interview with former senior officer with experience at Pacific Command, September 7, 2017.
33. Interview with former Defense Department senior civilian, June 7, 2018.
34. Interview with former diplomat, May 15, 2018.

35. Interview with retired military officer and military strategist, May 2, 2018; Interview with former member of the national security staff, September 29, 2017.
36. Interview with a former senior State Department official with East Asia experience, May 2, 2018; Interview with former Defense Department senior civilian, August 1, 2018.
37. Interview with former Defense Department senior civilian, June 7, 2018.
38. Interview with former diplomat, May 15, 2018.
39. Email communication with Peter Wilson, January 9, 2019.
40. The word ally, in this book, refers to both treaty allies and partners, or nations that share interests with the United States but with which there is no formal military obligation.
41. Interview with a former senior military officer, September 15, 2017
42. Interview with former diplomat, November 17, 2017.
43. Interview with a former senior State Department official with East Asia experience, May 2, 2018; Interview with former senior Defense Department official, April 16, 2018; Interview with former Defense Department senior civilian, June 1, 2018.
44. Christensen, "A Strong and Moderate Taiwan." Thomas Christensen was then a Deputy Assistant Secretary of State in the bureau of East Asian and Pacific affairs.
45. Interview with former national security staff member with Asia-related responsibility, September 6, 2017; Interview with former diplomat, May 7, 2018.
46. Interview with a former senior State Department official with East Asia experience, May 2, 2018; Interview with a former senior officer with Pacific Command experience, May 7, 2018.
47. Interview with a former senior officer with Pacific Command experience, May 7, 2018.
48. Interview with former senior Defense Department official, April 16, 2018. At least seven interviewees expressed strong support for this position. Additionally, none of the other interviewees disagreed with this position.
49. Interview with former diplomat, November 17, 2017; Interview with former Defense Department senior civilian, June 7, 2018.
50. Interview with a former senior State Department official, December 14, 2017.
51. Interview with former diplomat, November 17, 2017.
52. Interview with former Defense Department senior civilian, June 1, 2018.

53. Interview with a former senior officer with experience at Pacific Command, October 29, 2017; Interview with former Defense Department senior civilian, August 1, 2018; Interview with a former senior officer with Pacific Command experience, May 7, 2018; Interview with former diplomat, May 15, 2018; Interview with a former senior military officer, September 15, 2017; Interview with former senior officer with experience at Pacific Command, September 7, 2017.
54. Interview with former Defense Department senior civilian, August 1, 2018.
55. Interview with former Defense Department senior civilian, June 1, 2018.
56. Interview with former Defense Department senior civilian, June 1, 2018; Interview with a former senior officer with Pacific Command experience, May 7, 2018.
57. Interview with former diplomat, November 17, 2017.
58. Interview with retired military officer and military strategist, May 2, 2018.
59. Interview with former senior officer with experience at Pacific Command, September 7, 2017; Interview with former Defense Department senior civilian, June 7, 2018.
60. Interview with former senior Defense Department official, April 16, 2018.
61. Interview with a former senior State Department official with East Asia experience, May 2, 2018.
62. Interview with former national security staff member with Asia-related responsibility, September 6, 2017.
63. Interview with a former senior officer with Pacific Command experience, May 7, 2018.
64. Interview with former diplomat, November 17, 2017.
65. Interview with a former senior officer with experience at Pacific Command, October 29, 2017.
66. Interview with a former senior military officer, September 15, 2017.

CHAPTER 6

Peering into the Future, Part II

A Scenario-Based Survey

To complement the historical case studies, this chapter investigates how willing a sample of American national-security and foreign-policy experts are to recommend mainland strikes across a variety of US-China wartime scenarios. Eighty-five American national-security professionals, largely drawn from eight prominent American think tanks, roleplayed as an American national security advisor and answered questions related to their willingness to recommend conventional strikes on the Chinese mainland in a variety of scenarios. These future-oriented, scenario-based interviews and the survey experiment, which constitute an approach that might be called synthetic history, sidesteps charges of strained historical analogies, the weakness of historical case studies.

These results suggest useful guidelines for military planners and defense analysts preparing for a potential US-China conflict. Importantly, mainland strikes are a contingent phenomenon, but this contingency arises from more than randomness. Elite willingness to recommend mainland strikes will depend on whether China attacks US forces and the comprehensives of the proposed strikes. Advisor backgrounds (partisanship and age especially) and beliefs (related to Taiwan's importance and Chinese nuclear weapons) will also matter. Therefore planners and strategists should consider developing plans and the operational concepts and supporting forces that enable American forces to fight and win with and without mainland strikes.

SURVEY METHODOLOGY

The survey examines the effect of scenario characteristics and a national-security professional's demographic background and foreign-policy beliefs on their willingness to recommend mainland strikes in a hypothetical US-China war. Although surveys, including elite surveys,[1] have long been employed in international relations research, survey experiments have recently grown in popularity among political scientists.[2] The merits of an elite survey experiment include using a sample with relevant knowledge and expertise, asking close-ended questions that enable quantitative comparison, and possessing control over the randomized treatment. The most significant disadvantage is the artificiality of the scenarios. This section describes the sampling procedures, the survey questionnaire, and the analytic methods employed.

The Sample

The survey sampling procedure attempted to gather the views of American national-security elites, that is, experienced foreign- and defense-policy professionals, both civilian and military, Democrat and Republican. To this end, the sample plan involved asking staff at seven private American public policy research institutions and one US Department of Defense strategy research organization to participate in the study. The private public-policy research institutions ("thinktanks") are the American Enterprise Institute, the Brookings Institution, the Center for a New American Security, the Center for Strategic and Budgetary Assessments, the Center for Strategic and International Studies, the

Heritage Foundation, and the RAND Corporation. The Department of Defense organization is the Institute for National Strategic Studies at the National Defense University.

These organizations were chosen because of their partisan diversity (including conservative, liberal, and non-partisan institutions) and notable foreign policy and defense policy staffs. A senior staff member working at each of these think tanks emailed their colleagues with foreign- and defense-policy experience and requested that they voluntarily take the survey. This email requested that the respondent not forward the email. Respondents could then take an anonymous online survey. Of note, to increase the sample size, some additional recruiting was done via channels other than through these research organizations. Table 1 documents the number of potential participants contacted via each organization or method. The survey window spanned January to March 2019.

Table 1. Number of Potential Participants Contacted by Organization and Method.

Organization and Method	Potential Participants Contacted
AEI	12
Brookings	10
CNAS	27
CSBA	28
CSIS	15
Heritage	62
RAND	50
NDU	47
Other	20
Total	271

The survey sample eventually included 85 persons for a participation rate of 31 percent. A later section will provide quantitative details about the demographics of this sample. No information is available on the actual number of surveys completed by the staff of any particular organization; the survey intentionally did not ask a question about organization affiliation in order to preclude participant cross-identification via a combination of organizational affiliation and demographic information.

The Survey Instrument

The survey instrument—found in appendix F—evolved from a series of operational vignettes that were field-tested during the interview process into a structured series of scenarios built into a survey experiment. All scenarios involved a wartime scenario set in 2020 involving the United States, China, and Taiwan; the decision to orient the vignettes around this scenario resulted from an interview finding that many national-security elites considered mainland strikes inappropriate in a South China Sea scenario.

All participants were asked to play the role of the US national security advisor in this hypothetical scenario. This subsection describes how the survey was administered, the survey scenarios including the survey experiment, the demographic questions, and the foreign-policy belief questions.

Participants accessed the survey via a website that provided participation information and survey instructions. Appendix D contains an image of the survey website landing page. When a participant clicked on the "next" button of the landing page to proceed to the survey itself, the participant was then randomly assigned one of four surveys, explained further later. These surveys were all created with SelectSurvey technology.[3]

The first level of randomization involved assigning half of the participants to scenarios in which the participant was told that China initiated an amphibious invasion of Taiwan because "peaceful unification with Taiwan had been advancing too slowly." This language was meant to place responsibility for the war on the Chinese government and will be henceforth referred to as the China "at fault" condition. The other half of participants were assigned scenarios in which the responsibility for the war was shared between Taiwanese and Chinese leaders. The key statements in the "ambiguous fault" scenarios include "intelligence indicates China is attempting an invasion of Taiwan after several months of military posturing and hostile statements by both sides" and that "US intelligence analysts find it difficult to judge who is more 'at fault.'" See appendix E for further explanation.

This "at fault" condition was selected because six of the interviewees indicated that the extent to which China or the ally was at fault was a fundamental node in their decision-making logic. No condition in which Taiwan was entirely "at fault" for the war was included in the survey experiment; because the United States government might not intervene at all in such a situation, this scenario was judged insufficiently important by interviewees to merit inclusion.

All participants then sequentially completed questions related to four scenarios. See table 2 for a summary of the four scenarios. The first two scenarios proposed only relatively limited strikes against targets on the Chinese mainland. The participants were given this proposal:

> At a National Security Council meeting, the Chairman of the Joint Chiefs proposes strikes on military targets adjacent to the Taiwan Strait. These strikes would be on Chinese military units located at the staging site for the anticipated amphibious invasion such as air defense sites, Chinese ships and naval bases and aircraft and air bases.

This "limited" target set was intended to involve targets geographically close to the military theater of operations and likely unrelated to Chinese nuclear systems. In scenarios three and four, the respondents were offered a more "comprehensive" target set. The survey described the comprehensive target set with this language:

> At a National Security Council meeting, the Chairman of the Joint Chiefs proposes strikes on military targets throughout China.

These strikes would be on both Chinese military units located at the staging site for the anticipated amphibious invasion and on units located elsewhere in China that will likely support the invasion. The expanded category of targets includes Chinese intelligence centers, command centers, over-the-horizon radars, Chinese ballistic missiles, and anti-satellite weapon launch sites.

This comprehensive target set was intended to represent targets across a wide geography of China, to include inland targets and targets that are potentially associated with Chinese nuclear systems. This wider target set is meant to be similar in scope to the targets discussed in the Center for Strategic and Budgetary Assessment's 2010 report *AirSea Battle: A Point-of-Departure Operational Concept*.[4] This distinction also stemmed from the interviews in which interviewed elites expressed a much greater willingness to recommend strikes on coastal targets compared to deep inland targets and treated targets such as radars and anti-satellite weapon launch sites located deep inland as members of a special category of sensitive targets.

Table 2. The Four Scenarios and Associated Scenario Characteristics.

	No Attack on U.S. Forces	Chinese Attack on U.S. Forces at Kadena Air Base
Limited Mainland Strikes	Scenario 1	Scenario 2
Comprehensive Mainland Strikes	Scenario 3	Scenario 4

The two scenarios associated with each target set can be subdivided. Scenarios one and three specified that there had been no attack on US forces; the respondents were explicitly told, "China has not attacked any US forces or bases." In scenarios two and four, China has attacked US forces at Kadena Air Base in Okinawa, Japan. The scenario states, "China attacked American forces at Kadena Air Base in Okinawa, Japan with ballistic missiles launched from the Chinese mainland. The commander reports severe damage to the runways, two dozen damaged US aircraft, and scores of American casualties." Adding a Chinese attack on US forces allowed the analysis to determine if such an attack was an important threshold affecting respondent willingness to authorize mainland strikes.

This further subdivision of scenarios reflects the views of many of the interviewees: "if they attack Kadena [the US air base in Japan], they would be attacking the United States," stated one interviewee.[5] Other interviewees suggested that Chinese strikes on US forces in Asia would "chang[e] the calculus" and that it would "trigger" serious consideration of mainland strikes.[6]

After each scenario, the survey taker responded to this question: "under these circumstances, how likely are you to recommend to the president strikes on at least these targets?" Respondents then chose an option from a six-point scale: very unlikely, unlikely, somewhat unlikely, somewhat likely, likely, very likely. The phrase "at least these targets" was added to the question to reduce the probability that respondents who preferred broader, more expansive target sets would voice opposition to a given option.

Respondents then completed a section about potentially relevant foreign-policy beliefs and attitudes and another section related to demographic information and professional background. The foreign-policy beliefs section contained a randomization component: half of the participants received questions with a positive framing, and the other half of participants received questions with an alternative framing. This approach allowed the analysis to determine if the statistical results were robust to question wording. See table 3 for a list of all questions and the positive and alternative framings. All respondents faced the same five-point scale for each belief and attitude question: strongly disagree, disagree, neutral, agree, and strongly agree.

Table 3. Positive and Alternative Framing of Foreign-Policy Belief and Attitude Questions.

	Positive Framing	**Alternative Framing**
Taiwan Question	Defending Taiwan is a vital U.S. interest.	Defending Taiwan is not a vital U.S. interest.
Generals Question	I believe that once a war starts, the generals should be in charge.	I believe that once a war starts, civilians (not generals) should be in charge.
Goals Question	When force is used, military rather than political goals should determine its application.	When force is used, political rather than military goals should determine its application.
Decisive Force Question	Force should be used only if the U.S. military is allowed to decisively defeat the enemy.	Force should sometimes be used even if the United States is not prepared to decisively defeat its enemy.
Military Initiative Question	Military operations must emphasize seizing the initiative from the enemy.	Military operations do not need to emphasize seizing the initiative from the enemy.
Chinese Nukes Questions	Chinese possession of nuclear weapons makes me less willing to authorize strikes on the Chinese mainland.	Chinese possession of nuclear weapons does not affect my willingness to authorize strikes on the Chinese mainland.
Misperception Question	Chinese leaders will interpret any strikes on Chinese mainland targets as an attempt to destroy Chinese nuclear weapons.	Strikes on Chinese mainland targets will not be interpreted by Chinese leaders as an attempt to destroy Chinese nuclear weapons.

A positive and alternative question framing experiment was useful because these questions are not validated: their psychometric validity in survey research has not been proven through a rigorous battery of tests. Therefore, to reduce criticism of these survey questions, this survey used two framings. Some of the alternative framings are nearly equivalent to the inverse of the positive framing. For instance, the positive frame statement related to Taiwan is "defending Taiwan is a vital US interest." Its alternative frame simply adds a "not" after "is." Other statements lack an obvious inverse, however, and therefore the alternative framing is not an inverse. The decisive force, military initiative, and misperception questions possess this quality. The alternative framing in these cases should be viewed as a second analytical attempt to reveal an underlying belief or attitude.

Table 4. Demographic and Professional Background Questions and Response Options.

	Question	Response Options
Age	What is your age?	20-29, 30-39, 40-49, 50-59, 60+
Career Length	How long have you been working in the foreign policy or national security field?	0-5 years, 6-10 years, 11-20 years, 20+ years
Gender	What is your gender?	Female, Male, Other
Professional Background	What is your professional background? (Check all that apply.)	Military, Government – Civilian, Think-tank, Academia, Business, Other
Political Party	With what political party do you identify?	Democrat, Republican, Neither
Asia Expertise	Would you describe yourself as a subject matter expert on Asia?	No, Only a little, Moderately so, Yes
The questions below only pertained to those with who checked "military" in response to the professional background question.		
Active Duty	Are you currently on active-duty?	Yes, No
Military Branch	In what branch of the military did you or do you serve?	Army, Navy, Air Force, Marine Corps
Military Length	For how long have you served/did you serve in the military? (Count from year you first joined.)	0-5 years, 6-10 years, 11-19 years, 20 years or more

The respondents also answered questions related to their demographic information and professional background. See table 4 for these questions and possible responses.

Analysis

There are three analytical stages: descriptive statistics of the survey sample, an examination of the effects of different scenarios on respondent willingness to recommend mainland strikes, and an investigation of individual characteristics on respondent willingness to recommend mainland strikes. The descriptive statistics section uses histograms to document the characteristics of those who took the survey.

The scenario analysis section examines whether scenario characteristics affect respondent willingness to recommend mainland strikes. The first subsection determines whether attributing blame for starting the war solely to China versus China and Taiwan affects respondent willingness. Because this scenario characteristic was randomized, relatively simple statistical comparison can reveal whether blame attribution changes respondent willingness. In particular, this analysis uses chi-squared tests and Fisher's exact tests because the response variable is categorical. Fisher's exact test also compensates for the small sample size. As an additional check given the small sample size, this sub-analysis verifies if recoding answers into three categories—low willingness, medium willingness, and high willingness—changes the analytical results. The second and third subsections examine whether Chinese attacks on US forces and different potential target sets effect respondent willingness. Because these statistical tests compare the same respondents across scenarios (a so-called paired comparison), the analysis employs McNemar's test.[7] This test determines whether the distribution of responses to a question (sometimes called "marginal homogeneity") changes when the scenario changes. This analysis employs the recoded three category response variable given the small sample size and the low expected values in each cell.

The individual characteristics section assesses the effect of demographic characteristics and foreign-policy beliefs and attitudes on respondent willingness to recommend mainland strikes. The demographic background analysis section uses several statistical tests (Fisher's exact test, a t-test, and multiple linear regression) to examine the effect of military service, party affiliation, gender, age, and Asia-related expertise level on participant willingness to recommend mainland strikes across the scenarios. A final analytical section assesses the effect of several foreign-policy beliefs—categorized into national interest beliefs, use of force beliefs, and nuclear beliefs—on participant willingness to recommend mainland strikes. Because the framing of these belief-related questions varied randomly among participants, all analyses are done separately for those who received the positively framed questions and those who received the alternative framing. The statistical tests used for this last section include correlation, multiple linear regression, and a principal-components analysis of the questions related to use of force.

Survey Sample Descriptive Statistics
The sample includes a diverse selection of experienced national-security and foreign-policy professionals.

Figure 1. Survey Respondents by Age Group.

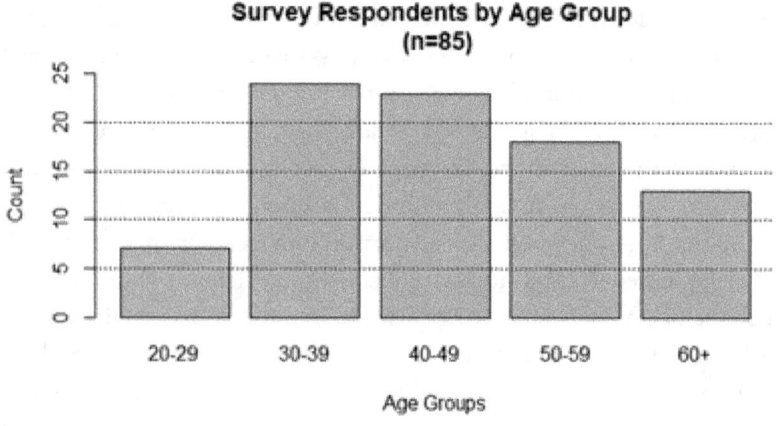

Age

Figure 1 demonstrates that the majority of respondents are forty or older. This age distribution is consistent with a sample largely composed of mid-career to late-career professionals.

Figure 2. Survey Respondents by Career Length.

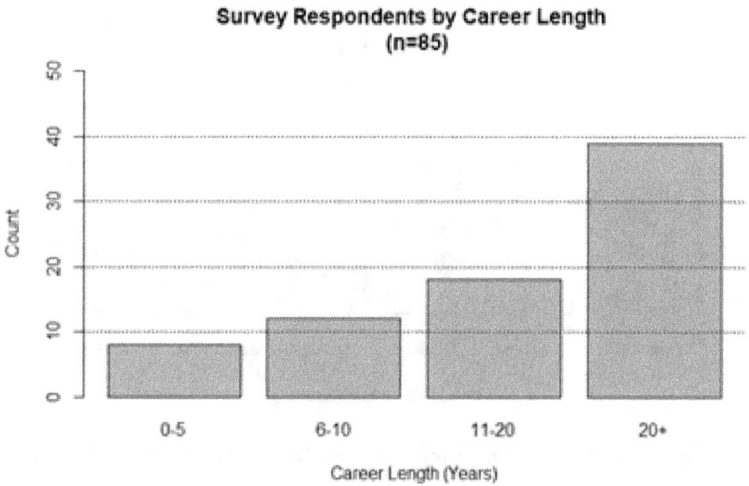

Career Length

The majority of respondents also have had careers in national security for longer than ten years. See figure 2 for a graphical analysis of career length among respondents. In fact, nearly half the sample has had a career in national security for twenty or more years. The exact question asked of respondents was: "how long have you been working in the foreign policy or national security field?"

Figure 3. Survey Respondents by Professional Background.

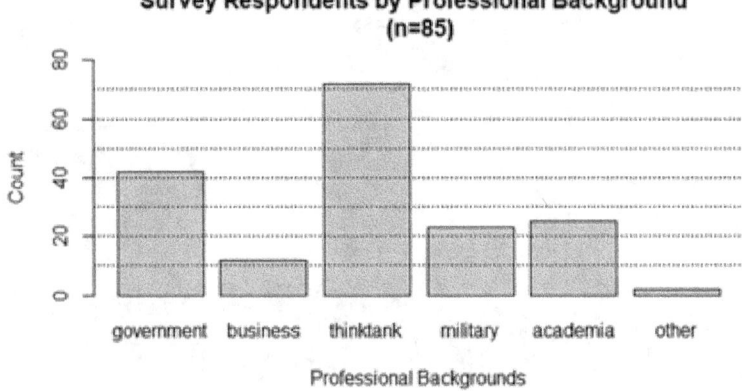

Note. Respondents checked all experiences that apply. The count therefore does not sum to 85.

Professional Background

The vast majority of respondents have spent some time working at a thinktank. See figure 3. That so many respondents share this background confirms that the survey sampling strategy, which focused on a number of prominent research organizations, achieved its main goals. Because respondents checked all professional experiences that applied, the survey reveals that respondents have had diverse experiences beyond a career in the think-tank industry. Nearly half of the respondents have served in the government and a quarter in the military.

Figure 4. Survey Respondents by Political Party (Self-Identified).

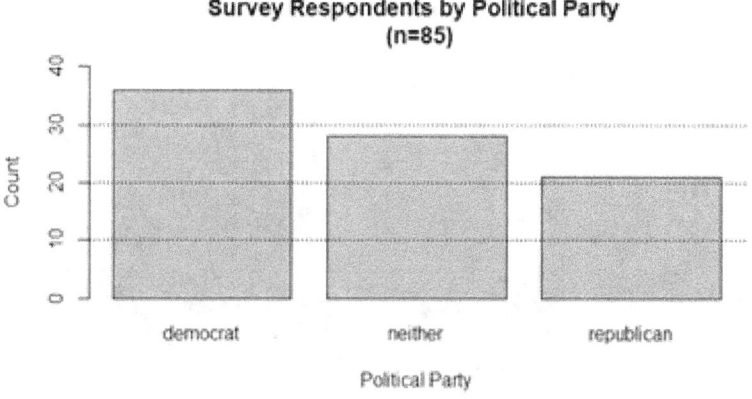

Party

Figure 4 shows that the respondent sample includes a variety of political affiliations. All respondents answered the question "with what political party do you identify?" A plurality (42 percent) identified with the Democratic party, a third chose neither party, and a minority (25 percent) of survey takers identified themselves with the Republican party. This distribution differs some from Gallup's 2018 poll of Americans, which found that 31 percent of Americans identify as Democrat, 38 percent as independent, and 26 percent as Republican.[8] In particular, Democrats are overrepresented in my sample (42 percent) compared to Gallup's result (31 percent). The survey representation of Republicans was essentially identical to Gallup's finding (25 percent versus 26 percent). Of course, the distribution of partisanship among American think-tank staff could be different from the distribution of partisanship in the broader American public.

Figure 5. Survey Respondents by Gender.

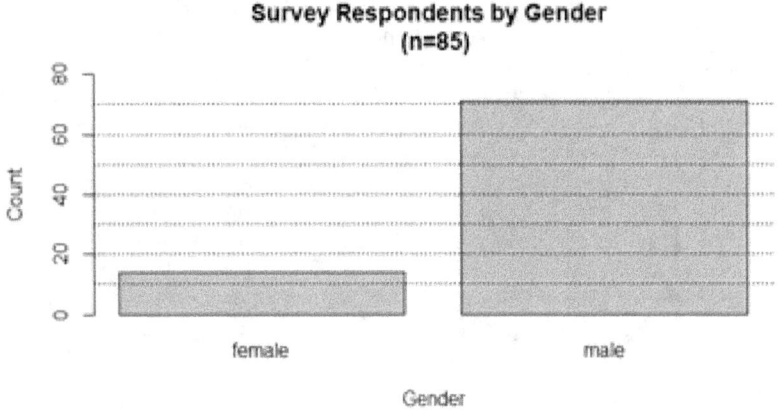

Gender
The survey sample, as indicated in figure 5, is composed primarily of male respondents. Less than twenty respondents were female. This relatively small sample of women limits the confidence a reader can have in any analytical results in this study related to gender.

Figure 6. Survey Respondents by Level of Asia Expertise.

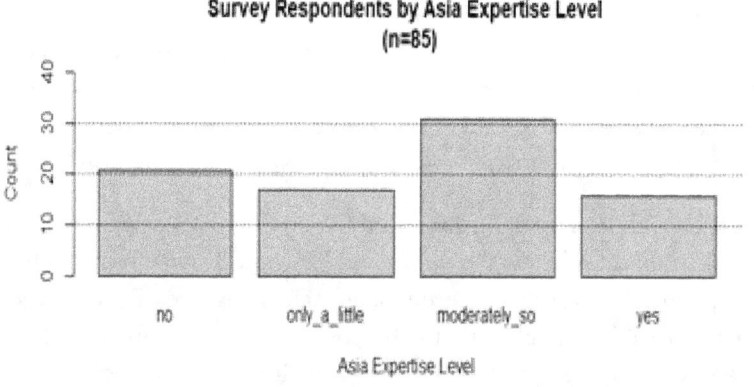

Asia Expertise

All respondents answered a question related to their expertise on Asian affairs: "would you describe yourself as a subject matter expert on Asia?" The survey respondents reported a range of Asia-related expertise. Figure 6 indicates that all four possible responses include at least fifteen respondents.

Summary of Sample

Although it is hard to determine if the sample is "representative," the demographic data at least suggests that the sample truly did capture national-security and foreign-policy elites and that these respondents are diverse in several key dimensions including, importantly, partisan affiliation.

SCENARIO RESULTS

There are three central findings. First, altering the scenario such that China and Taiwan share the blame for causing the war—rather than solely China provoking the war—does not reduce the willingness of participants to recommend mainland strikes. Second, Chinese attacks on a US air base (Kadena) in Japan dramatically increase participant willingness to recommend mainland strikes of all types. Third, expanding the target set from limited strikes to comprehensive strikes substantially reduces participant willingness to recommend mainland strikes whether China has attacked an American air base or not. Figure 7 displays the distribution of responses across all four scenarios and between experimental conditions.

Simple analytical methods produced the finding that assigning blame for conflict onset solely to China versus China and Taiwan has no effect on respondent willingness to recommend mainland strikes. First, in order to ensure that this result is not the function of improper randomization, the analysis checked for balance between the two groups on all key demographic and background characteristics; there are no statistically significant differences between the respondents assigned to the two conditions.[9] Second, a chi-squared test and Fisher's exact test were performed for each scenario to determine if altering political blame changed respondent willingness to recommend mainland strikes. The experiment produced a statistical null effect. Third, because the sample size is relatively small, which results in relatively few respondents for each answer response, an additional, coarsened analysis was performed.[10] The respondent willingness to recommend mainland strikes was simplified to three categories: less willing (those who answered "very unlikely" or "unlikely"), somewhat willing (those who answered "somewhat unlikely" or "somewhat likely"), and more willing (those who answered "likely" or "very likely"). A chi-squared and Fisher's exact test were then performed for each scenario and compared the responses of those that received the different conflict onset blame conditions. Again, there were no statistically significant differences. Of note, several survey participants used the end-of-survey comment box to explain what impact blame attribution had on their decision-making. One comment potentially illuminates the thinking of many respondents and explains this null finding: "I was not concerned with whose fault it was once China started launching missiles." That said, several participants did note that if Taiwan has been clearly and solely at fault for initiating the conflict, these respondents would have been unwilling to recommend mainland strikes or (potentially) any American action. The survey-design decision to not include a scenario in which Taiwan was solely to blame for conflict onset therefore also potentially explains the null finding.

A similar method determined that Chinese strikes on Kadena Air Base dramatically increase respondent willingness to recommend mainland strikes. The analysis that produced the result used a generalized McNemar's test: a matched-pair test for comparing changes in the distribution of a categorical variable.[11] Because McNemar's test assumes a relatively high number of responses per answer category, this analysis uses the coarsened willingness response discussed earlier. There were two separate statistical comparisons: 1) the limited strikes, no Chinese attack on Kadena scenario versus the limited strikes, Chinese attack on Kadena scenario and 2) the comprehensive strikes, no Chinese attack on Kadena scenario versus comprehensive strikes, Chinese attack on Kadena scenario. Both comparisons produced evidence of a statistically significant increase of respondent willingness to recommend mainland strikes; both p-values were less than .01. In the limited strike scenarios, an attack on Kadena Air Base leads to over 80 percent of respondents rating themselves as likely or very likely to recommend mainland strikes. In the comprehensive strike scenario, an attack on Kadena Air Base produces a statistically significant increase in willingness, but there is not the same high level of willingness found in the limited strikes scenario. In fact, the comprehensive strikes, attack on Kadena scenario is statistically indistinguishable—using McNemar's test—from the limited strikes, no attack on Kadena scenario: there is a wide range of willingness levels in both scenarios.

Figure 7. Willingness to Recommend Mainland Strikes by Scenario.

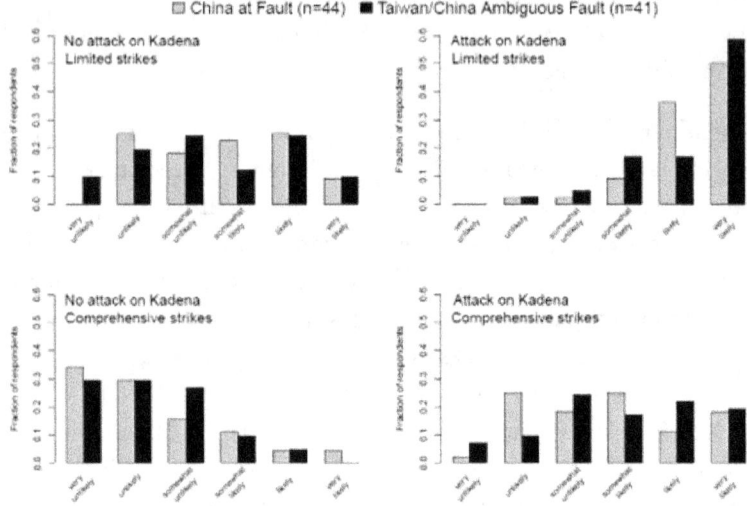

Note. Each respondent answered the same question after every scenario: "under these circumstances, how likely are you to recommend to the president strikes on at least these targets?" The histogram heights are the fraction of respondents selecting each answer by experimental condition, either the China "at fault" condition or the "ambiguous fault" condition.

Using the same methods, analysis reveals that expanding the target set from limited strikes to comprehensive strikes statistically significantly reduces respondent willingness to recommend mainland strikes. Especially without a Chinese attack on Kadena, a comprehensive target set leads to significant reluctance to recommend mainland strikes. In a scenario without Chinese strikes on Kadena, over 60 percent of respondents express that they are "unlikely" or "very unlikely" to recommend comprehensive mainland strikes. If China has struck Kadena Air Base, however, comprehensive strikes still statistically significantly reduce respondent willingness to recommend mainland strikes, although moderate levels of support remain for comprehensive strikes. It is worth noting that several survey respondents used the comment box at the end of the survey to elaborate on their thinking related to the composition of the target set. While several participants expressed serious concern that American attacks on targets such as Chinese command and control centers could potentially lead to Chinese fears of nuclear decapitation, a greater number mentioned that mainland strikes could be designed to reduce this potential Chinese fear by, for instance, avoiding "inland" targets and by judiciously choosing targets unrelated to Chinese nuclear weapons. Interestingly, respondents disagreed about which targets are sensitive: some singled out Chinese over-the-horizon radars and anti-satellite weapon launch sites as sensitive and as targets that should be avoided while others deemed strikes on these targets as unlikely to lead to Chinese nuclear use.

The scenario characteristics analysis therefore finds that one condition—whether China alone or China and Taiwan jointly were responsible for the outbreak of conflict—mattered little in respondent willingness to recommend mainland strikes. The other conflict conditions mattered greatly, though. A Chinese attack on Kadena lead to dramatic increases in respondent willingness to recommend both limited and mainland strikes while expanding the target set from limited to comprehensive strikes reduced respondent willingness to recommend mainland strikes whether China had attacked Kadena or not.

INDIVIDUAL RESULTS

Additional analysis also examined whether a respondent's background and beliefs influenced their willingness to recommend mainland strikes. Among the respondent's background characteristics, only partisan affiliation and age appear to systematically affect respondent willingness. Older, Democrat-leaning respondents were less willing to recommend mainland strikes, though this finding suggests only a modest tendency, not an absolute rule. Military service, gender, and level of Asia expertise were unrelated to respondent willingness to recommend mainland strikes. Among foreign-policy beliefs, attitudes on Taiwan and nuclear weapons appear nearly unambiguously related to respondent willingness to recommend mainland strikes. Respondents who view Taiwan as a vital American national interest and express little fear of Chinese nuclear use are more likely to recommend mainland strikes. There is mixed evidence on the relationship of beliefs about the use of force to willingness to recommend mainland strikes. The relationship only holds when using the data from the positive framing questions; analysis with data from the alternative framing questions found no relationship between these attitudes and willingness to recommend mainland strikes.

Respondent Background

To determine if the respondent's background influenced their willingness to recommend mainland strikes, this analysis performed three statistical tests. Fisher's exact test analyzes whether the distribution of categorical answers (i.e., "very unlikely", "unlikely", etc.) is statistically significantly different between two groups. A t-test and multiple linear regression treat the outcome as a six-point numeric scale ("very unlikely" corresponding to one and "very likely" corresponding to six) and test whether different characteristics increase or decrease, on average, respondent willingness to recommend mainland strikes. All three analytical tests are applied across all four scenarios. The t-test and regression approach also examine the effect of characteristics on the "scenario mean," a respondent's willingness to recommend mainland strikes averaged across all four scenarios. Finally, to simplify statistical testing, all characteristics have been converted to binary variables: a variable denoting either some or no prior military experience, another indicating that a respondent is a Democrat or is not a Democrat, a binary gender variable, an age variable converted to a dummy variable with 1 corresponding to a respondent being 50 or older, and an Asia expert variable for all respondents who answered "yes" or "moderately so" when asked if they are an Asia expert. See appendix G for regression output for these results.

Figure 8. Relationship between Individual Characteristics and Willingness to Recommend Mainland Strikes by Scenario.

	1: No attack Limited strikes			2: Chinese attack Limited strikes			3: No attack Comprehensive strikes			4: Chinese attack Comprehensive strikes			Scenario Mean		
	Fisher's exact	t-test	Combined regression	Fisher's exact	t-test	Combined regression	Fisher's exact	t-test	Combined regression	Fisher's exact	t-test	Combined regression	Fisher's exact	t-test	Combined regression
Military				■											
Democrat											−	−		−	−
Gender															
Age (50+)		−	−					−	−		−	−		−	−
Asia Expert															

Note. Statistical significance is defined as p < .1. A positive association and negative association are only noted for the t-test and regression results; the Fisher's exact test does not produce positive or negative associations. All variables related to participant characteristics have been converted to binary variables: military signifies any military experience; Democrats are compared to non-Democrats; gender is a binary (male or female) for this analysis; the age variable denotes that a participant is either fifty or older or younger than fifty; and Asia experts have been categorized as such if they responded with "yes" or "moderately so" to the Asia expertise question. The t-test and combined regression analyses treat the outcome variable as continuous on a six-point scale. The combined mean variable is the mean willingness of a respondent to recommend mainland strikes across all four scenarios. The combined regression includes all five variables and a dummy variable for whether the survey-taker received the survey version that assigned blame for conflict onset to China only or to Taiwan and China.

Figure 8 displays the results of these three tests applied to five respondent characteristics across all scenarios. Three null findings stand out: prior military service, gender, and Asia expertise are unrelated to respondent willingness to recommend mainland strikes.[12] With the exception of a single significant finding for prior military service for scenario 2, all three tests on these variables produced uniformly null results. Two statistically significant findings emerge. Democrats (compared to non-Democrats) are less willing to recommend mainland strikes, though only in scenario 4 and averaging across scenarios and only using the t-test and multiple linear regression.[13] Being a Democrat reduced the mean willingness to recommend mainland strikes by approximately .5 units on the six-point willingness scale. Also, those younger than fifty were more willing to recommend mainland strikes in the majority of scenarios, though Fisher's exact test only finds that difference exists for scenario 4.[14]

In sum, the null findings are strong; military experience, gender, and Asia expertise, according to three separate tests, are unrelated to respondent willingness to recommend mainland strikes. The positive findings are more tentative. Democrat-leaning respondents and older respondents were less willing to recommend mainland strikes, though different tests and different scenarios vary in their results.

Respondent Beliefs and Attitudes
The final survey analysis section assessed whether respondent beliefs and attitudes predict their willingness to recommend mainland strikes. Simple correlations between each respondent's average willingness to recommend mainland strikes and their answers to a series of foreign-policy belief questions enabled this assessment. The questions asked of each respondent span three topics: the perceived importance of Taiwan, use of force beliefs, and beliefs about Chinese nuclear weapons. An additional check is provided by examining whether changing the question framing changes the correlation coefficient. Therefore figure 9 reports two correlation coefficients for each question: one coefficient for those respondents who received the positive framing and one coefficient for

those who received the alternative framing. See table 3 for a side-by-side comparison of each question. The positive framing and alternative framings are sometimes mirror images of each other. In these cases, if there is a relationship between the underlying construct and respondent willingness to recommend mainland strikes, the two coefficients should be of similar magnitude but opposite sign. In other cases, the alternative framing asks a related but distinct question. Because there are four questions related to use of force beliefs, this section also performs a principal components analysis to examine if the underlying construct also predicts use of force beliefs.

The findings are three-fold. First, those who view Taiwan as a vital US national interest are more willing to recommend mainland strikes. Both correlation coefficients associated with this question are statistically significant and are of similar magnitude but opposite sign.[15] Second, the use-of-force beliefs—with the exception of military goals—are related to willingness to recommend mainland strikes in the portion of the sample that received the positive framing, but this relationship does not hold for those respondents who received the alternative framing. It bears mentioning that the alternative frame for the "decisive force" question was awkward and likely led to confusion among respondents. This could explain the null finding for the alternative wording of the "decisive force" question. The conflicting results lower the confidence a reader can have in the relationship between the use of force questions and respondent willingness to recommend mainland strikes. Third, some respondents acknowledged that Chinese possession of nuclear weapons reduced their willingness to recommend mainland strikes (in the positive framing) or that Chinese nuclear weapons affects their willingness to recommend mainland strikes (in the alternative framing). Furthermore, the more a respondent agreed that Chinese nuclear weapons reduced their willingness to recommend mainland strikes, the less likely that respondent was to recommend mainland strikes.[16] Additionally, some respondents did worry that *some* strikes on Chinese mainland targets would be interpreted by Chinese leaders as an attempt to destroy Chinese nuclear weapons (see the misperception question negative framing results), and this belief is negatively correlated with a willingness to recommend mainland strikes.[17]

These findings are consistent with the interview evidence. Recall one interviewee, a former senior Department of Defense civilian official, who cautioned that mainland strikes would be "escalatory" and that "launching thousands of strikes into Beijing or mainland China elsewhere doesn't seem like the smartest way to keep things constrained and below the nuclear threshold."[18] Chinese nuclear weapons clearly deeply affected the thinking of these elites. But there were also elites who showed relatively little concern for Chinese nuclear weapons, again consistent with the wide range of views uncovered by the survey.

Figure 9. Relationship between Foreign Policy Beliefs and Attitudes and Willingness to Recommend Mainland Strikes.

Category of Beliefs	Belief	Correlation	
		Positive Wording	Alternative Wording
National Interest	Taiwan	.31	-.34
Use of Force Beliefs	Generals	.40	
	Military Goals		
	Decisive Force	.28	
	Initiative	.39	
Nuclear Beliefs	Chinese Nukes	-.31	.25
	Chinese Misperceptions		.35

Note. Statistical significance is defined as p < .1. The reported values within each cell are the correlation coefficients. For the survey questions and their alternative wordings, refer back to table 3.

As an additional check on the influence of use-of-force beliefs on respondent willingness to recommend mainland strikes, a final subanalysis examined whether the use-of-force beliefs could be decomposed into underlying beliefs that predict respondent willingness to recommend mainland strikes. A principal-components analysis—an analysis able to determine if several similar questions are actually related to a single underlying latent belief—tested whether the use-of-force questions represent an underlying latent use of force belief. The results suggest that the positive frame use-of-force questions do tap an underlying belief; the first principal component explains 51 percent of the variance and is strongly associated with an increased willingness to recommend mainland strikes (with a coefficient of .45 and a p-value of .004). The negative frame questions, however, do not appear to readily decompose into an underlying belief; the first principal component explains only 35 percent of the variance, and there is no statistically significant relationship between these attitudes and respondent willingness to recommend mainland strikes. Therefore, once again, the evidence on whether use-of-force attitudes predict willingness to recommend mainland strikes is mixed.

Strategists seeking to understand whether a given national-security elite is more or less likely to recommend mainland strikes are therefore advised to focus on that person's attitudes on Taiwan and beliefs about Chinese nuclear weapons. Foreign-policy professionals who perceive the defense of Taiwan as a vital American interest and who are relatively unconcerned about Chinese nuclear use are more willing to recommend mainland strikes. Use-of-force beliefs appear less salient in explaining elite willingness to recommend mainland strikes.

LIMITS OF A SCENARIO-BASED SURVEY OF FOREIGN POLICY ELITES

There are several important limitations to the analysis presented earlier. To be sure, the scenarios had limited strategic context, and respondents did not have an array of policy options.[19] These survey design decisions, which helped ensure that the survey could be completed in five–10 minutes and thus minimized survey fatigue, do mean that the scenario was unlike the situation-room scenario a future US president will face in a potential US-China conflict. A scenario described with pages of detail would certainly be richer but would also open the survey to the charge that any findings are limited to a specific, detailed scenario. The relatively general, spare description of the scenario employed in the survey therefore potentially increases the generalizability of my findings. The survey also excluded the wide menu of policy options that a president would be able to wield in a future conflict. Several survey participants indicated in their survey comments that the exclusion of cyber- and economic-related policy options was especially limiting. This is true, but it is unclear if those options are necessary to achieve the survey's key analytical objective: to compare the desirability of mainland strikes across scenarios and between participants. Additionally, creating a wide range of options would have lengthened the survey and dramatically increased cognitive complexity, and it is likely that no matter what option set was presented, many participants would be bothered by the exclusion of yet another unconsidered option. Finally, survey participants found the negative phrasing of attitude-related questions confusing. This aspect of the survey, conceived as a feature, was perceived as a bug by participants.

The survey sample was also not drawn from a universally recognized list of foreign-policy experts. Strictly speaking, it is therefore not possible to gauge how representative it is. But the survey sample does meet several criteria that provide it with more than just face validity. The sample is largely drawn from seasoned foreign-policy and national-security professionals across major research organizations in Washington, DC. The sample contains Republicans, Democrats, and some persons affiliated with neither party. It also includes individuals with prior military experience. So, although it might not be representative, it is similar in composition, broadly speaking, to persons who move in and out of government at the highest levels of the US national-security agencies.

Peering into the Future, Part II 159

SUMMARY AND IMPLICATIONS

First, some details of the foreign-policy scenario matter greatly. A Chinese attack on Kadena Air Base (or potentially on another air base or an American aircraft carrier) would likely dramatically increase the willingness of advisors to recommend conventional strikes on the Chinese mainland. In one sense, this is good news for military planners; aggressive Chinese actions will likely loosen the rules of engagement. In another sense, this finding should alarm strategists; early in a conflict, before outright Chinese aggression against US forces, there might be less appetite for military steps such as conventional strikes on the Chinese mainland. The scope of the proposed conventional strikes on the Chinese mainland also matters. The more limited the strikes, the greater the willingness of elites to recommend them. Conversely, comprehensive strikes on targets that include command and control centers, intelligence centers, and other targets, some of which might be entangled with Chinese nuclear forces, are likely to meet some opposition. Readers who view comprehensive strikes as essential to American military success in a future war will view this finding with concern. Those who see limited strikes as sufficient to achieve operational goals will evince less concern.

But not all scenario details matter. Surprisingly, a foreign-policy situation in which Chinese leaders and Taiwanese leaders share blame for initiating the conflict is unlikely to dampen American support for mainland strikes. Proponents of mainland strike strategies should see this as evidence that their preferred strategy is not as susceptible to political circumstances as some detractors worry.

An individual's background and beliefs also matter, though there are more individual characteristics that do not matter than many experts might have predicted. Younger, Republican-leaning respondents are more likely to recommend mainland strikes. But military background, gender, and Asia expertise do not seem to matter. The fault lines are therefore not what one might expect: the generals and admirals are not as bent on tactical escalation as the theorizing of Betts would predict, and Asia expertise doesn't reduce respondent willingness to recommend mainland strikes. Military strategists who view mainland strikes as imperative during a future US-China conflict should therefore be most concerned that an older, Democrat-leaning foreign-policy team would favor tighter rules of engagement regarding mainland strikes. In contrast, experts worried about mainland strikes should be worried about a young, Republican-dominated administration.

Beliefs seem to play just as large or a larger role than an individual's background. Respondents who believe that Taiwan is a vital American interest express a greater willingness to recommend mainland strikes. Use of force beliefs are also potentially related to a willingness to recommend mainland strikes, but the conflicting findings that result when analyzing positively framed questions versus the alternative framing make this finding tentative at best. Beliefs related to nuclear weapons—that China might use nuclear weapons and a fear that Chinese leaders might perceive some conventional strikes on the Chinese mainland as part of a counterforce campaign—also reduce willingness to recommend mainland strikes. Strategists trying to understand the likelihood of mainland strikes are therefore also advised to consider the foreign-policy beliefs of high-level policy advisors.

In sum, advocates and opponents of mainland strikes strategies will both find some evidence in favor of their beliefs. Mainland strikes are conceivable, especially should China attack Kadena Air Base or other American forces and particularly if the presidential advisors are younger, Republican, believe that Taiwan is a vital American interest, or doubt that China would use nuclear weapons or that Chinese leaders might perceive mainland strikes as part of a counterforce campaign. Conversely, there are factors that mitigate against the employment of at least some forms of mainland strikes. Calling for mainland strikes before a direct Chinese attack on US forces is likely to meet some resistance, especially if the strikes are comprehensive. Furthermore, older, Democrat-leaning strategists who see Taiwan as less than a vital interest or fear Chinese use of nuclear weapons and potential Chinese misperceptions are also relatively less willing to recommend mainland strikes. Of course, these conditions will change over time as American administrations change and will also vary according to Chinese actions. In other words, mainland strikes are contingent, but this contingency is not purely random. Instead, military planners can understand some potential patterns related to the likelihood of the employment of mainland strikes. This understanding can then be an analytical input into planning for a potential future conflict with China and inform the pursuit of a suite of capabilities to deter or defeat potential future Chinese aggression.

Notes

1. Holsti and Rosenau, *The Foreign Policy Leadership Project*; Avey and Desch, "What Do Policymakers Want from Us?"; Hafner-Burton, LeVeck, Victor, Fowler, "Decision Maker Preferences for International Legal Cooperation."
2. Quek and Johnston, "Can China Back Down?"; Press, Sagan, Valentino, "Atomic Aversion"; Reddie, Goldblum, Lakkaraju, Reinhardt, Nacht, and Epifanovskaya, "Next-Generation Wargames."
3. The homepage for ClassApps.com, the owner of SelectSurvey, can be found here: http://www.classapps.com/, accessed March 26, 2019.
4. Tol, Gunzinger, Krepinevich, and Thomas, *AirSea Battle*.
5. Interview with former senior Defense Department official, April 16, 2018. At least seven interviewees expressed strong support for this position. Additionally, none of the other interviewees disagreed with this position.
6. Interview with former diplomat, November 17, 2017; Interview with former Defense Department senior civilian, June 7, 2018.
7. To be precise, the statistical test is a generalization of McNemar's test. McNemar's test was designed to be used for 2x2 contingency tables. A generalized McNemar test, sometimes called the Stuart-Maxwell test, performs a similar function but for variables with more than two values. For an explanation of this generalized McNemar's test, see Sun and Yang, "Generalized McNemar's Test for Homogeneity of Marginal Distributions."
8. Pew Research Center, "Political Independents: Who They Are, What They Think."
9. Statistical tests included a chi-squared test and Fisher's exact test on age, career length, gender, political party, Asia expertise, thinktank experience, and military experience. No p-value on any test was less than .05. Career length did obtain a p-value of .077 for the chi-squared test and .079 for the Fisher's exact test. Given that I performed seven tests, it is not surprising that one obtained a p-value below .1.
10. A chi-squared test traditionally requires at least five respondents for each answer response per condition.
11. Sun and Yang, "Generalized McNemar's Test for Homogeneity of the Marginal Distributions."

12. Comparing respondents who responded "yes" to the Asia expertise question to all other respondents led to a different—though tentative—conclusion. The t-tests for scenario mean, scenario one and scenario two were all significant, though the p-values were between .05 and .1. The Fisher's exact tests all produced null results. Experts defined thusly were relatively more willing to recommend mainland strikes.
13. Comparing Democrats to only Republicans produces similar findings. T-tests reveal that Republicans are statistically significantly more likely (p < .05) to recommend mainland strikes in scenarios two and four. The t-test for the scenario mean also indicated that Republicans are statistically significantly relatively more willing to recommend mainland strikes. The t-tests for The Fisher's exact test—when comparing Democrats to Republicans—produces null results.
14. Comparing respondents younger than forty to respondents that are forty or older leads to similar, though slightly less strong, results. The t-tests and the Fisher's tests are only significant for the scenario mean and scenario four. An additional robustness check examined whether older respondents were simply more likely to have served in government and whether this government service explained the pattern. Adding in a government service dummy to the linear regressions did not change the statistically significant age coefficient in three of four regressions. Scenario 1's statistically significant negative coefficient on age did disappear after the addition of the government service dummy variable. As a side note, government service does appear to reduce respondent willingness to recommend mainland strikes.
15. Additionally, in exploratory multiple regression analysis, a participant's views toward Taiwan were consistently statistically significant despite the addition of other predictors and the small sample sizes.
16. Some respondents used their end-of-survey comments to further describe their views. One wrote, "The presence of [a] survivable nuclear arsenal held by the US and China will greatly inhibit the escalation options considered by the leadership in Washington and Beijing."
17. Of the forty-six respondents who received the negative framing question set, thirteen stated that they disagree and five stated that they strongly disagree with the proposition that strikes on Chinese mainland targets will *not* be interpreted as an attempt to destroy Chinese nuclear weapons. It is interesting to note that fourteen agreed with this statement and one strongly agreed. Thirteen were neutral.

18. Interview with former Defense Department senior civilian, August 1, 2018.
19. Several survey participants pointed out these limitations in the survey's free-text comment box. I am grateful for their constructive critique.

Chapter 7

Policy Recommendations

At the time of this writing, the term "great power competition" is in vogue, though "competition" means many things to many parties. For some, competition entails gray-zone tactics, that is, maneuvering below the threshold of armed conflict given that outright war would be too costly and so will be avoided by all sensible parties.[1] This lens identifies China as a shrewd competitor, aware of the red lines of the United States, and interested in using "salami slice" tactics to patiently accumulate advantages. One scholar, for instance, labels China a "cautious bully" given its coercive tactics that infrequently involve outright violence.[2] Such tactics include, for instance, the use of so-called maritime militias in the South China Sea and the construction of artificial islands. These analysts concerned with this version of great power competition call for managing alliance dynamics and adjusting American diplomacy to make sure freedom of navigation operations never turn into the opening phase of war. Gray zone tactics are, after all, not about preparing for war. Military force planning and military war planning often get short shrift when analysts use this perspective. Analyses of this variety simply see war as out of the question, a rung on the escalation ladder that no participant wishes to grab.

For others, competition entails technological rivalry.[3] The United States and China, in this view, are angling for the commanding heights of technological mastery in a range of emerging fields such as artificial intelligence, quantum computing, and biotechnology. To compete, the United States needs to invest in this next generation of technologies to avoid missing out on what has been called the "fourth industrial revolution." At the time of writing, semiconductors have become an especially important part of this discourse.[4] The technological rivalry lens has contributed to policies that emphasize the building of crucial technology supply chains either in the United States or in countries that are friendly to the United States and beyond the reach of Chinese aggression. Even conservative, pro-market thinkers have embraced what might be called "industrial policy" in the name of this perspective. Policies that restrict the purchase of Huawei telecommunications gear can also be placed in this conceptual camp. Although commentators sometimes do see these technologies as contributing to the military power of the United States and shaping the broader military balance, many analyses focus more on long-term patterns of economic growth and the potential for economic coercion or digital espionage.

Still others see the competition as one involving values and whether American or Chinese political values will prevail in the future. Analysts who worry about digital authoritarianism are, in part, invoking this version of competition. Similarly, observers worried about the Chinese export of telecommunications equipment and of facial recognition technology are similarly concerned that Chinese political values will be exported along with these goods. Debates about US policy related to Xinjiang and the mass detention of Uyghurs and even about whether to ban TikTok, the wildly popular social media app owned by a Chinese company, feature within this discourse. Organizing a coalition of like-minded democracies is often seen as the necessary corrective to these initiatives. War is not a central concern.

The Chinese state as a mercantilist economic threat has also been an important framing of the "China problem." Perhaps most closely associated with the administration of Donald Trump, this perspective emphasizes the harms inflicted upon US workers, firms, and the economy due to Chinese trade restrictions, illegal business practices, and infringement of the intellectual property of US companies.[5] Although not necessarily dismissive of the need for American military preparations, this lens views conflict as economic in nature. These commentators often call for the US government to fight fire with fire and to employ retaliatory or defensive international trade practices.

These perspectives, and others too, have merit. There is another perspective though, an older and more pessimistic perspective, one that some may see as outmoded: war is possible between the United States and China, and the United States should prudently prepare for a potential conflict. War is competition by violent means, and it is hard to have much faith in precise predictions about the likelihood of war between China and the United States. Predicting international politics, especially the outbreak of war, is difficult.[6] So why not be prudent? The Russian invasion of Ukraine in early 2022 unfortunately supports this pessimistic perspective and has notably pushed the "competition" debate back toward this perspective.

This final perspective is why this book began by noting that in 2010 a public debate emerged over the growth of Chinese military power and the appropriate American military response. The participants in this strategic debate often referenced mainland strikes, wartime attacks on military targets located on the Chinese mainland with non-nuclear (i.e., conventional) weapons. Some strategists assumed that an American president and their advisors would be willing to authorize or recommend mainland strikes in a future war with China; these strategists consequently recommended designing a military force capable of carrying out these attacks. Other strategists assumed a president and their advisors would be extremely unwilling to recommend mainland strikes; these strategists called for building and training a military force capable of operational tasks other than mainland strikes. This research has been designed to test these competing assumptions about conventional escalation, nuclear weapons, and American military strategy toward China.

Historical research on the Korean and Vietnam Wars and interviews and surveys of American national-security elites enabled this testing. The contribution of this research should be measured by its ability to help American military planners better understand the course of a future —and hopefully unlikely—US-China war. The findings ought to assist American military planners in crafting war plans that are robust whether or not a president authorizes mainland strikes early or at all in a conflict. It also offers insights for Department of Defense leaders as they design, program, and advocate for future strategies and forces.

The remainder of this chapter is divided into key findings. Each finding references supporting evidence and spells out policy recommendations for US military strategy toward China.

Chinese Nuclear Weapons And Mainland Strikes

A central concern in the mainland strikes debate has been the relationship between nuclear weapons and conventional escalation (specifically mainland strikes) during war. This project described three theoretical models that could characterize this relationship: the caution model predicts that nuclear weapons dampen intra-war conventional escalation, the null model predicts no effect, and the emboldenment model predicts that mutual nuclear possession could increase conventional escalation.

Based on an analysis of American decision-making during the Korean and Vietnam Wars and the views of modern American national-security elites concerning potential Chinese nuclear use via interviews and a survey, this research finds support for the null and caution model, while casting some doubt on the emboldenment model. Mainland strikes,

Policy Recommendations

judging from this nuclear-related evidence, are therefore possible but not guaranteed.

All three methods provide at least some support for the null model. Mutual nuclear possession does not entirely dampen conventional escalation during war. In the Korean War and Vietnam War, members of the enemy coalition possessed nuclear weapons, yet there is remarkably little historical evidence that this influenced patterns of American choices regarding conventional escalation. Tight rules of engagement, such as foregoing bombing runs in China during the Korean War, arose from factors beyond adversary coalition nuclear weapons. To be sure, some readers who view these wars as unlike a future US-China one will object to this historical evidence given the significant differences that exist between them, especially the Chinese possession of a substantial nuclear arsenal. Skeptics should not, however, overlook that the interviews and surveys also produced a similar finding. There were at least some interviewees and survey participants who evinced relatively little fear that Chinese nuclear use might result from US conventional strikes on the Chinese mainland. The survey data especially showed that in a scenario in which China attacks an American airbase and the US military plan calls for relatively limited strikes, American national-security professionals are willing to recommend mainland strikes. In sum, Chinese nuclear possession does not appear to preclude mainland strikes.

But that does not mean that Chinese nuclear weapons have no effect on American conventional escalation decisions. In fact, two of the methods also produced evidence for the caution model. The interviews and the surveys uncovered participants who were quite worried about Chinese nuclear use, especially as a result of American conventional strikes against Chinese targets entangled with Chinese nuclear forces. In the survey, many elites even directly conceded that Chinese nuclear weapons reduced their willingness to recommend mainland strikes. Those same elites were then less willing to recommend mainland strikes across the different operational scenarios. Additionally, some elites worried that

Chinese leaders might misinterpret mainland strikes as an attempt to destroy Chinese nuclear weapons, setting off a dangerous use-it-or-lose-it situation for Chinese leaders. Even though some analysts think the danger of this use-it-or-lose-it situation is overblown, many US national-security elites, during the survey, disagreed.[7] This fear of misperception was then negatively correlated with willingness to authorize mainland strikes.

The emboldenment model received no support from any method employed. Senior leaders of the US government during the Korean and Vietnam Wars did not appear to perceive nuclear superiority, let alone use that nuclear superiority to achieve their conventional war aims. Additionally, the interviewees either did not believe the United States possessed nuclear superiority vis-à-vis China or did not think that superiority enabled American conventional escalation in the form of mainland strikes.

How can both the caution and null model simultaneously receive support? The answer seems to lie in the fact that attitudes and beliefs about nuclear weapons vary greatly among national-security elites. Some interviewees were escalation pessimists who expressed a strong worry that mainland strikes could lead to a US-China nuclear war, whereas others were escalation optimists who thought American nuclear possession ensured no Chinese leader would ever pull the nuclear trigger. Some survey takers stated that Chinese nuclear weapons reduced their willingness to recommend mainland strikes, and some stated that Chinese nuclear weapons had little bearing on their willingness to recommend mainland strikes. The ability of Chinese nuclear weapons to reduce American intra-war conventional escalation therefore might depend on the particular advisors involved. This is not part of standard theorizing on nuclear weapons and international politics. The power of nuclear weapons is not, in conventional analytic narratives, meant to be in the eye of the beholder. This finding therefore supports the idea that when it comes to conventional escalation in a potential US-China conflict, the effect of Chinese nuclear weapons is what American leaders make of it, and most surveyed national-security elites expressed attitudes consistent with the caution model or null model.

These findings on the relationship between nuclear weapons and conventional escalation neither rule out nor guarantee mainland strikes in a future US-China war. Chinese nuclear weapons will likely reduce the willingness of advisors to recommend mainland strikes, but a reduced willingness should not be confused with an absolute unwillingness. This finding points to the likelihood that other factors, either the details of the war or of the advisors involved, will have an important bearing on the likelihood of mainland strikes.

One US air force lieutenant colonel has described the broad outlines of how this finding should affect US military strategy. "The military services," he writes, "should ensure they are prepared to present viable options that offer lower risks of miscalculation and escalation" in addition to approaches that rely on mainland strikes.[8] When planners are drawing up war plans and analysts are modeling combat outcomes, leaders should ensure that these plans and analyses not only include scenarios in which mainland strikes are curtailed or delayed but that the alternative plans stand a fighting chance of operational success. For instance, those proposing denial strategies that focus on destroying a Chinese amphibious invasion force without mainland strikes should examine the likelihood of military success.[9] Viable, non-mainland strike approaches will then need to be turned into procurement plans and operational exercises.

For analysts who view mainland strikes, especially comprehensive mainland strikes early in a conflict, as essential to US plans, these findings should be a wake-up call. Chinese nuclear weapons do curb American conventional escalation options, at least in the eyes of some interviewed and surveyed American national-security elites. That said, this research does not support a recommendation that all approaches related to mainland strikes be scrapped and, with those plans, forces like stealthy bombers. Senior national-security leaders might want to keep this arrow in their quiver. Analysts now have evidence to counter those advocates who believe Chinese nuclear weapons virtually eliminate the possibility of mainland strikes. Some elites do sometimes reveal that some scenarios, in their minds, justify some forms of mainland strikes.

Scenarios and Mainland Strikes

All three research approaches turned up evidence concerning the importance of scenario characteristics in predicting the willingness of leaders and advisors to engage in acts of conventional escalation. The details of a future US-China war matter when it comes to predicting the likelihood of mainland strikes.

The interviews of national-security elites amassed overwhelming evidence that leaders would be extremely reluctant to employ mainland strikes in a scenario related to a dispute in the South China Sea. Although there is a diversity of opinions on the importance of American stakes in the South China Sea, the interviews revealed that even a thought experiment involving US-China conflict in the South China induced strong skepticism among the interviewees. Most interviewees thought that the stakes involved in a US-China conflict related to conflict in the South China Sea were incommensurate with the nuclear escalation risks associated with mainland strikes. A conflict over Taiwan, though, was much more likely to result in a decision to employ mainland strikes. Participants generally viewed the defense of Taiwan as a top-tier American national interest.

The methods also created convergent evidence that whether China attacked American forces first and whether mainland strikes were limited or comprehensive would exert a strong influence on the likelihood of mainland strikes. The scenario-based survey uncovered clear evidence that a Chinese missile attack on Kadena Air Base would greatly increase the willingness of advisors to recommend mainland strikes. Mainland strikes before this threshold is breached will likely encounter relatively more resistance. Interviewed national-security elites emphatically agreed, and the patterns of escalation in the Korean War and Vietnam War are consistent with this finding. Especially in the Vietnam War, the escalation of American bombing operations was gradual and predicated on enemy forces escalating first. Additionally, limiting the target set of mainland strikes to targets near the theater of operation, relatively close to the Chinese coast, and unentangled with Chinese nuclear capabilities, according to the survey results, also greatly increases the willingness of potential advisors to recommend mainland strikes. Conversely, attacking targets far from the theater of operation, far inland in China, and potentially related to Chinese nuclear capabilities will likely reduce the willingness of elites to employ mainland strikes. In-depth interviews with American national-security elites corroborated this logic. Mainland strikes are therefore, according to these findings, not all the same. It is therefore simplistic to analyze the likelihood of mainland strikes without subdividing this action into a range of discrete military options.

The experiment embedded in the elite survey demonstrated that attributing conflict onset to China versus China and Taiwan does not appreciably affect the willingness of potential advisors to recommend mainland strikes. This result might seem to conflict with the finding derived from the interviews that some provocative Taiwanese actions would dramatically reduce the interview participant's willingness to recommend mainland strikes. This mixed finding can be partially resolved because interview respondents likely imagined a scenario in which Taiwanese leaders were believed to be entirely responsible for the onset of a conflict between Taiwan and China. In this situation, there would likely be a greatly reduced willingness for American leaders and advisors to embrace mainland strikes. The scenario-based survey did not present a scenario in which only Taiwanese leaders were at fault for the onset of a conflict. This conflict between methods is therefore more apparent than real. Nonetheless, it is indeed surprising that an ambiguous situation in which Taiwan and China share the fault for conflict onset did not reduce the willingness of respondents to recommend mainland strikes. This finding suggests that although scenario characteristics matter, not all permutations matter equally.

The historical case studies also detected a range of additional scenario-related considerations, including initial uncertainty about adversary intentions, the possibility of civilian casualties, public opinion, and armistice negotiations. The prevalence of these extra-military considerations suggests that many factors beyond battlefield conditions could hang over a mainland strikes decision. Military leaders should be advised that these additional factors, in the context of a potential US-China conflict, are a potential occupational hazard. Preparing plans that dampen the battlefield effects of these political consideration should be a top priority.

Scenario factors will therefore likely have an important influence on a future American decision to employ mainland strikes. Whether these factors will facilitate or impede a decision to employ mainland strikes depends on one's assessment of each individual factor's likelihood. Analysts who view a Chinese conventional first strike on American forces as likely and also believe that limited mainland strikes could serve important operational goals will likely be heartened; authorization of limited mainland strikes after a Chinese attack on American forces seems likely. But should a wartime scenario demand early, comprehensive strikes, there might be noticeably little support for mainland strikes.

American military planners should therefore consider and advocate for wartime plans that are viable no matter the vagaries of the different scenarios. For instance, Caitlin Talmadge has suggested creating plans and forces capable of geographically constrained operations. She has also recommended a "serious peacetime effort to develop target sets inside China that do not have nuclear functions."[10] This recommendation is certainly consistent with the analysis presented earlier.

Individual Characteristics and Mainland Strikes

The surveys found that some individual characteristics and beliefs —though far from all the examined beliefs—explain variation in the willingness of American national-security elites to recommend mainland strikes.

Political party and age appear to be weakly correlated with willingness to recommend mainland strikes, at least according to the survey results. Democrats and relatively older respondents (fifty or older) were both relatively less willing to recommend mainland strikes. Neither prior military service, nor gender, nor level of Asia-related expertise provide a reliable guide to an elite's willingness to recommend mainland strikes. That prior military service provides no insight is surprising. Theorists have often argued that prior military experience either reduces an individual's willingness to recommend force or that once a war starts, persons with a military background become more willing to recommend conventional escalation, but this finding supports neither argument. Those with and without military experience, according to survey analysis, appear to hold similar attitudes on mainland strikes. Although there is no prior published research on the determinants of attitudes towards mainland strikes, many parties have informally offered the opinion that military officers are more inclined to support mainland strikes given the bureaucratic preferences and worldview of these officers. Though a larger interview sample or survey sample might bear this out, this evidence suggests that civilian and military attitudes, at least among national-security elites, are surprisingly similar.

Survey respondents and interviewees who view defending Taiwan as a vital American interest are more willing to recommend mainland strikes. The converse is also true: national-security elites who view defending Taiwan as less than a vital interest (a noticeable portion) are less willing to recommend mainland strikes. Perhaps the most surprising aspect of this finding is that there are in fact differences among US national-security elites in attitudes toward supporting Taiwan. In public and mainstream forums, it can sometimes be hard to detect anything but consensus on US policy toward Taiwan. The survey, conducted anonymously, found not only wide variation in this attitude but also that this attitude lead to differences in willingness to support mainland strikes. Those commentators who believe that widespread support of Taiwan among American national-security elites will bolster American conventional escalation options may need to revise their opinions, although a post-coronavirus change in attitudes is also possible.

A respondent's views on the use of force have an uncertain relationship with a willingness to recommend mainland strikes; the results are sensitive to question wording, and therefore no definitive finding is possible. This finding is again surprising. In a manner similar to the result that military experience appears to have no effect on attitudes toward mainland strikes, it is possible that there is also simply too little variation in attitudes toward the use of force, no matter whether the participant has served in the military or not. The surveyed elites appear more similar to each other than some analysts might expect.

At least some background characteristics and beliefs of the president and their presidential advisors are therefore likely to have an important influence on the likelihood of mainland strikes. Because these characteristics and beliefs are likely to vary from one administration to another and even within an administration, strategists ought to be humble in their prediction of the likelihood of mainland strikes. Also, given that preferences about mainland strikes could vary, defense planners also ought to incorporate a discussion of mainland strikes into strategic conversations with new presidential administrations and during the preparation of the annual Defense Planning Guidance.

THE NEED FOR AN UPDATED MENTAL MODEL

This analysis provides broad guidance for American military strategists creating and comparing war plans, capabilities, and weapons systems. This research proposed that there are three possibilities for American military strategy toward China: a strategy that emphasizes mainland strikes, a maritime denial strategy that focuses on attacking offensive

Chinese maneuver forces, and a naval blockade strategy. To be clear, these analytical results do not resolve which strategy is superior. The findings do, however, provide some additional means to analyze these strategies.

Most importantly, any strategy that features mainland strikes prominently should be conceptually divided into strategies that emphasize limited versus comprehensive strikes and strategies that require strikes before a Chinese attack on US forces and those that do not. The scenario-based survey results indicate that comprehensive strikes before an attack on American forces—even if China is already attacking an American partner—are likely to meet stiff resistance from top presidential advisors. Conversely, limited strikes after a Chinese attack on American forces will likely receive overwhelming support from top advisors.

Additionally, Chinese nuclear weapons do not preclude American conventional escalation against China, specifically mainland strikes, at least according to the survey results and to my reading of the Korean War and Vietnam War evidence. But Chinese nuclear weapons, based on the interview and survey results, do lessen the appetite of American national-security elites to recommend conventional strikes on the Chinese mainland. American national-security elites do perceive striking the Chinese mainland with conventional weapons as raising the specter of nuclear escalation, especially inadvertent nuclear escalation, and will therefore only reach for this option as a last resort.

The findings also do lend some support to those who worry that plans that rely heavily on a mainland strikes strategy should be avoided. Numerous authors have warned that a strategy dependent on mainland strikes could leave a future American president grasping for alternative courses of action during a future war with China, alternatives that do not involve mainland strikes or involve only a circumscribed version of mainland strikes. These alternatives include an increased emphasis on sea denial via a larger attack submarine force, sea-mine laying capabilities and the creation of a small surface combatant fleet with anti-ship missiles, a de-emphasis of aircraft carriers, and a host of other options. Many analysts also emphasize the importance of a large stockpile of anti-ship munitions, long-range aircraft that can carry these munitions, and a sensor network capable of tracking Chinese naval forces that have left port. The analysis did not determine which of these particular maritime denial strategies is best. It does however suggest that a president and their advisors might want more flexibility than a mainland strike-centric war plan offers. The willingness to recommend mainland strikes can substantially differ from situation to situation and, importantly, from advisor to advisor. Military leaders should consider the willingness of leaders to authorize a course of action when considering procuring capabilities and technological systems that support a given course of action. That said, mainland strikes, contrary to the writings of the most ardent skeptics, are not unthinkable, at least according to the evidence presented earlier, and many national-security elites can imagine plausible scenarios in which they would be willing to recommend mainland strikes.

These research findings also have implications for US military strategy toward other nuclear-armed powers, but these inferences must be treated more tentatively. Strategists writing about a potential conflict between the United States and Russia, North Korea, or a future nuclear-armed Iran have examined how American military strategy affects the likelihood of adversary nuclear use and steps the United States could take to reduce the likelihood of adversary nuclear use. These writings have pointed out, for instance, that "intensive air campaigns" may be "less appropriate" for war against nuclear-armed powers and that, for instance, the risk of Russian nuclear use might force the United States and its NATO allies to acquiesce to Russian conventional aggression.[11] Others worry that American conventional strikes on military targets on Russian territory could create a dangerous risk of Russian nuclear use. As a result of these potential escalation dangers, these thinkers have called for shifts in planning, procurement, and doctrine. Elbridge Colby summarizes what he views as the needed conceptual shift:

> US defense decision-makers need to be keenly aware that preparing to take on potential adversaries cannot be thought of merely as a conventional force problem, with the possibility of escalation to the nuclear level seen as something so improbable that it can be ignored or relegated to an afterthought.[12]

This research supports Colby's line of argument and adds empirical evidence that can enrich the debate. Adversary nuclear weapons can indeed dampen the willingness of American elites to recommend strikes on the homeland of a nuclear adversary. In the interviews and the surveys, some American national-security elites did express a fear of Chinese nuclear use, despite American possession of nuclear weapons. This evidence suggests that nuclear weapons do not simply "cancel each other out." Instead, mutual nuclear possession can, at least sometimes, induce caution. An American war with any other nuclear-armed power could demonstrate similar dynamics. A fearful American leadership might curb conventional military operations, preventing strikes in certain geographies (like the homeland of an adversary) or on certain targets in a war with a nuclear-armed power. This could reduce the operational effectiveness of an American military campaign, a type of operational warfare that has emphasized conventional strikes on a wide range of military targets throughout the enemy's homeland.

That said, all lines of evidence in this research also support the view that adversary nuclear weapons *do not completely* constrain American freedom of action and the willingness of American leaders to engage in higher levels of conventional escalation. In the Korean and Vietnam Wars, despite there being a nuclear shadow cast by the arsenals of adversary alliances, President Truman and then President Johnson were willing to contemplate higher levels of conventional escalation. Furthermore, interviewees and survey participants also identified situations in which they would be willing to recommend a conventional strike on the homeland of a nuclear power.

Final Words

Studying a potential decision about US conventional strikes on the Chinese mainland in a possible future US-China war is, to understate the challenge, difficult. Such a conflict has not and hopefully will not occur. But this research and analysis challenge, contrary to popular wisdom, can be overcome. This book has shown that two historical cases, the Korean and Vietnam Wars, are similar enough that their histories reveal interesting and useful parallels to a future mainland strikes decision. In addition to retrospective historical analysis, the earlier analysis also employed more prospective methods in the field of synthetic history. Interviews and a scenario-based survey conducted with American national-security elites helped assess the role of nuclear weapons, scenarios, and individuals in a future mainland-strikes decision.

What resulted from all this research? Several findings have great salience for planners and decision-makers. Conventional strikes on the Chinese mainland by US forces in a future US-China war are possible, but they are also far from guaranteed. Chinese nuclear weapons do reduce, though only moderately, the likelihood of mainland strikes. A Chinese attack on US forces increases the likelihood that advisors will recommend mainland strikes. If American military commanders propose a broad target set on the Chinese mainland, advisors are less likely to recommend mainland strikes. And on top of this uncertainty, there are some systematic differences between individuals. American military planners have strong operational reasons to see mainland strikes as necessary, but they would be wise to prepare alternative plans and the forces to execute to them. Even in highly stressing scenarios, there are conditions in which the president might deny permission to strike the homeland of a nuclear power. To recast a piece of traditional military wisdom, some war plans do not even survive first contact with one's own leaders.

Notes

1. Morris, Mazarr, Hornung, Pezard, Binnendijk, and Kepe, *Gaining Competitive Advantage in the Gray Zone.*
2. Zhang, "Cautious Bully."
3. Darby and Sewall, "The Innovation Wars: America's Eroding Technological Advantage."
4. Miller, *Chip War;* Scharre, *Four Battlegrounds.*
5. Navarro, *Crouching Tiger.*
6. Tetlock, *Expert Political Judgment.*
7. Kroenig and Massa, "Are Dual-Capable Weapon Systems Destabilizing?"
8. MacLean, "Reconsidering Attacks on Mainland China," 216.
9. Montgomery, "Kill 'Em All?"
10. Talmadge, "Preventing Nuclear Escalation in US-China Conflict."
11. Ochmanek and Schwartz, *The Challenge of Nuclear-Armed Regional Adversaries,* 49; Morgan, "Dancing with the Bear," 39.
12. Colby, *Nuclear Weapons in the Third Offset Strategy,* 9.

Appendices

Appendix A: Interview Questions

- What was your role in policy related to what was called AirSea Battle?
- Do you have an opinion, in any direction, toward AirSea battle?
- In your opinion, what is your current assessment of US-China relations? [Probe: What are the sticking points?]
- [Assuming a relevant scenario comes up] Could you assess the danger of escalation in that scenario?
- More generally, how likely do you assess that a conventional war between China and the United States could turn into a nuclear war?
- Some strategists think that strikes on mainland Chinese targets are unlikely to be authorized by the president. You might know their writings. T.X. Hammes of the National Defense University is in this camp. Others believe that a president is very likely to authorize these strikes. Elbridge Colby, formerly of the Center for a New American Security, is often associated with this view.
- If you were in a presidential advisor role, what would be your strategic and tactical considerations? How would you prioritize these considerations?
- Can you help me understand your basic mental model for how to structure your decision-making?
- How does the scenario matter to you? [Taiwan invasion, Taiwan blockade, South China Sea dispute, Diaoyu-Senkaku Island dispute]
- How does the type of target matter to you? [Air defense vs. command and control vs. ballistic missiles, etc.]
- How does Chinese possession of nuclear weapons affect your decision-making?
- How does American possession of nuclear weapons affect your decision-making?

- How do US-China trade ties affect your decision-making?
- How does the probability of victory with and without mainland strikes affect your decision?
- Is there a possibility that you would recommend deferring a decision about mainland strikes for several days during the early stages of the war?
- If you were advocating for X policy in the inter-agency process, who would be your allies? Your enemies? Why? What would be their views?
- What would this conversation look like if it were part of the National Security Council, instead of just a one-on-one conversation between us?
- Would your views be affected if you were in one of your past professional roles?
- Attacks on North Korea have been in the news recently. Are there considerations in that conflict that are similar, or more importantly, different in that scenario?
- Is there anything I have not asked about that you would like to add?
- If I referred to you in my analysis in a past professional role of yours, what language would you like me to use? For instance, an Air Force officer (colonel), who previously worked in J-5?

Appendix B: Interview Vignettes

Taiwan Scenario A

Vignette 1: Comprehensive mainland strikes, no US base hit
China is attempting an invasion of Taiwan after Taiwan held a successful referendum to declare independence. Chinese missiles have already attacked Taiwan air bases, air defense systems, and command centers. US intelligence indicates that a Chinese amphibious invasion could begin in as soon as 48 hours; China has not yet attacked an American air base. A US National Security Council meeting is considering the appropriate American military response. A representative from the Joint Chiefs proposes immediate strikes by the Air Force and Navy not only on Chinese military units directly involved in the amphibious attempt (such as air defense sites, ballistic missile launchers, Chinese ships and naval bases and aircraft and air bases), but also on units indirectly involved (such as Chinese intelligence centers, command centers, over-the-horizon radars, and anti-satellite weapon launch sites).

Vignette 2: Comprehensive mainland strikes, US base hit
China is attempting an invasion of Taiwan after Taiwan held a successful referendum to declare independence. Chinese missiles have already attacked Taiwan air bases, air defense systems, and command centers. US intelligence indicates that a Chinese amphibious invasion could begin in as soon as 48 hours. China only an hour ago attacked Kadena Air Base on Okinawa with ballistic missiles. The commander reports severe damage to runways, two dozen damaged aircraft, and scores of casualties. A US National Security Council meeting is considering the appropriate American military response. A representative from the Joint Chiefs proposes immediate strikes by the Air Force and Navy not only on

Chinese military units directly involved in the amphibious attempt (such as air defense sites, ballistic missile launchers, Chinese ships and naval bases and aircraft and air bases), but also on units indirectly involved (such as Chinese intelligence centers, command centers, over-the-horizon radars, and anti-satellite weapon launch sites).

Vignette 3: Partial mainland strikes, no US base hit
China is attempting an invasion of Taiwan after Taiwan held a successful referendum to declare independence. Chinese missiles have already attacked Taiwan air bases, air defense systems, and command centers. US intelligence indicates that a Chinese amphibious invasion could begin in as soon as 48 hours. China has not yet attacked an American air base. A US National Security Council meeting is considering the appropriate American military response. A representative from the Joint Chiefs proposes immediate strikes by the Air Force and Navy on Chinese military units directly involved in the amphibious attempt (such as air defense sites, ballistic missile launchers, Chinese ships and naval bases and aircraft and air bases).

Vignette 4: Partial mainland strikes, US base hit
China is attempting an invasion of Taiwan after Taiwan held a successful referendum to declare independence. Chinese missiles have already attacked Taiwan air bases, air defense systems, and command centers. US intelligence indicates that a Chinese amphibious invasion could begin in as soon as 48 hours. China only an hour ago attacked Kadena Air Base on Okinawa with ballistic missiles. The commander reports severe damage to runways, two dozen damaged aircraft, and scores of casualties. A US National Security Council meeting is considering the appropriate American military response. A representative from the Joint Chiefs proposes immediate strikes by the Air Force and Navy on Chinese military units directly involved in the amphibious attempt (such as air defense sites, ballistic missile launchers, Chinese ships and naval bases and aircraft and air bases).

Taiwan Scenario B

Vignette 5: Comprehensive mainland strikes, no US base hit
China is attempting an invasion of Taiwan after Beijing decided that efforts for a peaceful unification with Taiwan were advancing too slowly. Chinese missiles have already attacked Taiwan air bases, air defense systems, and command centers. US intelligence indicates that a Chinese amphibious invasion could begin in as soon as 48 hours. China has not yet attacked an American air base. A US National Security Council meeting is considering the appropriate American military response. A representative from the Joint Chiefs proposes immediate strikes by the Air Force and Navy not only on Chinese military units directly involved in the amphibious attempt (such as air defense sites, ballistic missile launchers, Chinese ships and naval bases and aircraft and air bases), but also on units indirectly involved (such as Chinese intelligence centers, command centers, over-the-horizon radars, and anti-satellite weapon launch sites).

Vignette 6: Comprehensive mainland strikes, US base hit
China is attempting an invasion of Taiwan after Beijing decided that efforts for a peaceful unification with Taiwan were advancing too slowly. Chinese missiles have already attacked Taiwan air bases, air defense systems, and command centers. US intelligence indicates that a Chinese amphibious invasion could begin in as soon as 48 hours. China only an hour ago attacked Kadena Air Base on Okinawa with ballistic missiles. The commander reports severe damage to runways, two dozen damaged aircraft, and scores of casualties. A US National Security Council meeting is considering the appropriate American military response. A representative from the Joint Chiefs proposes immediate strikes by the Air Force and Navy not only on Chinese military units directly involved in the amphibious attempt (such as air defense sites, ballistic missile launchers, Chinese ships and naval bases and aircraft and air bases), but also on units indirectly involved (such as Chinese intelligence centers,

command centers, over-the-horizon radars, and anti-satellite weapon launch sites).

Vignette 7: Partial mainland strikes, no US base hit

China is attempting an invasion of Taiwan after Beijing decided that efforts for a peaceful unification with Taiwan were advancing too slowly. Chinese missiles have already attacked Taiwan air bases, air defense systems, and command centers. US intelligence indicates that a Chinese amphibious invasion could begin in as soon as 48 hours. China has not yet attacked an American air base. A US National Security Council meeting is considering the appropriate American military response. A representative from the Joint Chiefs proposes immediate strikes by the Air Force and Navy on Chinese military units directly involved in the amphibious attempt (such as air defense sites, ballistic missile launchers, Chinese ships and naval bases and aircraft and air bases).

Vignette 8: Partial mainland strikes, US base hit

China is attempting an invasion of Taiwan after Beijing decided that efforts for a peaceful unification with Taiwan were advancing too slowly. Chinese missiles have already attacked Taiwanese air bases, air defense systems, and command centers. US intelligence indicates that a Chinese amphibious invasion could begin in as soon as 48 hours. China only an hour ago attacked Kadena Air Base on Okinawa with ballistic missiles. The commander reports severe damage to runways, two dozen damaged aircraft, and scores of casualties. A US national security council meeting is considering the appropriate American military response. A representative from the Joint Chiefs proposes immediate strikes by the Air Force and Navy on Chinese military units directly involved in the amphibious attempt (such as air defense sites, ballistic missile launchers, Chinese ships and naval bases and aircraft and air bases).

Appendix B: Interview Vignettes

South China Sea Scenario

Vignette 9: Comprehensive mainland strikes, no US carrier struck

The Philippines begins to exploit oil and gas resources in the South China Sea. China denounces Manila's "provocative behavior" and begins to harass Philippine ships and platforms. The Philippines reinforces its position in the Spratly Islands, especially on Thitu Island, and China responds by dispatching naval forces and violently occupying the island, killing several dozen Filipino marines and destroying several Filipino ships. After the United States dispatches a carrier battle group to the area, a US surveillance aircraft is destroyed by Chinese naval surface-to-air missiles, and the United States decides to eject Chinese forces from Thitu. A US National Security Council meeting is considering the appropriate American military response. A representative from the Joint Chiefs proposes immediate strikes by the Air Force and Navy on Chinese military units directly involved in the attack (such as Chinese aircraft and Chinese ships) as well as Chinese military units on the Chinese mainland that are not directly involved (such as Chinese naval bases, air bases, intelligence centers, command centers, over-the-horizon radars, and anti-satellite weapon launch sites).

Vignette 10: Comprehensive mainland strikes, US carrier hit

The Philippines begins to exploit oil and gas resources in the South China Sea. China denounces Manila's "provocative behavior" and begins to harass Philippine ships and platforms. The Philippines reinforces its position in the Spratly Islands, especially on Thitu Island, and China responds by dispatching naval forces and violently occupying the island, killing several dozen Filipino marines and destroying several Filipino ships. After the United States dispatches a carrier battle group to the area, a US surveillance aircraft is destroyed by Chinese naval surface-to-air missiles. Soon thereafter, a US aircraft carrier battle group is attacked by Chinese submarines and Chinese missiles. There are hundreds of casualties and the carrier sustains serious damage, rendering it incapable of further missions. The United States decides to eject Chinese forces from Thitu. A US National Security Council meeting is considering the appropriate American military response. A representative from the Joint Chiefs proposes immediate strikes by the Air Force and Navy on Chinese military units directly involved in the attack (such as Chinese aircraft and Chinese ships) as well as Chinese military units on the Chinese mainland that are not directly involved (such as Chinese naval bases, air bases, intelligence centers, command centers, over-the-horizon radars, and anti-satellite weapon launch sites).

Vignette 11: Partial mainland strikes, No US carrier hit
The Philippines begins to exploit oil and gas resources in the South China Sea. China denounces Manila's "provocative behavior" and begins to harass Philippine ships and platforms. The Philippines reinforces its position in the Spratly Islands, especially on Thitu Island, and China responds by dispatching naval forces and violently occupying the island, killing several dozen Filipino marines and destroying several Filipino ships. After the United States dispatches a carrier battle group to the area, a US surveillance aircraft is destroyed by Chinese naval surface-to-air missiles, and the United States decides to eject Chinese forces from Thitu. A US National Security Council meeting is considering the appropriate American military response. A representative from the Joint Chiefs proposes immediate strikes by the Air Force and Navy on Chinese military units directly involved in the attack (such as Chinese aircraft and Chinese ships).

Vignette 12: Partial mainland strikes, US carrier hit
The Philippines begins to exploit oil and gas resources in the South China Sea. China denounces Manila's "provocative behavior" and begins to harass Philippine ships and platforms. The Philippines reinforces its position in the Spratly Islands, especially on Thitu Island, and China responds by dispatching naval forces and violently occupying the island,

killing several dozen Filipino marines and destroying several Filipino ships. After the United States dispatches a carrier battle group to the area, a US surveillance aircraft is destroyed by Chinese naval surface-to-air missiles. Soon thereafter, a US aircraft carrier battle group is attacked by Chinese submarines and Chinese missiles. There are hundreds of casualties and the carrier sustains serious damage, rendering it incapable of further missions. The United States decides to eject Chinese forces from Thitu. A US National Security Council meeting is considering the appropriate American military response. A representative from the Joint Chiefs proposes immediate strikes by the Air Force and Navy on Chinese military units directly involved in the attack (such as Chinese aircraft and Chinese ships).

Appendix C: Qualitative Coding Tree

1. Nuclear Weapons

1.1. Likelihood of Nuclear War: Any statement that references the possibility of nuclear war happening and doesn't specifically specify either China or the United States "starting" nuclear use.

1.2. Nuclear Weapons Cancelling Each Other Out: Any statements that discuss whether Chinese and American nuclear weapons "cancel" each other out. In other words, statements that suggest China would never use nuclear weapons because the United States possesses them and therefore American decision-makers will not fear Chinese nuclear weapons.

1.3. Intelligence on Chinese Nuclear Weapons Doctrine: Statements that suggest the importance of intelligence on Chinese nuclear weapons doctrine for assessing the possibility of Chinese nuclear weapons use.

    1.3.1. Chinese No-First Use Doctrine: Statements concerning China's No-First Use doctrine.

    1.3.2. Importance of Intelligence on Chinese Nuclear Doctrine: Statements suggesting that understanding Chinese nuclear doctrine is important for making a recommendation about mainland strikes.

- Example: "What's really important is the intelligence that underpins the calculus...now shifting back to the mainland and China, if we have, and I would hope we would, if we have good intelligence about what their reaction might be, actually, that would incredibly instructive, in terms of how risky it is."

    1.3.3. Impossibility of Knowing Chinese Nuclear Doctrine: Statements that suggest that learning about Chinese nuclear doctrine would be helpful for making a recommendation about mainland strikes but that knowledge about Chinese doctrine is impossible to acquire.

1.4. Nuclear Other: Statements about nuclear weapons that don't fall into one of the other categories.

2. Scenario-Related Factors
2.1. Geographic Scope of Chinese Attacks on US: Any statements that US strikes on the mainland—their timing and scope—depends on the geographic scope of past Chinese attacks.

    2.1.1. Attacks on US Bases: Statements that specifically reference whether the decision to authorize US mainland strikes depends on whether there have been attacks on US bases, especially ones in East Asia.

    2.1.2. Attacks on US Territory: Statements that specifically reference whether the decision to authorize US mainland strikes depends on whether there have been attacks on targets that are on US territory, in particular, Guam.

    2.1.3. Attacks on the US Homeland: Statements that specifically reference whether the decision to authorize US mainland strikes depends on whether there have been attacks on the US homeland, including Hawaii and Alaska.

    2.1.4. Attacks only on Taiwan: Statements that specifically reference whether the decision to authorize US mainland strikes depends on whether the Chinese have attacked only Taiwan.

2.2. Timing of Mainland Strikes within Conflict: Any statement that addresses the likelihood of mainland strikes at a specific time during a US-China conflict.

    2.2.1. Attacks Early or Late in Conflict: Statements that discuss the likelihood of mainland strikes early or late in a conflict.

    2.2.2. Preemptive Attack on Mainland: Statements that discuss the advisability of mainland strikes before direct attacks on US forces.

2.3. US Relationship with Ally: Any statement that discusses how relationships with allies or partners bear on a decision about mainland strikes.

Appendix C: Qualitative Coding Tree

2.3.1. Ally as the Cause of Conflict: Statements that discuss an ally "starting" or "causing" a conflict and the impact of this action on the decision about mainland strikes.

2.3.2. China as the Cause of Conflict: Statements that discuss China "starting" or "causing" a conflict and the impact of this action on the decision about mainland strikes.

2.3.3. Preferences of the Ally Regarding Mainland Strikes: Statements that discuss whether and how the preferences of allied leaders would bear upon the decision to authorize mainland strikes.

2.4. Target Characteristics: Any statement that discusses how the type of target to be attacked affects the likelihood of authorization.

2.4.1. Attacks on Directly Involved Chinese Forces: Statements about attacks on Chinese forces that are directly involved in an attack on either US or allied forces and mainland strikes.

2.4.2. Attacks on Targets with No Nuclear Connection: Statements about attacks on targets that have no relationship with Chinese nuclear forces and US mainland strikes.

2.4.3. Attacks on Targets Near or In Theater of Conflict: Statements about attacks on targets that are geographically in the theater of conflict and mainland strikes.

2.4.4. Comprehensive vs. Limited Strikes: Statements that address whether attacks would be broader or narrower in scope and the relationship of this decision to mainland strikes.

2.4.5. Attacks on Specific Military Target Categories: Statements about whether attacks on a particular type of military weapon (naval forces, missile launchers) are related to mainland strikes.

2.5. Relative US and Chinese Interests During a Conflict: Statements that discuss whether the United States or China has a greater interest in a particular scenario and the relationship of this balance of interests to a mainland strike decision.

2.6. US-China Economic Relationship and Mainland Strikes: Statements that discuss any aspect of the US-China economic relationship and its bearing on a mainland strike decision.

2.7. US Domestic Politics Considerations: Statements that discuss US domestic politics—any aspect—and its likely bearing on a mainland strike decision.

2.8. Chinese Foreign Policy and Military Strategy: Statements that discuss Chinese foreign policy and its relationship to the mainland strike decision.

- Example: "They have a pretty wicked record of not caring for mass losses, and so does that calculus give them a little more freedom of maneuver."

2.9. Perceived strength of Chinese air defense: Applies to any statements or quotes referencing the strength (or weakness) of Chinese air defenses and how this strength should be considered in military calculations.

2.10. Standard Operating Procedure: Statements that suggest that mainland strikes are a standard operating procedure for the US military.

- Example: "It is illogical to me that if we committed to defending Taiwan, that we wouldn't as a matter of course...[attack] those missiles."

2.11. Overall Chinese Military Power: Applies to any statements referencing the implications of Chinese military strength for US decision-making.

- Example: "Things are getting worse from the Chinese over the next three to five years, and therefore the operational design is going to have less and less flexibility for not conducting mainland strikes."

2.12. Comparing mainland strikes to other options (e.g. a blockade): Statements referencing or comparing mainland strikes with other options.

2.13. Costs imposed on Chinese forces

2.13.1. Wartime Cost Imposition: Statements that support forcing Chinese forces *during a war* to counter a variety of US tactics, including strikes on mainland targets.

2.13.2. Peacetime Cost Imposition: Forcing China *before a war* to invest in air defense and other activities required to counter mainland strikes.

Appendix D:
Survey Website Landing Page

Research Survey

Participation Information

Your participation in this survey is voluntary and anonymous. The survey does not request your name or email address. The survey takes no longer than 10 minutes.

This survey is being conducted by John Speed Meyers of the Pardee RAND Graduate School as part of his dissertation. For questions about the survey, please contact him at jmeyers@rand.org. If you have questions about your rights as a research participant or need to report a concern, you can contact RAND's Human Subjects Protection Committee at (868)697-5620 or by emailing hspcinfo@rand.org.

Scenario Instructions

The following survey asks you to play the role of the U.S. national security adviser in a hypothetical scenario involving the United States and China. This scenario occurs in the year 2020.

Your task is to use your expertise, judgment, and the information provided in the scenarios to answer questions related to your willingness to authorize different courses of action.

There will be four scenarios. Each scenario will have the same background. The situation and the proposed course of action will vary. These changes in the scenario will help the project to understand how the context affects your recommendations. A final section will ask about your foreign policy attitudes and demographic info to aid the project in assessing the relationship between individual differences and recommended actions.

Highlighted sections in the scenarios indicate new information.

[Next]

Appendix E: China "At Fault" Condition versus China-Taiwan "Ambiguous Fault" Condition.

Scenario 1/4

1. **Background**
   - Intelligence indicates China is attempting an invasion of Taiwan after several months of military posturing and hostile statements by both sides.
   - U.S. intelligence analysts find it difficult to judge who is more "at fault."
   - Hundreds of Chinese missiles have attacked Taiwanese military targets.
   - Intel indicates an amphibious invasion could begin in the next 48 hours.

   Situation: China has not attacked any U.S. forces or bases.

   Proposal:
   - At a national security council meeting, the Chairman of the Joint Chiefs proposes strikes on military targets adjacent to the Taiwan Strait.
   - These strikes would be on Chinese military units located at the staging site for the anticipated amphibious invasion such as air defense sites, Chinese ships and naval bases and aircraft and airbases.

   Under these circumstances, how likely are you to recommend to the president strikes on at least these targets?

   ○ Very likely
   ○ Likely
   ○ Somewhat likely
   ○ Somewhat unlikely
   ○ Unlikely
   ○ Very unlikely

   [Next]

Scenario 1/4

1. **Background**
   - Intelligence indicates China is attempting an invasion of Taiwan after several months of military posturing and hostile statements by both sides.
   - U.S. intelligence analysts find it difficult to judge who is more "at fault."
   - Hundreds of Chinese missiles have attacked Taiwanese military targets.
   - Intel indicates an amphibious invasion could begin in the next 48 hours.

   Situation: China has not attacked any U.S. forces or bases.

   Proposal:
   - At a national security council meeting, the Chairman of the Joint Chiefs proposes strikes on military targets adjacent to the Taiwan Strait.
   - These strikes would be on Chinese military units located at the staging site for the anticipated amphibious invasion such as air defense sites, Chinese ships and naval bases and aircraft and airbases.

   Under these circumstances, how likely are you to recommend to the president strikes on at least these targets?

   ○ Very likely
   ○ Likely
   ○ Somewhat likely
   ○ Somewhat unlikely
   ○ Unlikely
   ○ Very unlikely

   [Next]

Appendix F: Survey Questionnaire

First, this survey was actually four surveys (1A, 1B, 2A and 2B). I performed a survey experiment and assigned participants to one of four surveys. These surveys all used hypothetical scenarios involving the United States and China in a scenario related to Taiwan's defense. I manipulate two conditions, which each have two values, and thus have four surveys. One dimension is the degree to which "blame" is assigned on the party the US is defending (Taiwan) versus the opponent (China); this is the difference between survey 1 and survey 2. There is language in the scenario that manipulates this condition. The second condition is the wording of attitudinal questions; this is the difference between version A and version B of each survey. I created a positive wording version and a negative wording version in order to determine if the wording affects conclusions. A full written survey instrument (survey version 1A) comes later. A final section explains in detail the differences between surveys 1 and 2 and versions A and B.

FULL SURVEY (Survey 1A)

Your participation in this survey is voluntary and anonymous. The survey does not request your name or email address.

The survey takes no longer than 10 minutes.

This survey is being conducted by John Speed Meyers of the BLANK as part of his dissertation. For questions about the survey, please contact him at BLANK.

If you have questions about your rights as a research participant or need to report a concern, you can contact RAND's Human Subjects Protection Committee at (868)697-5620 or by emailing hspcinfo@rand.org.

The following survey asks you to play the role of the US national security advisor in a hypothetical scenario involving the United States and China. This scenario occurs in the year 2020.

Your task is to use your expertise, judgment, and the information provided in the scenarios to answer questions related to your willingness to authorize different courses of action.

There will be four scenarios. Each scenario will have the same background. The situation and the proposed course of action will vary. These changes in the scenario will help the project to understand how the context affects your recommendations.

Highlighted sections in the scenarios indicate new information.

First Scenario

Background

- China is attempting an invasion of Taiwan because peaceful unification with Taiwan had been advancing too slowly.
- Hundreds of Chinese missiles have attacked Taiwanese military targets.
- Intel indicates an amphibious invasion could begin in the next 48 hours.

Situation

China has not attacked any US forces or bases.

Proposal

- At a National Security Council meeting, the Chairman of the Joint Chiefs proposes strikes on military targets adjacent to the Taiwan Strait.
- These strikes would be on Chinese military units located at the staging site for the anticipated amphibious invasion such as air

defense sites, Chinese ships and naval bases and aircraft and air bases.

Question alias: scenario_1

Under these circumstances, how likely are you to recommend to the president strikes on at least these targets?

Options: Very likely, Likely, Somewhat likely, Somewhat unlikely, Unlikely, Very unlikely

SECOND SCENARIO

Same Background

- China is attempting an invasion of Taiwan because peaceful unification with Taiwan had been advancing too slowly.
- Hundreds of Chinese missiles have attacked Taiwanese military targets.
- Intel indicates an amphibious invasion could begin in the next 48 hours.

New Situation

China attacked American forces at Kadena Air Base in Okinawa, Japan with ballistic missiles launched from the Chinese mainland.

The commander reports severe damage to runways, two dozen damaged US aircraft, and scores of American casualties.

Same Proposal

- At a National Security Council meeting, the Chairman of the Joint Chiefs proposes strikes on military targets adjacent to the Taiwan Strait.
- These strikes would be on Chinese military units located at the staging site for the anticipated amphibious invasion such as air

defense sites, Chinese ships and naval bases and aircraft and air bases.

Under these circumstances, how likely are you to recommend to the president strikes on at least these targets?

Options: Very likely, Likely, Somewhat likely, Somewhat unlikely, Unlikely, Very unlikely

Third Scenario

Same Background

- China is attempting an invasion of Taiwan because peaceful unification with Taiwan had been advancing too slowly.
- Hundreds of Chinese missiles have attacked Taiwanese military targets.
- Intel indicates an amphibious invasion could begin in the next 48 hours.

Original Situation

China has not attacked any US forces or bases.

New Proposal

- At a National Security Council meeting, the Chairman of the Joint Chiefs proposes strikes on military targets throughout China.
- These strikes would be on both Chinese military units located at the staging site for the anticipated amphibious invasion and on units olcated elsewhere in China that will likely support the invasion.
- This expanded category of targets includes Chinese intelligence centers, command centers, over-the-horizon radars, Chinese ballistic missiles, and anti-satellite weapon launch sites.

Under these circumstances, how likely are you to recommend to the president strikes on at least these targets?

Appendix F: Survey Questionnaire

Options: Very likely, Likely, Somewhat likely, Somewhat unlikely, Unlikely, Very unlikely

FOURTH SCENARIO

Same Background

- China is attempting an invasion of Taiwan because peaceful unification with Taiwan had been advancing too slowly.
- Hundreds of Chinese missiles have attacked Taiwanese military targets.
- Intel indicates an amphibious invasion could begin in the next 48 hours.

New Situation

- China attacked American forces at Kadena Air Base in Okinawa, Japan with ballistic missiles launched from the Chinese mainland.
- The commander reports severe damage to runways, two dozen damaged US aircraft, and scores of American casualties.

New Proposal

- At a National Security Council meeting, the Chairman of the Joint Chiefs proposes strikes on military targets throughout China.
- These strikes would be on both Chinese military units located at the staging site for the anticipated amphibious invasion and on units located elsewhere in China that will likely support the invasion.
- This expanded category of targets includes Chinese intelligence centers, command centers, over-the-horizon radars, Chinese ballistic missiles, and anti-satellite weapon launch sites.

Under these circumstances, how likely are you to recommend to the president strikes on at least these targets?

Options: Very likely, Likely, Somewhat likely, Somewhat unlikely, Unlikely, Very unlikely

Attitude and Belief Questions

Please indicate the extent to which you agree or disagree.

Options: Very likely, Likely, Somewhat likely, Somewhat unlikely, Unlikely, Very unlikely

Positive wording: Defending Taiwan is a vital US interest.
Negative wording: Defending Taiwan is not a vital US interest.

Positive wording: I believe that once a war starts, the generals should be in charge.
Negative wording: I believe that once a war starts, civilians (not generals) should be in charge.

Positive wording: When force is used, military rather than political goals should determine its application.
Negative wording: When force is used, political rather than military goals should determine its application.

Positive wording: Force should be used only if the US military is allowed to decisively defeat the enemy.
Negative wording: Force should sometimes be used even if the United States is not prepared to decisively defeat its enemy.

Positive wording: Military operations must emphasize seizing the initiative from the enemy.
Negative wording: Military operations do not need to emphasize seizing the initiative from the enemy.

Positive wording: Chinese possession of nuclear weapons makes me less willing to authorize strikes on the Chinese mainland.
Negative wording: Chinese possession of nuclear weapons does not affect my willingness to authorize strikes on the Chinese mainland.

Positive wording: Chinese leaders will interpret any strikes on Chinese mainland targets as an attempt to destroy Chinese nuclear weapons.

Appendix F: Survey Questionnaire

Negative wording: Strikes on Chinese mainland targets will not be interpreted by Chinese leaders as an attempt to destroy Chinese nuclear weapons.

BACKGROUND QUESTIONS

Demographic Info

What is your age?
Options: 20–29, 30–39, 40–49, 50–59, 60+

How long have you been working in the foreign policy or national security field?
Options: 0–5 years, 6–10 years, 11–20 years, 20+ years

What is your gender?
Options: Female, Male, Other

What is your professional background? (Check all that apply.)
Options: Military, Government—Civilian, Think-tank, Academia, Business, Other

With what political party do you identify?
Options: Democrat, Republican, Neither

Would you describe yourself as a subject matter expert on Asia?
Options: No, Only a little, Moderately so, Yes

[These questions were only shown to the participants who selected military as one of the answers for "What is Your Professional Background?" question.]

Are you currently on active-duty?
Options: Yes, No

In what branch of the military did you or do you serve?
Options: Army, Navy, Air Force, Marine Corps

For how long have you served/did you service in the military? (Count from year you first joined.)
Options: 0–5 years, 6–10 years, 11–19 years, 20 years or more

Final Question
(Optional) Please write any thoughts you would like to share about the scenarios and their impact on your answers.

The Difference between Survey 1 and Survey 2

Survey 1 attributes "the blame" for the conflict on China. The language in the background section of the scenarios read: "China is attempting an invasion of Taiwan because peaceful unification with Taiwan had been advancing too slowly."

Survey 2 attributes "the blame" for the conflict on both China and Taiwan; the fault of either party is meant to be ambiguous. The language in the background section has changed to: "Intelligence indicates China is attempting an invasion of Taiwan after several months of military posturing and hostile statements by both sides. US intelligence analysts find it difficult to judge who is more 'at fault.'"

The Difference between A and B Versions of the Survey

The A and B versions differ in their wording of belief and attitude questions on pages 7 and 8. The A version, shown earlier, uses a "positive" wording. The statements are worded in the positive form without negation. The B version uses negative wordings. The meaning of the questions is negated.

Appendix G: Regression Results

	Results				
	Dependent variable:				
	Scenario 1	Scenario 2	Scenario 3	Scenario 4	Scenario Mean
	(1)	(2)	(3)	(4)	(5)
Prior Military	0.152	-0.106	-0.196	-0.241	-0.098
	(0.361)	(0.253)	(0.330)	(0.357)	(0.264)
Male	0.238	0.359	0.386	0.276	0.315
	(0.440)	(0.308)	(0.402)	(0.434)	(0.322)
China at fault	0.160	-0.011	-0.038	-0.334	-0.056
	(0.312)	(0.218)	(0.285)	(0.308)	(0.228)
Democrat	0.309	0.310	0.307	0.801**	0.432*
	(0.313)	(0.219)	(0.286)	(0.309)	(0.229)
50+	0.844**	0.391	0.644**	0.984***	0.716***
	(0.347)	(0.243)	(0.317)	(0.342)	(0.254)
Asia Expert	-0.506	-0.041	-0.046	0.191	-0.101
	(0.319)	(0.224)	(0.292)	(0.315)	(0.233)
Constant	2.825***	4.596***	1.526***	2.671***	2.904***
	(0.546)	(0.382)	(0.499)	(0.539)	(0.399)
Observations	85	85	85	85	85
R^2	0.110	0.072	0.082	0.216	0.151
Adjusted R^2	0.041	0.001	0.012	0.156	0.085
Residual Std. Error (df = 78)	1.400	0.980	1.279	1.381	1.023
F Statistic (df = 6; 78)	1.602	1.009	1.166	3.580***	2.304**
Note:				*$p<0.1$; **$p<0.05$; ***$p<0.01$	

Note: Dependent variable is willingness to recommend mainland strikes in a particular scenario.

Bibliography

Aberbach, Joel D., and Bert A. Rockman. "Conducting and Coding Elite Interviews." *PS: Political Science and Politics* 35, no. 4 (2002): 673–676.

Acton, James M. "Escalation through Entanglement: How the Vulnerability of Command-and-Control Systems Raises the Risks of an Inadvertent Nuclear War." *International Security* 43, no. 1 (2018): 56–99.

Allison, Graham, and Philip Zelikow. *Essence of Decision: Explaining the Cuban Missile Crisis, 2nd Edition*. New York: Addison-Wesley, 1999.

Arena, Philip, and Glenn Palmer. "Politics or the Economy? Domestic Correlates of Dispute Involvement in Developed Democracies." *International Studies Quarterly* 53, no. 4 (2009): 955–975.

Asal, Victor, and Kyle Beardsley. "Proliferation and International Crisis Behavior." *Journal of Peace Research* 44, no. 2 (2007): 139–155.

Avey, Paul, and Michael C. Desch. "What Do Policymakers Want from Us? Results from a Survey of Current and Former National Security Decision-Makers." *International Studies Quarterly* 58, no. 2 (2014): 227–246.

Barrett, David M. "'Doing Tuesday Lunch' at Lyndon Johnson's White House: New Archival Evidence on Vietnam Decisionmaking." *Political Science and Politics* 24, no. 4 (1991): 676–679.

Bartels, Elizabeth M., Igor Mikolic-Torreira, Steven W. Popper, and Joel B. Predd. *Do Differing Analyses Change the Decision?* Santa Monica, CA: RAND Corporation, 2019.

Basrur, Rajesh M., Michael D. Cohen, and Ward Wilson. "Correspondence: Do Small Arsenals Deter?" *International Security* 32, no. 3 (2007/2008): 202–214.

Beardsley, Kyle, and Victor Asal. "Winning with the Bomb." *Journal of Conflict Resolution* 53, no. 2 (2009): 278–301.

Beckley, Michael. "The Emerging Military Balance in East Asia: How China's Neighbors Can Check Chinese Naval Expansion." *International Security* 42, no. 2 (2017): 78–119.

Berry, Jeffrey M. "Validity and Reliability Issues in Elite Interviewing." *PS: Political Science and Politics* 35, no. 4 (2002): 679–682.

Bell, Mark S., and Nicholas L. Miller. "Questioning the Effect of Nuclear Weapons on Conflict." *Journal of Conflict Resolution* 59, no. 1 (2015): 74–92.

Bertoli, Andrew, Allan Dafoe, and Robert F. Trager. "Is There a War Party? Party Change, the Left-Right Divide, and International Conflict." *Journal of Conflict Resolution* 63, no. 4 (2019): 950–975.

Betts, Richard. *Soldiers, Statesmen, and Cold War Crises.* New York: Columbia University Press, 1977.

Biddle, Stephen, and Ivan Oelrich. "Future Warfare in the Western Pacific: Chinese Antiaccess/Area Denial, US AirSea Battle, and Command of the Commons in East Asia." *International Security* 41, no. 1 (2016): 7–48.

Blair, Bruce. *Strategic Command and Control.* Washington, D.C.: The Brookings Institution Press, 1985.

Blair, Bruce, Chen Yali, and Eric Hagt. "The Oil Weapon: Myth of China's Vulnerability. " *China Security* (Summer 2006): 32–63.

Blair, Dennis C., and Caitlin Talmadge. "Would China Go Nuclear?" *Foreign Affairs* 98, no. 1 (January/February 2019).

Blechman, Barry M., and Stephen S. Kaplan. *Force without War: U.S. Armed Forces as a Political Instrument.* Washington, DC: The Brookings Institution Press, 1978.

Bonds, Timothy M., Joel B. Predd, Timothy R. Heath, Michael S. Chase, Michael Johnson, Michael J. Lostumbo, James Bonomo, Muharrem Mane, and Paul S. Steinberg, *What Role Can Land-Based, Multi-Domain Anti-Access Forces Play in Deterring or Defeating Aggression?*, Santa Monica: RAND Corporation, 2017.

Boot, Max. *War Made New: Weapons, Warriors, and the Making of the Modern World.* New York: Gotham Books, 2006.

Bibliography

Bowie, Christopher. *The Anti-Access Threat and Theater Air Bases.* Washington, DC: Center for Strategic and Budgetary Assessments, 2002.

Bracken, Paul. *The Command and Control of Nuclear Forces.* New Haven: Yale University Press, 1983.

Brands, Hal, and William Inboden. "Wisdom without Tears: Statecraft and the Uses of History." *Journal of Strategic Studies* 41, no. 7 (2018): 916–946.

Brands, H. W. *The General vs. the President: MacArthur and Truman at the Brink of Nuclear War.* New York: Doubleday, 2016.

Brands, Hal, and Zack Cooper. "After the Responsible Stakeholder, What? Debating America's China Strategy." *Texas National Security Review* 2, no. 2 (2019): 69–81.

Brodie, Bernard. *Strategy in the Missile Age.* Princeton: Princeton University Press, 1959.

Brooks, Deborah Jordan, and Benjamin Valentino. "A War of One's Own: Understanding the Gender Gap in Support for War." *Public Opinion Quarterly* 75, no. 2 (2011): 270–286.

Builder, Carl H. *The Icarus Syndrome: The Role of Air Power Theory in the Evolution and Fate of the US Air Force.* New York, NY: Transaction Publishers, 1989.

———. *Masks of War: American Military Styles in Strategy and Analysis.* Baltimore: The Johns Hopkins University Press, 1993.

Byman, Daniel L., and Kenneth M. Pollack. "Let Us Now Praise Great Men: Bringing the Statesmen Back In." *International Security* 25, no. 4 (2001): 107–146.

Chase, Michael S., Jeffrey Engstrom, Tai Ming Cheung, Kristen Gunness, Scott W. Harold, Susan Puska, and Samuel K. Berkowitz. *China's Incomplete Military Transformation: Assessing the Weaknesses of the People's Liberation Army (PLA).* Santa Monica: RAND, 2015.

Cheung, Tai Ming. *Fortifying China: The Struggle to Build a Modern Defense Economy.* Ithaca: Cornell University Press, 2008.

Christensen, Thomas J. *The China Challenge: Shaping the Choices of a Rising Power.* New York: W. W. Norton and Company, 2015.

———. "Posing Problems without Catching Up: China's Rise and Challenges for US Security Policy." *International Security* 25, no. 4 (2001): 5–40.

———. "A Strong and Moderate Taiwan." speech delivered at the 2007 US-Taiwan Business Council, Defense Industry Conference, Annapolis, Maryland, September 11, 2007.

———. "The Meaning of the Nuclear Evolution: China's Strategic Modernization and US-China Security Relations." *Journal of Strategic Studies* 35, no 4 (2012): 447–487.

Cliff, Roger. *China's Military Power: Assessing Current and Future Capabilities.* New York: Cambridge University Press, 2015.

Cliff, Roger, Mark Burles, Michael Chase, Derek Eaton, and Kevin Pollpeter. *Entering the Dragon's Lair: Chinese Antiaccess Strategies and Their Implications for the United States.* Santa Monica: RAND Corporation, 2007

Clodfelter, Mark. *The Limits of Airpower: The American Bombing of North Vietnam.* New York: Free Press, 1989.

Cohen, Eliot A. *Supreme Command: Soldiers, Statesmen, and Leadership in Wartime.* New York: The Free Press, 2002.

Colby, Elbridge. *America Must Prepare for 'Limited War.'* Washington, DC: Center for a New American Security, 2015

———. "Don't Sweat AirSea Battle." *The National Interest,* July 31, 2013.

———. "If You Want Peace, Prepare for Nuclear War." *Foreign Affairs* 97, no. 6 (November/December 2018).

———. *Nuclear Weapons in the Third Offset Strategy: Avoiding a Nuclear Blind Spot in the Pentagon's New Initiative.* Washington, D.C.: Center for a New American Security, 2015.

———. "The War over the War with China," *The National Interest,* August 15, 2013.

Collins, Gabriel B. "A Maritime Oil Blockade Against China: Tactically Tempting but Strategically Flawed." *Naval War College Review* 71, no. 2 (2018).

Bibliography

Collins, Gabriel B., and William S. Murray. "No Oil for the Lamps of China?" *Naval War College Review* 61, no. 2 (2008).

Crane, Conrad. *American Airpower Strategy in Korea, 1950–1953.* Lawrence, KS: University Press of Kansas, 2000.

Cropsey, Seth, Bryan G. McGrath, and Timothy A. Walton. *Sharpening the Spear: The Carrier, the Joint Force, and High-End Conflict.* Washington, DC: The Hudson Institute, 2015.

Cunningham, Fiona S. "The Maritime Rung on the Escalation Ladder: Naval Blockades in a US China Conflict." *Security Studies* 29, no. 4 (2020): 730-768.

Dafoe, Allan and Devin Caughey. "Honor and War: Southern US Presidents and the Effects of Concern for Reputation." *World Politics* 68, no. 2 (2016): 341–381.

Desch, Michael C. *Civilian Control of the Military: The Changing Security Environment.* Baltimore: Johns Hopkins University Press, 2001.

DeWeerd, Harvey A. *The Triumph of the Limiters: Korea.* Santa Monica: RAND Corporation, 1968.

Dobbs, Michael. *One Minute to Midnight: Kennedy, Khrushchev, and Castro on the Brink of Nuclear War.* New York: Vintage, 2009.

Dougherty, Christopher M. *Why America Needs a New Way of War.* Washington, DC: Center for a New American Security, 2019.

Dube, Oeindrila and S.P. Harish. "Queens." *Journal of Political Economy* 128, no. 7 (2020): 2579–2652.

Eichenberg, Richard. "Gender Differences in Public Attitudes toward the Use of Force by the United States, 1990–2003." *International Security* 28, no. 1 (2003): 110–141.

Erickson, Andrew. "Raining Down: Assessing the Emergent ASBM Threat." *Jane's Navy International,* 2016.

Erickson, Andrew S., Evan Braden Montgomery, Craig Neuman, Stephen Biddle, and Ivan Oelrich. "Correspondence: How Good Are China's Antiaccess/Area-Denial Capabilities?" *International Security* 41, no. 4 (2017): 202–213.

Etzioni, Amitai. "The Air-Sea Battle 'Concept': A Critique." *International Politics* 51, no. 5 (2014): 577--596.

Fallows, James. "The Tragedy of the American Military," *The Atlantic,* January/February 2015.

Feaver, Peter D. *Armed Servants: Agency, Oversight, and Civil-Military Relations.* Cambridge, MA: Harvard University Press, 2005.

Fisher, Richard D., Jr. *China's Military Modernization: Building for Regional and Global Reach.* Santa Barbara: Praeger Security International, 2008.

Foot, Rosemary. *The Wrong War: American Policy and the Dimensions of the Korean Conflict, 1950–1953.* Ithaca: Cornell University Press, 1985.

Foreign Relations of the United States, 1951. Volume I, National Security Affairs; Foreign Economic Policy. Washington, DC: US Government Printing Office, 1979.

Fravel, Taylor. "Threading the Needle: The South China Sea Disputes and US-China Relations." *Social Science Research Network,* August 10, 2016. Available at https://papers.ssrn.com/sol3/papers.cfm?abstract_id=2826109, accessed January 8, 2019.

Friedberg, Aaron L. *Beyond Air-Sea Battle: The Debate over US Military Strategy in Asia.* New York: Adelphi Series, International Institute for Strategic Studies, 2014.

———. *A Contest for Supremacy: China, American, and the Struggle for Mastery in Asia.* New York: W. W. Norton and Company, 2011.

———. "Ripe for Rivalry: Prospects for Peace in a Multipolar Asia." *International Security* 18, no. 3 (1993): 5–33.

Futrell, Robert F. *The United States Air Force in Korea 1950–1953.* Washington, D.C.: Air University Press, 1983.

Gacek, Christopher M. *The Logic of Force: The Dilemma of Limited War in American Foreign Policy.* New York, NY: Columbia University Press, 1994.

Gaddis, John Lewis. "The Long Peace: Elements of Stability in the Postwar International System." *International Security* 10, no. 4 (Spring 1986): 99–142.

———. *Strategies of Containment: A Critical Appraisal of American National Security Policy During the Cold War (expanded edition)*. Oxford, UK: Oxford University Press, 2005.

Gartzke, Erik and Dong-Joon Jo. "Bargaining, Nuclear Proliferation, and Interstate Disputes," *Journal of Conflict Resolution* 53, no. 2 (2009): 209–233.

Garver, John. *Face Off: China, the United States, and Taiwan's Democratization*. Seattle: University of Washington Press, 1997.

Gavin, Frank. *Nuclear Statecraft: History and Strategy in America's Atomic Age*. Ithaca, NY: Cornell University Press, 2012

Geist, Edward M. *Two Worlds of Civil Defense: State, Society, and Nuclear Survival in the USA and USSR, 1945–1991*, PhD diss., University of North Carolina at Chapel Hill, 2013.

Gelpi, Christopher, and Peter D. Feaver. "Speak Softly and Carry a Big Stick? Veterans in the Political Elite and the American Use of Force." *The American Political Science Review* 96, no. 4 (2002): 779–793.

George, Alexander, and Richard Smoke. *Deterrence in American Foreign Policy: Theory and Practice*. New York: Columbia University Press, 1974.

Glaser, Charles L. "A US-China Grand Bargain? The Hard Choice between Military Competition and Accommodation." *International Security* 39, no 4 (2015): 49–90.

Goldstein, Kenneth. "Getting in the Door: Sampling and Completing Elite Interviews." *PS: Political Science and Politics* 35, no. 4 (2002): 669–672.

Goldstein, Lyle. "Do Nascent WMD Arsenals Deter? The Sino-Soviet Crisis of 1969." *Political Science Quarterly* 118, no. 1 (2003): 53–80.

Goldstein, Lyle. "The US-China Naval Balance in the Asia-Pacific: An Overview." *China Quarterly* 232, (2017): 904–931.

Goldstein, Lyle. *Meeting China Halfway: How to Defuse the Emerging US-China Rivalry*. Washington, DC: Georgetown University Press, 2015.

Gompert, David. "Sea Power and American Interests in the Western Pacific." Santa Monica: RAND, 2013.

Gompert, David, and Terrence Kelly. "Escalation Cause." *Foreign Policy*, August 3, 2013.

Gompert, David, Astrid Cevallos, and Cristina L. Garafola. "War with China: Thinking Through the Unthinkable." Santa Monica: RAND Corporation, 2016.

Goodwin, Doris Kearns. *Lyndon Johnson and the American Dream*. New York, NY: St. Martin's Press, 1976.

Gries, Peter Hayes. *The Politics of American Foreign Policy: How Ideology Divides Liberals and Conservatives over Foreign Affairs*. Stanford: Stanford University Press, 2014.

Hagen, Jeff. "Potential Effects of Chinese Aerospace Capabilities on US Air Force Operations." US-China Economic and Security Review Commission, May 10, 2010.

Hafner-Burton, Emilie M., Brad L. LeVeck, David G. Victor, and James H. Fowler. "Decision Maker Preferences for International Legal Cooperation." *International Organization* 68, no. 4 (2014): 845–876.

Halperin, Morton H. "The Limiting Process in the Korean War." *Political Science Quarterly* 78, no. 1 (1963): 13–39.

———. *Limited War in the Nuclear Age*. New York: Jon Wiley and Sons, 1963.

———. "The 1958 Taiwan Strait Crisis: A Documented History." Santa Monica: RAND Corporation, 1966.

———. "Nuclear Weapons and Limited War." *Journal of Conflict Resolution* 5, no. 2 (1961): 146–166.

Hammes, T.X. *Offshore Control: A Proposed Strategy for an Unlikely Conflict*, Washington, DC: National Defense University, Institute for National Strategic Studies, Strategic Forum, 2012.

———. "Offshore Control: A Proposed Strategy." *Military Strategy Magazine* 2, no. 2 (Spring 2012): 10–14.

———. "Offshore Control: A Proposed Strategy for an Unlikely Conflict." National Defense University, Strategic Forum, June 2012.

———. "Offshore Control vs. AirSea Battle: Who Wins?" *The National Interest,* August 21, 2013.

———. "Strategy and AirSea Battle." *War on the Rocks,* July 23, 2013.

———. "Sorry, AirSea Battle is No Strategy." *The National Interest,* August 7, 2013.

Healey, Jason, ed. *A Fierce Domain: Conflict in Cyberspace, 1986 to 2012.* Cyber Conflict Studies Association, 2013.

Heginbotham, Eric, Michael Nixon, Forrest E. Morgan, Jacob L. Heim, Jeff Hagen, Sheng Li, Jeffrey Engstrom, Martin C. Libicki, Paul DeLuca, David A. Shlapak, David R. Frelinger, Burgess Laird, Kyle Brady, and Lyle J. Morris. *The U.S-China Military Scorecard: Forces, Geography, and the Evolving Balance of Power, 1996–2017.* Santa Monica: RAND Corporation, 2015.

Heginbotham, Eric and Jacob L. Heim. "Deterring without Dominance: Discouraging Chinese Adventurism under Austerity." *The Washington Quarterly* 38, no. 1 (2015): 185–199.

Heim, Jacob L. *Missiles for Asia? The Need for Operational Analysis of US Theater Ballistic Missiles in the Pacific.* Santa Monica: RAND, 2016.

Herring, George. *America's Longest War: The United States and Vietnam, 1950–1975 (4th edition).* New York: McGraw-Hill, 2002.

Hendrix, Jerry. *Retreat from Range: The Rise and Fall of Carrier Aviation.* Washington, DC: Center for a New American Security, 2015.

Hoffman, Stanley. *Gulliver's Troubles: Or, the Setting of American Foreign Policy.* New York: McGraw-Hill, 1968.

Holloway, David. *Stalin and the Bomb.* New Haven: Yale University Press, 1996.

Holsti, Ole R., and James N. Rosenau. *American Leadership in World Affairs: Vietnam and the Breakdown of Consensus.* Winchester: George Allen & Unwin Publishers, 1984.

Horowitz, Michael, Rose McDermott, and Allan C. Stam. "Leader Age, Regime Type, and Violent International Relations." *Journal of Conflict Resolution* 49, no. 5 (2005): 661–685.

Horowitz, Michael C., and Allan C. Stam. "How Prior Military Experience Influences the Future Militarized Behavior of Leaders." *International Organization* 68, no 3 (2014): 527–559.

Horowitz, Michael C., and Matthew Fuhrmann. "Studying Leaders and Military Conflict: Conceptual Framework and Research Agenda." *Journal of Conflict Resolution* 62, no. 1 (2018): 2072–2086.

Huntington, Samuel. *The Soldier and the State.* Cambridge, MA: The Belknap Press of Harvard University Press, 1957.

Huth, Paul, and Bruce Russett. "Deterrence Failure and Crisis Escalation." *International Studies Quarterly* 32, no.1 (1988): 29–45.

———. "What Makes Deterrence Work? Cases from 1900 to 1980." *World Politics* 36, no. 4 (1984): 496–526.

Inboden, William. "Statecraft, Decision-Making, and the Varieties of Historical Experience: A Taxonomy." *Journal of Strategic Studies* 37, no. 2 (2014): 291–318.

Jervis, Robert. *The Illogic of American Nuclear Strategy.* Ithaca: Cornell University Press, 1984.

———. *Perception and Misperception in International Politics.* Princeton: Princeton University Press, 1976.

———. "The Political Effects of Nuclear Weapons: A Comment." *International* Security 13, no. 2 (1988): 80–90.

———. *The Meaning of the Nuclear Revolution: Statecraft and the Prospect of Armageddon.* Ithaca: Cornell University Press, 1989.

Johnson, Dominic D. P., Rose McDermott, Emily S. Barrett, Jonathan Cowden, Richard Wrangham, Matthew H. McIntyre, and Stephen Peter Rosen. "Overconfidence in Wargames: Experimental Evidence on Expectations, Aggression, Gender and Testosterone." *Proceedings of the Royal Society: Biological Sciences* 273, no. 1600 (2006): 2513–2520.

Johnson, Dominic D. P., Rose McDermott, Jon Cowden, and Dustin Tingley, "Dead Certain: Confidence and Conservatism Predict Aggression in Simulated International Crisis Decision-Making." *Human Nature,* 23, no. 1 (2012): 98–126.

Johnson, Lyndon Baines. *The Vantage Point: Perspectives of the Presidency 1963–1969.* New York, NY: Holt, Rinehart, and Winston, 1971.

Kapur, S. Paul. "India and Pakistan's Unstable Peace: Why Nuclear South Asia Is Not Like Cold War Europe." *International Security* 30, no. 2 (2006): 127–152.

Karnow, Stanley. *Vietnam: A History.* Middlesex, England: Penguin Books, 1984.

Kennedy, Paul. *The Rise and Fall of Great Powers: Economic Change and Military Conflict from 1500–2000.* New York: Random House, 1987.

Khalizad, Zalmay, Abram N. Shulsky, Daniel Byman, Roger Cliff, David T. Orletsky, David A. Shlapak, and Ashley J. Tellis. *The United States and a Rising China: Strategic and Military Implications.* Santa Monica: RAND Corporation, 1999.

Kent, Glenn A., and David Ochmanek. "A Framework for Modernization within the United States Air Force." Santa Monica, CA: RAND Corporation, 2003.

King, Gary, Robert O. Keohane, and Sidney Verba. *Designing Social Inquiry: Scientific Inference in Qualitative Research.* Princeton: Princeton University Press, 1994.

Kline, Jeffrey E., and Wayne P. Hughes Jr. "Between Peace and the Air-Sea Battle: A War at Sea Strategy." *Naval War College Review* 65, no. 4 (2012).

Kreis, John F. *Air Warfare and Air Base Air Defense 1914–1973.* Washington, D.C.: Office of Air Force History, United States Air Force, 1988.

Krepinevich, Andrew, Barry Watts, and Robert Work. *Meeting the Anti-Access and Area-Denial Challenge.* Washington, DC: The Center for Strategic and Budgetary Assessments, 2003.

Krepenevich, Andrew F. *Why AirSea Battle?* Washington, DC: The Center for Strategic and Budgetary Assessments, 2010.

Kristensen, Hans M., and Robert S. Norris. "Chinese Nuclear Forces, 2016." *Bulletin of the Atomic Scientists* 72, no. 4 (2016): 77–84.

———. "Global Nuclear Weapons Inventories, 1945–2013." *Bulletin of the Atomic Scientists* 69, no. 5 (2013): 75–81.

Kristensen, Hans M., Matt Korda, Eliana Johns, and Kate Kohn. "Status of World Nuclear Forces." Federation of American Scientists. March 31, 2023.

Kroenig, Matthew. *The Logic of American Nuclear Strategy*. New York: Oxford University Press, 2018.

———. "Nuclear Superiority and the Balance of Resolve: Explaining Nuclear Crisis Outcomes." *International Organization* 67, no. 1 (2013): 141–171.

Kroenig, Matthew and Mark J. Massa. "Are Dual-Capable Weapon Systems Destabilizing? Questioning Nuclear-Conventional Entanglement and Inadvertent Escalation." Washington, DC: *The Atlantic Council*, 2021.

Kugler, Jacek. "Terror without Deterrence: Reassessing the Role of Nuclear Weapons." *Journal of Conflict Resolution* 28, no. 3 (1984): 470–506.

Lambeth, Benjamin S. *The Transformation of American Air Power*. Ithaca: Cornell University Press, 2000.

Lebow, Richard Ned. *Between Peace and War: The Nature of International Crisis*. Baltimore: The Johns Hopkins University Press, 1981.

Leech, Beth L. "Asking Questions: Techniques for Semistructured Interviews." *PS: Political Science and Politics* 35, no. 4 (2002): 665–668.

Legro, Jeffrey W. *Cooperation Under Fire: Anglo-German Restraint During World War II*. Ithaca: Cornell University Press, 1995

———. "Military Culture and Inadvertent Escalation." *International Security* 18, no. 4 (1994): 108–142.

LeMay, Curtis E. with MacKinlay Kantor. *Mission with LeMay: My Story*. Garden City: Doubleday, 1965.

Lewis, John Wilson, and Xue Litai. *China Builds the Bomb*. Palo Alto: Stanford University Press, 1991.

Lewy, Guenter. *American in Vietnam*. New York: Oxford University Press, 1978.

Lin-Greenberg, Erik. "Wargame of Drones: Remotely Piloted Aircraft and Conflict Escalation." *Journal of Conflict Resolution* 66, no. 10 (2022): 613–626.

Lustick, Ian S. "History, Historiography, and Political Science: Multiple Historical Records and the Problem of Selection Bias." *American Political Science* Review 90, no. 3 (1996): 605–618.

Mahnken, Thomas G., ed. *Competitive Strategies for the 21st Century: Theory, History, and Practice.* Stanford: Stanford University Press, 2012.

———. "A Maritime Strategy to Deal with China." *Proceedings* 148, no. 2 (2022).

Mahnken, Thomas G., Travis Sharp, Billy Fabian, and Peter Kouretsos. *Tightening the Chain: Implementing a Strategy of Maritime Pressure in the Western Pacific.* Washington, DC: Center for Strategic and Budgetary Assessments, 2019.

Macdonald, Julia, and Jacquelyn Schneider. "Presidential Risk Orientation and Force Employment Decisions: The Case of Unmanned Weaponry." *Journal of Conflict Resolution* 61, no. 3 (2017): 511–536.

Manzo, Vincent A. "After the First Shots: Managing Escalation in Northeast Asia." *Joint Forces Quarterly* 77, no. 2 (2015): 91–100.

Mastro, Oriana Skylar, and Ian Easton. *Risk and Resiliency: China's Emerging Air Base Strike* Threat. Arlington: Project 2049 Institute, 2017.

McDermott, Rose, and Jonathan A. Cowden. "The Effects of Uncertainty and Sex in a Crisis Simulation Game." *International Interactions* 27, no. 4 (2001): 353–380.

McDermott, Rose, Dominic Johnson, Jonathan Cowden, and Stephen Rosen. "Testosterone and Aggression in a Simulated Crisis Game." *Annals of the American Academy of Political and Social Science* 614, no.1 (2007): 15–33.

McDermott, Rose, and Peter K. Hatemi. "The Relationship Between Physical Aggression, Foreign Policy, and Moral Choices: Phenotypic and Genetic Findings." *Aggressive Behavior* 43, no 1 (2017): 37–46.

McIntyre, Matthew H., Emily S. Barret, Rose McDermott, Dominic D. P. Johnson, Jonathan Cowden, and Stephen P. Rosen. "Finger Length Ratio (2D:4D) and Sex Difference in Aggression During a Simulated War Game." *Personality and Individual Differences* 42, no. 4 (2007): 755–764.

McNamara, Robert S. "The Military Role of Nuclear Weapons: Perceptions and Misperceptions." *Foreign Affairs* 62, no. 1 (1983).

Mead, Walter Russell. *Special Providence: American Foreign Policy and How It Changed the World/* New York: Routledge, 2002.

Meyers, John Speed. "The Real Problem with Strikes on Mainland China." *War on the Rocks*, August 4, 2015.

———. "Will a President Approve Air-Sea Battle? Learning from the 1958 Taiwan Strait Crisis." *Military Strategy Magazine* 4, no. 4 (2015): 40–48.

Miller, Chris. *Chip War: The Fight for the World's Most Critical Technology.* New York: Scribner, 2022.

Millett, Allan R., and Peter Maslowski. *For the Common Defense: A Military History of the United States of America.* New York, NY: Free Press, 1984.

Millot, Marc Dean, Walter Perry, Preston Niblack, Beth Lachman, Corinne Replogle, and Jeannette Van Winkle. *Response to Warning: Making Decision on Strategic Force Readiness.* Santa Monica: RAND Corporation, 1993.

Mirski, Sean. "Stranglehold: The Context, Conduct, and Consequences of an American Naval Blockade of China." *Journal of Strategic Studies* 36, no. 3 (2013): 385–421.

Moise, Edwin E. *Tonkin Gulf and the Escalation of the Vietnam War.* Chapel Hill: University of North Carolina Press, 1996.

Monteiro, Nuno P., and Alexandre Debs. "The Strategic Logic of Nuclear Proliferation." *International Security* 39, no. 2 (2014): 7–51.

Montgomery, Evan Braden. "Breaking Out of the Security Dilemma: Realism, Reassurance, and the Problem of Uncertainty." *International Security* 31, no. 2 (2006): 151–185.

———. "Contested Primacy in the Western Pacific: China's Rise and the Future of US Power Projection." *International Security* 38, no. 4 (2014): 115–149.

———. "Reconsidering a Naval Blockade: A Response to Mirski." *Journal of Strategic Studies* 36, no. 4 (2013): 615–623.

Morgan, Forrest E., Karl P. Mueller, Evan S. Medeiros, Kevin L. Pollpeter, and Roger Cliff. *Dangerous Thresholds: Managing Escalation in the 21st Century.* Santa Monica: RAND Corporation, 2008.

Morgan, Forrest E. "Dancing with the Bear: Managing Escalation in a Conflict with Russia." Paris, France: Institut Francais Relations Internationales, 2012.

Mueller, John. "The Essential Irrelevance of Nuclear Weapons." *International Security* 13, no. 2 (1988): 55–79.

———. "Nuclear Weapons Don't Matter: But Hysteria Does." *Foreign Affairs* 97, no. 6 (November/December 2018).

———. *Retreat from Doomsday.* New York: Basic Books, 1989.

Narang, Vipin. "Posturing for Peace? Pakistan's Nuclear Postures and South Asian Stability." *International Security* 34, no. 2 (2009/2010): 38–78.

———. "What Does It Take to Deter? Regional Power Nuclear Postures and International Conflict." *Journal of Conflict Resolution* 57, no. 3 (2013): 478–508.

Navarro, Peter. *Crouching Tiger: What China's Militarism Means for the World.* Amherst: Prometheus Books, 2015.

Neustadt, Richard E., and Ernest R. May. *Thinking in Time.* New York: Free Press, 1988.

Oakes, Amy. *Diversionary War: Domestic Unrest and International Conflict.* Stanford: Stanford University Press, 2012.

Oberholtzer, Jenny, Abby Doll, David Frelinger, Karl Mueller, and Stacie Pettyjohn. "Applying Wargames to Real-World Policies." *Science* 363, no. 6434 (2019): 1406.

Ochmanek, David, and Lowell H. Schwartz. *The Challenge of Nuclear-Armed Regional Adversaries.* Santa Monica, CA: RAND Corporation, 2008.

Ochmanek, David. *Sustaining US Leadership in the Asia-Pacific Region: Why a Strategy of Direct Defense Against Antiaccess and Area Denial Threats is Desirable and Feasible.* Santa Monica, CA: RAND Corporation, 2015.

O'Hanlon, Michael E., and James Steinberg. *A Glass Half Full?: Rebalance, Reassurance, and Resolve in the US-China Strategic Relationship.* Washington, DC: Brookings Institution Press, 2017.

Organski, A. F. K., and Jacek Kugler. *The War Ledger.* Chicago: The University of Chicago Press, 1980.

O'Rourke, Ronald. *China Naval Modernization: Implications for U.S Navy Capabilities—Background and Issues for Congress.* Washington, DC: Congressional Research Service, August 1, 2018.

Osgood, Robert E. *Limited War: The Challenge to American Strategy.* Chicago: University of Chicago Press, 1957.

Osgood, Robert E. *Limited War Revisited.* Boulder: Westview Press, 1979.

Palmer, Glenn, Tamar London, and Patrick Regan. "What's Stopping You?: The Sources of Political Constraints on International Conflict Behavior in Parliamentary Democracies." *International Interactions* 30, no. 1 (2004): 1–24.

Pauly, Reid B. C. "Would US Leaders Push the Button? Wargames and the Sources of Nuclear Restraint." *International Security* 43, no. 2 (2018): 151–192.

Peifer, Douglas C. "China, the German Analogy and the New AirSea Operational Concept." *Orbis* 55, no. 1 (2011): 114–131.

Pettyjohn, Stacie L., and Jennifer Kavanagh. *Access Granted: Political Challenges to the US Overseas Military Presence, 1945–2014.* Santa Monica: RAND, 2016.

Podvig, Pavel (editor). *Russian Strategic Nuclear Forces.* Cambridge, MA: MIT Press, 2004.

Bibliography

Press, Daryl G., Scott D. Sagan, and Benjamin A. Valentino. "Atomic Aversion: Experimental Evidence on Taboos, Traditions, and the Non-Use of Nuclear Weapons." *American Political Science Review* 107, no. 1 (2013): 188–206.

Quek, Kai, and Alastair Iain Johnston. "Can China Back Down? Crisis De-escalation in the Shadow of Popular Opposition." *International Security* 43, no. 3 (Winter 2017/2018): 7–36.

Posard, Marek N., Jennifer Kavanagh, Kathryn Edwards, and Sonni Efron. *Millennial Perceptions of Security: Results from a National Survey of Americans.* Santa Monica: RAND, 2018.

Posen, Barry. *The Sources of Military Doctrine: France, Britain, and Germany Between the World Wars.* Ithaca: Cornell University Press, 1984.

Posen, Barry. *Inadvertent Escalation: Conventional War and Nuclear Risks.* Ithaca: Cornell University Press, 1991.

Rauchhaus, Robert. "Evaluating the Nuclear Peace Hypothesis." *Journal of Conflict Resolution* 53, no. 2 (2009): 258–277.

Reddie, Andrew W., Bethany L. Goldblum, Kiran Lakkaraju, Jason Reinhardt, Michael Nacht, and Laura Epifanovskaya. "Next-Generation Wargames." *Science* 362, no. 6421 (2018): 1362–1364.

Reddie, Andrew W., Bethany L. Goldblum, Jason Reinhardt, Kiran Lakkaraju, Laura Epifanovskaya, and Michael Nacht. "Applying Wargames to Real-World Policies—Response." *Science* 363, no. 6434 (2019): 1406–1407.

Riqiang, Wu. "Assessing China-US Inadvertent Nuclear Escalation." *International Security* 46, no. 2 (2022): 128–162.

Rivera, Sharon Werning, Polina M. Kozyreva, and Eduard G. Sarovskii. "Interviewing Political Elites: Lessons from Russia." *PS: Political Science and Politics* 35, no. 4 (2002): 683–688.

Rosen, Stephen Peter. "Vietnam and the American Theory of Limited War." *International Security* 7, no. 2 (Fall 1982): 83–113.

Rovner, Joshua. "Three Paths to Nuclear Escalation with China." *The National Interest,* July 19, 2012.

———. "Two Kinds of Catastrophe: Nuclear Escalation and Protracted War in Asia." *Journal of Strategic Studies* 40, no. 5 (2017): 676–730.

Sagan, Scott D. *The Limits of Safety: Organizations, Accidents, and Nuclear Weapons.* Princeton, NJ: Princeton University Press, 1993.

Sagan, Scott, and Kenneth N. Waltz. *The Spread of Nuclear Weapons: An Enduring Debate, 3rd Edition.* New York: W. W. Norton and Company, 2003.

Saunders, Elizabeth N. *Leaders at War: How Presidents Shape Military Interventions.* Ithaca: Cornell University Press, 2011.

Scharre, Paul. *Four Battlegrounds: Power in the Age of Artificial Intelligence.* New York: W. W. Norton & Company, 2023.

Schelling, Thomas C. *Strategy of Conflict.* Cambridge, MA: Harvard University Press, 1960.

Schlosser, Eric. *Command and Control.* New York: Penguin Books, 2014.

Schneider, Jacquelyn. *The Information Revolution and International Stability: A Multi-Article Exploration of Computing, Cyber, and Incentives for Conflict.* PhD diss., The George Washington University, 2017.

Schramm, Madison and Alexandra Stark. "Peacemakers or Iron Ladies? A Cross-National Study of Gender and International Conflict." *Security Studies* 29, no. 3 (2020): 515–548.

Scotto, Thomas J., and Jason Reifler. "Getting Tough with the Dragon? The Comparative Correlates of Foreign Policy Attitudes toward China in the United States and UK." *International Relationcs of the Asia-Pacific* 17, no. 2 (2017): 265–299.

Sharp, Travis, John Speed Meyers, and Michael Beckley, "Will East Asia Balance against Beijing?" *International Security* 43, no. 3 (2018/2019): 194–197.

Sharp, US Grant. *Strategy for Defeat: Vietnam in Retrospect.* Novato, CA: Presidio Press, 1978.

Shlapak, David, David Orletsky, and Barry Wilson. "Dire Strait? Military Aspects of the China-Taiwan Confrontation and Options for US Policy." Santa Monica, CA: RAND Corporation, 2000.

Shlapak, David, David Orletsky, Toy Reid, Murray Scott Tanner, and Barry Wilson. *A Question of Balance: Political Context and Military Aspects of the China-Taiwan Dispute.* Santa Monica: RAND Corporation, 2009.

Shugart, Thomas, and Javier Gonzales. *First Strike: China's Missile Threat to US Bases in Asia.* Washington, DC: Center for a New American Security, 2017.

Smeltz, Dina, Ivo Daalder, Karl Friedhoff, and Craig Kafura. *America Divided: Political Partisanship and US Foreign Policy, Results of the 2015 Chicago Council Survey of American Public Opinion and US Foreign Policy.* Chicago: The Chicago Council of Global Affairs, 2015.

———. *What Americans Think about America First: Results of the 2017 Chicago Council Survey of American Public Opinion and US Foreign Policy.* Chicago: The Chicago Council on Global Affairs, 2017.

Smoke, Richard. *National Security and the Nuclear Dilemma, Second Edition.* New York: Random House, 1988.

———. *War: Controlling Escalation.* Cambridge, MA: Harvard University Press, 1977.

Snyder, Glenn H. *Deterrence and Defense: Toward a Theory of National Security.* Princeton: Princeton University Press, 1961.

Snyder, Glenn. *Balance of Power.* Paul Seabury, ed. New York: Chandler Publishing Company, 1965.

Snyder, Glenn, and Paul Diesling. *Conflict Among Nations: Bargaining, Decision Making, and System Structure in International Crises.* Princeton: Princeton University Press, 1977.

Snyder, Jack. "Civil-Military Relations and the Cult of the Offensive, 1914 and 1984." *International Security* 9, no. 1 (1984): 108–146.

Stillion, John and David T. Orletsky. *Air Base Vulnerability to Conventional Cruise-Missile and Ballistic-Missile Attacks: Technology, Scenarios, and US Air Force Responses.* Santa Monica: RAND Corporation, 1999.

Suzuki, Akisato. "Is More Better or Worse? New Empirics on Nuclear Proliferation and Interstate Conflict by Random Forests." *Research and Politics* 2, no. 2 (2015).

Talmadge, Caitlin. "Would China Go Nuclear? Assessing the Risk of Chinese Nuclear Escalation in a Conventional War with the United States." *International Security* 41, no. 4 (2017): 50–92.

Tellis, Ashley J., C. Christine Fair, and Jamison Jo Medby. *Limited Conflicts Under the Nuclear Umbrella: Indian and Pakistani Lessons from the Kargil Crisis.* Santa Monica: RAND, 2001.

Tellis, Ashley J. *Balancing without Containment: An American Strategy for Managing China.* Washington, DC: Carnegie Endowment for International Peace, 2014.

Thrall, Trevor, Dina Smeltz, Erik Goepner, Will Ruger, and Craig Kafura. *The Clash of Generations? Intergenerational Change and American Foreign Policy Views.* Chicago: The Chicago Council on Global Affairs, 2018.

Tilford, Earl H., Jr. *Crosswinds: The Air Force's Setup in Vietnam.* College Station: Texas A&M University Press, 1993.

Trachtenberg, Marc. "A 'Wasting Asset': American Strategy and the Shifting Nuclear Balance, 1949–1954." *International Security* 13, no. 3 (1988/1989): 5–49.

———. "The Influence of Nuclear Weapons in the Cuban Missile Crisis." *International Security* 10, no. 1 (1985): 1371–163.

van Creveld, Martin. *Nuclear Proliferation and the Future of Conflict.* New York: Free Press, 1993.

van Evera, Stephen. "The Cult of the Offensive and the Origins of the First World War." *International Security* 9, no 1 (1984): 58–107.

Stillion, John, and David T. Orletsky. *Air Base Vulnerability to Conventional Cruise-Missile and Ballistic-Missile Attacks: Technology, Scenarios, and US Air Force Responses.* Santa Monica: RAND Corporation, 1999.

Tangredi, Sam. "Keep War Confined to the 'Seas'." *Proceedings* 148, no. 6 (June 2022).

Bibliography

Thomas, Jim. "Why the US Army Needs Missiles: A New Mission to Save the Service." *Foreign Affairs* 92, no. 3 (May/June 2013).

Van Evera, Stephen. *Guide to Methods for Students of Political Science.* Ithaca: Cornell University Press, 1997.

van Tol, Jan, Mark Gunzinger, Andrew F. Krepinevich, and Jim Thomas. *AirSea Battle: A Point-of-Departure Operational Concept.* Washington, DC: The Center for Strategic and Budgetary Assessments, 2010.

Vick, Alan J. *Air Base Attacks and Defensive Counters: Historical Lessons and Future Challenges.* Santa Monica: RAND Corporation, 2015.

Waltz, Kenneth. *Man, the State, and War.* New York, NY: Columbia University Press, 1959.

———. *The Spread of Nuclear Weapons: More May Be Better.* London: Adelphi Papers, no. 171, The International Institute for Strategic Studies, 1981.

Weigley, Russell F. *History of the United States Army.* New York: The Macmillan Company, 1967.

White, Hugh. *The China Choice: Why We Should Share Power.* Oxford: Oxford University Press, 2013.

Whitlark, Rachel Elizabeth. "Nuclear Beliefs: A Leader-Focused Theory of Counter-Proliferation." *Security Studies* 26, no. 4 (2017): 545–574.

Wilson, James Q. *Bureaucracy.* New York: Basic Books, 1989.

Wilson, Ward. *Five Myths about Nuclear Weapons.* New York, NY: Houghton Mifflin Harcourt, 2013.

Wolfers, Arnold. "'National Security' as an Ambiguous Symbol." *Political Science Quarterly* 67, no. 4 (1952): 481–502.

Woliver, Laura R. "Ethical Dilemmas in Personal Interviewing." *PS: Political Science and Politics* 35, no. 4 (2002): 677–678.

Yoshihara, Toshi, and James Holmes. *Red Star over the Pacific: China's Rise and the Challenge to US Maritime Strategy.* Annapolis, MD: Naval Institute Press, 2013.

Zhang, Ketian. "Cautious Bully: Reputation, Resolve, and Beijing's Use of Coercion in the South China Sea." *International Security* 44, no. 1 (2019): 117–159.

Zhang, Xiaoming. *Red Wings over the Yalu: China, the Soviet Union, and the Air War in Korea.* College Station: Texas A&M University Press, 2003.

Index

accidental nuclear war, 18–19, 108
Acheson, Dean, 53–56, 58–59, 61, 65, 68
active denial strategy, 6
AirSea Battle, 5, 13–14, 16, 43, 46, 64, 136, 162, 185
American air bases, 60, 62
   air base vulnerability problem, 5
   Andersen Air Force Base, 3
   Kadena Air Base, 3, 120, 137, 148–151, 159–160, 172, 187–190, 207, 209
American Enterprise Institute, 132
armistice, 56, 61, 68, 174
Asal, Victor, 20, 44
Atlee, Clement, 54
atomic bomb, 20, 51

Ball, George, 74, 77, 85
Bartels, Elizabeth, 37, 48
Beardsley, Kyle, 20, 44
Beckley, Michael, 4, 9, 12, 14, 98
Bell, Mark S., 23, 44–45
Blair, Bruce, 19, 44
Bracken, Paul, 19, 44
Bradley, Omar, 54–55, 65–66
Brands, H. W., 48, 51, 65
Brookings Institution, 132
Builder, Carl, 51, 65
Bundy, McGeorge, 77, 98–99
Bundy, William, 72

caution model, 18, 20, 23, 51, 56, 63, 89–90, 109–110, 116, 125, 168–169, 171

Center for a New American Security, 132, 185
Center for New American Security, 3
Center for Strategic and Budgetary Assessment (CSBA), 5–6, 8–10, 13, 16, 27, 136
Center for Strategic and International Studies, 132
Central Intelligence Agency (CIA), 53, 65, 67, 72, 88, 100
China
   anti-access/area-denial capabilities, 5, 13
   military power, 1–4, 167, 198
   missile attack on US base, 3, 172
   nuclear weapons, 1, 6, 8–9, 16–17, 19–20, 23–24, 26, 35, 39–40, 43, 49–57, 63, 70–71, 73–79, 88–95, 97–100, 105, 108–118, 121–123, 125, 128, 132, 135–136, 151–152, 154–157, 159–161, 163, 167–173, 177, 179–180, 185, 195, 197, 210–211
   surveillance and precision-strike capabilities, 4
   See also mainland strikes on China *and* US-China war
Clifford, Clark, 72, 98, 101–102
Clodfelter, Mark, 65, 67–68, 73, 78, 84, 88, 96–102
coercive diplomacy, 61, 83
   bombing as a form of, 82
Colby, Elbridge, 8, 13–14, 27, 43–44,

Colby, Elbridge (*continued*), 64, 178–179, 181, 185
Cold War, 3, 18, 20, 31, 44, 46, 59, 90, 96
conventional bombing, 38–39, 41, 61–62, 70–71, 90
conventional escalation, 15–16, 18–22, 24–31, 34, 39, 51, 56, 61, 71, 73, 75, 79, 89, 92–95, 109, 115–116, 125, 169, 171–172, 175–177, 179
    definition, 17
    intra-war, 17, 63, 70, 168, 170
Correlates of War, 20
Crane, Conrad, 52, 61, 64–65, 67–68
Cuban Missile Crisis, 20, 25, 39, 45, 90, 92
    parallels with future US-China war, 91

Department of Defense. *See* United States
Department of State. *See* United States
deterrence, 2, 16, 38, 43, 45–46, 103
    extended deterrence, 23

Eisenhower, Dwight, 51–52, 64, 76–77, 91, 99
emboldenment model, 18, 24–26, 56, 78, 109–110, 115–116, 168, 170
Europe, 59, 85

Fallows, James, 50, 64
Foot, Rosemary, 51, 56, 64–65, 67–68
Foreign Policy Analysis, 27, 46
fundamental military strategies, 5
Futrell, Robert Frank, 52, 64–65, 67–68

Gaddis, John Lewis, 44, 48, 65, 67, 73, 97
Gartzke, Erik, 23, 45
George, Alexander, 28
Goldberg, Arthur, 74, 85
Gompert, David, 10, 14
Goodwin, Doris Kearns, 72–73, 96–97
great power competition, 165

Hagen, Jeff, 3, 12
Haiphong Harbor. *See* Vietnam
Hammes, T. X., 6, 9–10, 13–14, 16, 27, 43, 46, 50, 64, 92, 103, 185
Hanoi. *See* Vietnam
Heginbotham, Eric, 3, 6, 9, 12–14
    US-China Military Scorecard, The, 2
Heim, Jacob, 6, 9, 12–14
Heritage Foundation, 133
historical case studies, 15, 17, 20, 24, 26, 36, 38–40, 42, 131, 174
Ho Chi Minh, 83
Hughes, Wayne, 6, 9–10, 13–14
Huth, Paul, 23, 45

inadvertent nuclear use, 18–19, 109, 113
India, 22, 44, 46, 93–95, 103
Institute for National Strategic Studies. *See* National Defense University
intervention, 2, 52, 54, 58, 67, 73, 79, 89
    Chinese intervention, 50, 53, 56, 65, 71–72, 74–77

Japan, 3, 28, 32, 60, 120, 137, 148, 207, 209

Index

Jervis, Robert, 18, 25, 43–45, 47–48
Jo, Dong-Joon, 23, 45
Johnson, Harold Keith, 86
Johnson, Lyndon, 38, 47, 50, 71, 74–75, 78–90, 96–102, 179
   and Dwight Eisernhower, 76–77
   fear of Chinese and Soviet intervention, 72–73
Joint Chiefs of Staff, 25, 54–55, 58, 80, 106

Kargil War, 39, 93–95
Karnow, Stanley, 73, 96–97, 102
Kennedy, John F., 48, 92
Khalizad, Zalmay, 8, 14
Kline, Jeffrey, 6, 9, 13–14
Korean War, 31, 38–39, 41, 49–53, 56, 60–65, 67, 77–78, 90, 94–95, 168–170, 172, 177, 179–180
Kroenig, Matthew, 24–26, 45–46, 128, 181

Lebow, Richard Ned, 22–23, 44
Lemay, Curtis, 82
Lin-Greenberg, Erik, 37, 48

MacArthur, Douglas, 49, 51–52, 59, 65–66, 72
mainland strikes on China
   adversary perceptions, 88
   ally with domestic turmoil, 82
   American public opinion, 85
   attacks on US air base, 5, 81, 120–121, 137, 148–150, 160, 172
   considerations about civilian casualties, 84
   considerations about coercive diplomacy, 83
   "defensive" authorization, 81
   early in a conflict, 79, 89, 124,
mainland strikes on China
   early in a conflict (*continued*), 159, 171
   implications of Cuban Missile Crisis, 92
   implications of Korean War, 63
   implications of US maritime strategy in the 1980s, 93
   implications of Vietnam War, 89–90
   military value of different targets, 87
   tactical cost imposition role, 88
   and Taiwan, 28, 82, 91, 93, 117–118, 121, 124–125, 132, 134, 140, 147–149, 151–155, 157, 160, 172–173, 175–176, 185–186, 196
Manchuria, 53–56, 58–59, 61, 64–66, 68
maritime denial strategy, 6–7, 13, 176, 178
Marshall, George C., 52–55
May, Ernest, 36–37
McCone, John, 72, 100
McNamara, Robert, 22, 44, 72, 75–76, 80, 83–84, 86, 98–99, 101–102
   targeting decisions during the Vietnam War, 85
MiG. *See* Soviet Union
military balance, 2–5, 8, 12, 14, 25, 98, 166
Miller, Nicholas L., 23, 44–45, 181
Millot, Marc Dean, 38, 48
Muccio, John, 58
Mueller, John, 21–23, 43–45, 48

Narang, Vipin, 22, 44
National Defense University, 6, 13, 185

National Defense University (*continued*)
  Institute for National Strategic Studies, 133
National Security Council (NSC), 186
  documents, 53, 60, 99
  meetings, 53–56, 65–68, 74, 80, 85–86, 98, 100, 102, 135, 187–193, 206–209
national security elites (in survey)
  Asia-related expertise, 141, 147, 175
  career length, 143, 162
  interview protocol, 108
  interview sample, 107
  on American allies, 119
  on categories of mainland strikes, 122–123
  on Chinese actions, 121
  on Chinese nuclear weapons, 110–111, 114–116
  on South China Sea confrontation, 118
  on timing of mainland strikes, 124
  political affiliations, 145
  scenario-based survey, 15, 40, 131, 157, 172–173, 177, 180
  See also scenario-based survey
National Security Resources Board, 55–56
NATO, 20, 97, 178
naval blockade, 7, 13, 177
Neustadt, Richard, 36, 48
North Korea, 49, 53, 58–59, 64, 178, 186
nuclear superiority, 24–26, 45–46, 57, 110, 115–116, 128, 170
nuclear symmetry, 17–18, 24, 26
nuclear weapons, 9, 23, 35, 37–40,

nuclear weapons (*continued*), 43–45, 49–50, 52–55, 57, 64, 77–79, 90–91, 94–95, 97–98, 100, 103, 105, 108, 110–114, 128, 132, 151–152, 154–157, 160–161, 163, 172, 180–181, 185, 195–196, 210–211
  and conventional escalation, 15–22, 24–26, 51, 56, 63, 70–71, 73, 75, 89, 92–93, 109, 115–116, 125, 168–171, 177, 179
  Chinese acquisition, 71
  Soviet possession, 20, 51, 71
null model, 21–24, 45, 57, 63, 71, 73, 78, 89, 109–110, 113–114, 116, 125, 168–171

Ochmanek, David, 8, 14, 181
Offshore Control, 6, 13, 43, 103
Operation Pierce Arrow, 80
Operation Rolling Thunder, 69–74, 78, 82, 90, 96, 100
  American public opinion, 84–85
  bombing pauses, 83
  civilian casualties, 83–84
  tactical cost imposition, 87
  tit-for-tat retaliation, 79–81

Pakistan, 22, 44, 46, 93–95, 103
Pauly, Reid, 37, 48
Philippines, 28, 117, 191–192
political values, 166

RAND Corporation, 2–3, 8, 12, 33, 38, 43, 51, 118, 133, 205
Rauchhaus, Robert, 20, 23, 26, 44, 46
reconnaissance, 5–6, 55
Reddie, Andrew, 37, 48, 162

Index

restraint, 20, 63, 71, 90, 94–95, 120
  American, 39, 62, 67, 83
  Chinese, 60, 62
  mutual, 60
  studied, 83
Rovner, Joshua, 9, 14, 44, 98
Rusk, Dean, 25, 72, 78, 84
Russett, Bruce, 23, 45, 101–102
Russia, 64, 70, 72–73, 76, 93, 100, 167, 178

Sagan, Scott, 19, 43–44, 162
sanctuary status, 5, 8, 10, 12, 49–50, 60, 64
scenario characteristics, 160
  ally actions and preferences, 28
  enemy actions, 27–29
  foreign-policy tools, 29
  operational aspects, 13, 27, 29
scenario-based survey, 15, 40, 131, 172–173, 177, 180
  analytical stages, 140–141
  "at fault" condition, 134–135, 150, 203
  central findings, 148, 150–151
  comprehensive target set, 135–136, 150
  Fisher's exact test, 140–141, 148, 152–154, 162–163
  framing of foreign policy questions, 137–138, 155–156
  influence of respondent's background on decisions, 151–152, 154
  influence of respondent's beliefs on decisions, 154–157
  limitations of, 157
  "limited" target set, 121, 135
  McNemar's test, 140, 149, 162
  partisan diversity, 133
  randomization, 134, 137, 148

scenario-based survey (*continued*)
  South China Sea Scenario, 191–192
  Taiwan Scenario A, 187–188
  Taiwan Scenario B, 189–190
  See also national security elites
Schlosser, Eric, 19, 44
Schneider, Jacqueline, 38, 46, 48
Sherman, Forrest, 60
Shlapak, David, 2, 12, 14
Smith, Walter Bedell, 53, 65
Smoke, Richard, 16–17, 28, 43, 46, 48, 64, 92, 103
Snyder, Glenn, 25
South China Sea, 117–119, 124, 134, 165, 172, 185, 191–192
South Korea, 28, 60
Soviet Union, 20, 23, 25, 38–39, 46, 50–60, 62–64, 70–74, 76–80, 82, 88–93, 99–100
  MiG, 49, 75
stability-instability paradox, 25–26, 110, 115
Stennis, John, 84
Symington, Stuart, 56
synthetic history, 36–38, 40–41, 131, 180

Taiwan, 28, 46, 82, 93, 118–121, 124–125, 129, 132, 134–135, 140, 147–149, 151, 153–154, 163, 172–173, 176, 185, 187–190, 196, 198, 203, 205–209, 212
  as vital US interest, 139, 152, 155, 157, 160, 175, 210
  Taiwan Relations Act, 117
  Taiwan Strait Crisis, 39, 90–91, 103
Talmadge, Caitlin, 9, 14, 44, 92–93, 103, 174, 181
Tangredi, Sam, 6, 13

Taylor, Maxwell, 25, 85
technological rivalry, 166
Thompson, Llewelyn, 81
tit-for-tat retaliation, 79–81, 89
Trachtenberg, Marc, 25, 45, 65
Truman, Harry S., 38, 49–54, 56–57, 63–65, 179
   decision not to expand war to Chinese territory, 58–61
Trump, Donald, 167
Twining, Nathan, 60

U.S.-China Economic and Security Review Commission, 3
United Kingdom, 52
United Nations (UN), 49, 52–53, 56, 58–60, 74, 85
United States, 1–2, 5–6, 8–10, 12, 15–16, 19–21, 23, 27, 32, 39–41, 43–44, 46–50, 52–63, 65–69, 74–76, 78–89, 91–92, 94–95, 98–102, 108–109, 112–114, 117–126, 128–129, 131, 134–137, 139–140, 148, 155, 158–160, 162–163, 165–167, 169–172, 174–175, 177–181, 185–193, 195–199, 205–210, 212
   American aircraft carriers, 4
   Department of Defense, 37, 111, 132–133, 156, 168
   Department of State, 64, 77, 106
   maritime strategy, 14, 90, 93, 103
   US Navy, 3–4, 7, 93
US-China war
   caution on mainland strikes, 90
   Chinese strikes against US bases, 62
   and the Cuban Missile Crisis, 91
   Korean War analogy, 60
   parallels with Cuban Missile Crisis, 91

US-China war (*continued*)
   risk of misperception, 20
   similarities to historical case studies, 39
   US targeting Chinese nuclear forces, 92
US-China Military Scorecard, The. See Heginbotham, Eric
USS Constellation, 76

van Tol, Jan, 8, 13–14, 43, 46
Vandenberg, Hoyt, 60
Viet Cong, 70, 80, 84
Vietnam, 45, 50, 96–98, 103
   Haiphong Harbor, 69, 72–73, 76, 83–84
   Hanoi, 69, 82–84, 88, 99, 101–102
   North Vietnam, 69–73, 75, 77–84, 86–88, 99
   petroleum, oil, and lubricants (POL) targets, 72, 74, 86
   South Vietnam, 70, 81–82, 84–85, 88, 100
   Vietnam War, 31, 38–39, 41, 69, 71–72, 77–79, 85, 89–90, 94–95, 100, 168–170, 172–173, 177, 179–180
   See also Operation Pierce Arrow, Operation Rolling Thunder, Operation Flaming Dart

Waltz, Kenneth, 18, 27, 30, 43–44, 46
wargames, 37–38, 47–48, 118, 162
Weigley, Russell, 51, 65
Wheeler, Earle, 72, 84, 98
Whiting, Allen, 77–78

willingness to endorse
conventional escalation
and age, 33
and gender, 32

willingness to endorse
conventional escalation
(*continued*)
and military background, 30
and political party, 31
Wilson, Peter, 12, 44, 118, 129

About the Author

John Speed Meyers is the head of research and development at Chainguard, a software supply chain security startup. He holds a PhD from the Pardee RAND Graduate School and an MPA from Princeton University. Dr. Meyers has previously worked at In-Q-Tel, the RAND Corporation, and the Center for Strategic and Budgetary Assessments.

Cambria Rapid Communications in Conflict and Security Series

General Editor: Thomas G. Mahnken
(Founding Editor: Geoffrey R. H. Burn)

The aim of this series is to provide policy makers, practitioners, analysts, and academics with in-depth analysis of fast-moving topics that require urgent yet informed debate. Since its launch in October 2015, the RCCS series has the following book publications:

- *A New Strategy for Complex Warfare: Combined Effects in East Asia* by Thomas A. Drohan
- *US National Security: New Threats, Old Realities* by Paul R. Viotti
- *Security Forces in African States: Cases and Assessment* edited by Paul Shemella and Nicholas Tomb
- *Trust and Distrust in Sino-American Relations: Challenge and Opportunity* by Steve Chan
- *The Gathering Pacific Storm: Emerging US-China Strategic Competition in Defense Technological and Industrial Development* edited by Tai Ming Cheung and Thomas G. Mahnken
- *Military Strategy for the 21st Century: People, Connectivity, and Competition* by Charles Cleveland, Benjamin Jensen, Susan Bryant, and Arnel David
- *Ensuring National Government Stability After US Counterinsurgency Operations: The Critical Measure of Success* by Dallas E. Shaw Jr.
- *Reassessing U.S. Nuclear Strategy* by David W. Kearn, Jr.
- *Deglobalization and International Security* by T. X. Hammes
- *American Foreign Policy and National Security* by Paul R. Viotti

- *Make America First Again: Grand Strategy Analysis and the Trump Administration* by Jacob Shively
- *Learning from Russia's Recent Wars: Why, Where, and When Russia Might Strike Next* by Neal G. Jesse
- *Restoring Thucydides: Testing Familiar Lessons and Deriving New Ones* by Andrew R. Novo and Jay M. Parker
- *Net Assessment and Military Strategy: Retrospective and Prospective Essays* edited by Thomas G. Mahnken, with an introduction by Andrew W. Marshall
- *Deterrence by Denial: Theory and Practice* edited by Alex S. Wilner and Andreas Wenger
- *Negotiating the New START Treaty* by Rose Gottemoeller
- *Party, Politics, and the Post-9/11 Army* by Heidi A. Urben
- *Resourcing the National Security Enterprise: Connecting the Ends and Means of US National Security* edited by Susan Bryant and Mark Troutman
- *Subcontinent Adrift: Strategic Futures of South Asia* by Feroz Hassan Khan
- *The Next Major War: Can the US and its Allies Win Against China?* by Ross Babbage
- *Warrior Diplomats: Civil Affairs Forces on the Front Lines* edited by Arnel David, Sean Acosta, and Nicholas Krohley
- *Russia and the Changing Character of Conflict* by Tracey German
- *Planning War with a Nuclear China: US Military Strategy and Mainland Strikes* by John Speed Meyers

For more information, see **cambriapress.com**.

www.ingramcontent.com/pod-product-compliance
Lightning Source LLC
Chambersburg PA
CBHW051353290426
44108CB00015B/2000